Revival and Reaction

Revival and Reaction
The Right in Contemporary America

by

Gillian Peele

CLARENDON PRESS · OXFORD

Oxford University Press, Walton Street, Oxford OX2 6DP

Oxford New York Toronto
Delhi Bombay Calcutta Madras Karachi
Petaling Jaya Singapore Hong Kong Tokyo
Nairobi Dar es Salaam Cape Town
Melbourne Auckland
and associated companies in
Beirut Berlin Ibadan Nicosia

Oxford is a trade mark of Oxford University Press

Published in the United States
by Oxford University Press, New York

First published 1984
First issued as a paperback 1985
Reprinted 1987

British Library Cataloguing in Publication Data
Peele, Gillian
Revival and reaction: the right in contemporary America.
1. Conservatism—United States
I. Title
320.973   JA84.U5
ISBN 0–19–821132–5

Library of Congress Cataloging in Publication Data
Peele, Gillian, 1949–
Revival and reaction.
Bibliography: p.
Includes index.
1. Conservatism—United States.   2. United States—
Politics and government—1981–ย. I. Title.
JA84.U5P39   1985   320.5′2′0973   85–15304
ISBN 0–19–821132–5 (pbk.)

Printed in Great Britain
by J. W. Arrowsmith Ltd,
Bristol

For John and Leslie Francis

ACKNOWLEDGEMENTS

In the course of writing this book I have been helped by a very large number of institutions, organizations, and individuals.

Financial support for the work on which this book is based has been provided by the American Council of Learned Societies (in conjunction with the Fulbright Commission), which awarded me a scholarship enabling me to spend much of the academic year 1979–80 in the United States. In 1982 the Leverhulme Trust gave me an award which enabled me to complete the project. I should like to record my debt to the American Politics Group of the Political Studies Association and to the Burleson Fund, which exists within Lady Margaret Hall to promote research in the United States. I am grateful to all these bodies for their generous financial assistance, which has allowed me to spend a large amount of time in the United States over the past five years.

A number of academic institutions provided help and hospitality while I was engaged in the research. The Woodrow Wilson School of Public and International Affairs at the University of Princeton made me a Visiting Fellow for 1979–80 and provided a stimulating environment for my work. The University of Utah offered me hospitality as a Visiting Scholar in 1980. I am extremely grateful to these universities for the opportunity which they provided to spend time in such congenial academic surroundings. The Brookings Institution in Washington has over the past decade proved extremely helpful to me, and I benefited greatly from a short stay there in April 1983. I should especially like to thank Walter Beach, Jim Reichley, and Bruce Smith for their personal and academic help. A special debt of gratitude is owed to Margaret Latus, who was a major source of advice on the intricacies of Political Action Committees and the Federal Elections Commission.

Other organizations in the United States have facilitated my researches. Austin Ranney and his colleagues at the American Enterprise Institute have been generous with their time.

viii *Acknowledgements*

John O'Sullivan and other members of the Heritage Foundation have enhanced my understanding of key issues in
American politics. And a variety of groups and organizations
which appear in this book have been willing to answer
queries and provide material, often at very short notice.

To record my thanks to all the other individuals in the
United States who have helped me would take another
book. The dedication reflects my appreciation of two friends
and their families who have provided intellectual and social
stimulation in Washington, Salt Lake City, Los Angeles,
and Sacramento. Others who have cheerfully allowed me to
stay with them in various parts of the United States include
John and Margery O'Shaughnessy, John and Elsa Pickering,
John and Irene Francis, Morris and Carlen Abram, Richard
and Karen Warmer, Bruce and Anne Cain, Miles Kahler,
Leonard Barkan, Allan and Solveig Brownfeld, Elizabeth
Creighton, Archie and Suzelle Smith, Irving and Huguette
London, Norman and Rosalin Provizer, Tom Gee, Thomas
Laquer, Michael and Shelley Pinto-Duschinsky, Mary Skinner,
and Phyllis Thorburn.

In the United Kingdom I am deeply grateful to Lord
Beloff, who read the whole book with meticulous care and
good humour. I am also indebted to Philip Williams, who
read large portions of the manuscript and gave me the benefit
of his knowledge of American government. Other colleagues
who helped with portions of the manuscript include Nigel
Ashford, S. E. Finer, Catherine Jones, John Gray, John
Hogan, James Miller, Nicholas Shrimpton, Gabrielle Stoy, and
Frances Lannon. My colleagues Martin Holmes and Vernon
Bogdanor, apart from their help with other aspects of the
book, read the proofs with admirable care. John Bennett
produced the index. The errors that remain are of course mine
alone.

I am deeply grateful to the Principal and Fellows of Lady
Margaret Hall, who have provided a scholarly and congenial
environment for my academic work during the last nine
years. I am indebted to them especially for their support
in the finishing stages of this book. I should also like to thank
the College Office, and especially Mrs Tina Thomas and Miss
Deborah Janes. Their help with the production of the manu-

script and their cheerful willingness to rescue me from the idiosyncrasies of the word processor proved invaluable.

In the course of developing the themes outlined here I have been immensely helped by opportunities to discuss the issues with colleagues at other universities. I should like to thank the Universities of London, Edinburgh, Birmingham, and Hull for inviting me to participate in various meetings and seminars. I also benefited greatly from a conference at the Aspen Institute in Berlin in 1983. And I owe a special debt of gratitude to my graduate students, who willingly provided information and criticism on specific points. Robb London and Daniel Dreisbach were extremely acute critics. Chris Bailey and Nicol Rae were also a constant source of intellectual stimulation.

I have been especially grateful for the research assistance given by Timothy Brazy and Christopher Bloor over the past two years. And I have benefited in a number of ways from the help and encouragement given by Derek Leebaert both in the United States and the United Kingdom.

Finally, I must thank most sincerely my publishers and especially my editor, Ivon Asquith, whose kindness and forbearance were often, I fear, greatly strained.

G.R.P.

Lady Margaret Hall, Oxford
January 1984

Contents

Abbreviations — xii

Note on Interviews — xiv

Introduction — 1

I. Neo-conservatism — 19

II. The New Right — 51

III. The Religious Right — 80

IV. Republicans and the Right — 120

V. Reagan, the Right, and Social Policy — 146

VI. Reagan, the Right, and Foreign Policy — 167

Conclusion — 191

Notes — 195

Bibliographical Essay — 225

Index — 234

ABBREVIATIONS

ACLU	American Civil Liberties Union
ACU	American Conservative Union
AFDC	Aid to Families with Dependent Children
AFL – CIO	American Federation of Labor – Congress of Industrial Organisations
ALEC	American Legislative Exchange Council
APSA	Americal Political Science Association
AWACS	Airborne Warning and Control System
CETA	Comprehensive Education and Training Act
CIA	Central Intelligence Agency
CIO	Congress of Industrial Organisations
CSFC	Committee for the Survival of a Free Congress
CSIS	Center for Strategic and International Studies
DSG	Democratic Study Group
ERA	Equal Rights Amendment
FEC	Federal Election Commission
FECA	Federal Election Commission Act
GDP	Gross Domestic Product
GNP	Gross National Product
GOA	Gun Owners of America
GOP	Grand Old Party (Republican Party)
IRD	Institute for Religion and Democracy
IRS	Internal Revenue Service
LAPAC	Life Amendment Political Action Committee
MAD	Mutual Assured Destruction
NATO	North Atlantic Treaty Organization
NCC	National Council of Churches
NCPAC	National Conservative Political Action Committee
NEA	National Education Association
NRA	National Rifle Association

OMB	Office of Management and Budget
PAC	Political Action Committee
PAW	People for the American Way
RNC	Republican National Committee
SALT	Strategic Arms Limitation Talks
UNESCO	United Nations Educational, Scientific, and Cultural Organization
WCC	World Council of Churches
YAF	Young Americans for Freedom

NOTE ON INTERVIEWS

Although I have conducted a very large number of interviews in the course of my research on American politics, I have used the information gleaned from interviews primarily for background information. I have therefore not felt it incumbent on me to provide a list of persons interviewed. However, where I have relied upon interviews the end-notes indicate the nature of the interview. I should like to record my thanks to those individuals who spent time explaining their policies and attitudes, and generally illuminating my understanding of American politics.

INTRODUCTION

This book has been written with two broad purposes in mind. By focusing on some of the different strands of opinion and styles of political activity within the American right, I hope to make some contribution to the understanding of the contemporary conservative movement in the United States. The need to clarify the meaning of such terms as 'neo-conservative' and 'new right' as well as to explore the implications of these tendencies in American political life ought to be obvious for readers on both sides of the Atlantic. For the United States, developments on the right of the political spectrum reflect a fundamental questioning of many of the assumptions of post-war economic, social, and foreign policy, and they constitute concrete evidence of the extent to which the landscape of the country's politics has changed even in the past twenty years. For Britain, those developments have not only had, or may yet come to have, echoes in the politics of that country but seriously call into question such vital issues as the future of the Atlantic Alliance and the relationship between the defense of Europe and American nuclear strategy.[1] Thus, there is an obvious common interest in both democracies in such questions as the proper role of government in a free society and the correct balance between public and private provision of social services. And there is also a sense in which the impulses and concerns of the American right must be of direct and practical concern to the United Kingdom.

There is, however, another reason why a study of the American right may prove illuminating at this juncture. Ronald Reagan came to power with a set of policies which were extremely well defined, even ideological, by the standards of a political system which tends to eschew programmatic politics in favor of coalition-building, brokerage, and compromise. And in the first year his administration had a substantial impact on the course of American politics. Yet within two years of taking office the Reagan administration's policies appeared to many to have lost much of their coherence and direction, in a manner reminiscent of earlier administrations. Although this book is not intended primarily as a study of the peculiar weaknesses and strengths of the American system of government, reflection on the experience of the Reagan administration's attempt to translate its policies into practice may yield some insight into the more general problems of constitutional government in America.[2]

At first sight 1980 represented a major victory for the American right. Ronald Reagan, despite the handicaps of age and an image which lent itself to caricature, defeated an incumbent President and won all but six states of the Union. The Senate (which had last been controlled by the Republicans in 1953–4) lost several of its leading Democrats and was also captured by the Republican Party. The House of Representatives, it is true, remained in Democratic control, but two factors made that control precarious. First, the Republicans had gained seats from the Democrats, so that the overwhelming Democratic preponderance of the previous decade, which had led to a quickening of Congressional activism, was weakened.[3] Secondly, on a number of issues it was quite clear that opinion within the Democratic ranks had become more conservative than hitherto. For some Republicans this movement of opinion meant that they could again think in terms of a 'conservative coalition' built on the basis of largely southern and western support. Indeed, even before the 1980 election there had been some speculation about how, if the Republicans just failed to secure a majority, the House might be organized on coalition rather than party lines in order to reflect its ideological as opposed to its partisan majority.[4] Although the House did organize on normal party lines after the 1980 elections, the Democratic majority was conscious that it had to operate in a highly conservative political environment. And even when the results of the 1982 mid-term elections (as well as a certain amount of party discipline exercised against wayward Democrats) dispelled some of the optimism of the Republicans and reduced the effectiveness of the Conservative Democratic Forum, it remained clear that the preferences of most Democrats had moved away from the explicit support of high levels of federal spending on the domestic front.[5]

The dynamics of party factionalism took several new turns during the 1970s as far as both the Republicans and the Democrats were concerned. Division within the Democratic Party was not, of course, a new phenomenon in American politics. Race and civil liberties — the themes which had for so long separated southern Democrats and their liberal colleagues from the urban North-East and which formed a central plank of the southern strategy of earlier Republican theorists such as Kevin Phillips — were no longer the most important direct source of conservative bipartisanship, although issues such as law and order and welfare inevitably had racial overtones.[6] A broad panorama of issues ranging from defense and foreign policy and the level of federal expenditure to the newer regional issues and conflicts over energy policy divided the Democratic Party and provided opportunities for legislative coalitions. Although the coalition of conservative Democrats and Republicans began to unravel in 1982, it was crucial to Reagan's early success. The forty or so 'boll-weevils' of 1980 might seem like the Dixiecrats of an earlier generation; but since much of their emphasis was on economic policy rather than race, in so far as they constituted a durable faction they no longer reflected the isolation of southern political culture. Indeed, their activity in many ways represented the extent to which southern political culture had been absorbed into the broader identity of the sun-belt.[7] Ronald Reagan was very much a product of the sun-belt culture, so that his victory could be seen not merely as a triumph of Republicans over Democrats but as a power-shift from the Eastern Establishment to the country's Southern Rim. And in that movement there was a shift in political values which suggested that the United States would become less dominated by liberalism than it had appeared to be in the past.[8]

Developments behind what seemed in 1980 to be a dramatic alteration in the balance of political forces in the United States initially gave adherents of the right even more cause for self-congratulation. The conservative Republican Study Committee had consolidated its position within the House of Representatives to a point where roughly 80 per cent of the Republican members belonged to it.[9] And in the

Senate hawkish Jacksonian Democrats combined with new-right Republicans to change the direction of American foreign policy.[10] The national organization of the Republican Party had been enormously strengthened in the period immediately prior to the 1980 elections and, indeed, in those elections it took much of the credit for Republican successes at all levels of electoral competition. From a nadir in its fortunes in the aftermath of Watergate and the loss of the Presidency in 1976, William Brock, the Republican National Committee Chairman, had encouraged a revival of the party at the grass roots and stimulated a comprehensive process of policy reappraisal. Changes in electoral law had occasioned a readjustment of candidates' financial strategies, but the Republicans in 1980 had put in motion a coherent program designed both to maximize the party's help to their candidates and to secure a pool of experienced candidates. Direct mail had been used to place the Republicans on a sound financial footing and had helped to improve the Republican image by transforming the party into one which received most of its money from small donations of less than $100 rather than from the 'fat cats' who had been the source of funds in the past.[11] For the 1980 elections the Republican National Committee operated as a significant source of technical aid and advice to candidates and integrated the presidential, congressional, and state campaigns to a much greater extent than before.

The renewal of the Republican Party's organizational vitality was, however, paralleled by shifts which occurred outside the confines of orthodox party activity. The electoral success of November 1980 capped what had already been hailed as major changes in the climate of American public opinion generally and in policy debates. In effect, America was becoming more critical of the liberal public philosophy and rejecting much of the consensus which had seemed to support the continued extension of federal government activity. In part this alteration in the climate of American politics was the result of the activities of a small group of academics and politicians who had questioned the trends of existing governmental policies, and had voiced reservations about a number of the programs associated with the Great

Society legislation sponsored by Lyndon Johnson. Indeed, it would not be too much to say that the conservative politics of the 1970s and 1980s reflected on a number of levels the disillusion and doubts of both the policy élite and the general public in respect of the general direction of American government in those years.

The intellectual questioning of the assumptions behind the policies of the Great Society was itself diverse, and generated a number of critics who could not readily be placed in any school or grouping. However, one label which did emerge and stick (although it was originally used disparagingly by Michael Harrington) was the term 'neo-conservative'.[12] The individuals to whom this term was applied were for the most part academics and writers who had been Democrats but who rejected both the 'new politics' of the Democratic Party after 1968 and the assumptions which pervaded Democratic domestic and foreign policy thereafter.[13] Many neo-conservatives placed themselves firmly in the liberal Democratic Party tradition; but they believed that with the 1960s and the excesses, as they saw them, of the 'counter-culture' (the loose phrase used to describe the rebellion against established moral, social, and aesthetic values in the 1960s) and the peace movement, as well as the policy flaws of the Great Society programs, the Democratic Party had lost its way. Their trenchant reassessments both of the general goals of American federal policy and of specific themes in relation to such problems as crime and welfare did much to remold the agenda of American politics. While many of these neo-conservatives would claim that they were not and perhaps never could be Republicans, they inevitably contributed to the success of the Republican Party. And although many proclaimed their loyalty to the Roosevelt vision of the Democratic Party, they helped to produce an intellectual environment that was conducive to policies in a radically different vein from the New Deal–New Frontier–Great Society tradition.[14]

The neo-conservatives were not the only group of writers who were affecting the intellectual climate within which American politics was carried on in the 1970s and who helped to move the United States towards the right of the political spectrum. In the field of economic theory there was much criticism of Keynesianism in the United States, as elsewhere. At the University of Chicago, Milton Friedman's free-market and monetarist approach to economic policy won adherents both inside and outside of academic life and generated interest not only within the discipline of economics itself but also in related disciplines such as law and political science. This creed differed in a number of respects from that of the neo-conservatives; but it fed a general feeling that the movement of ideas was away from collectivism, as did the writings of men like Hayek and Nozick.

Also in opposition to traditional Keynesianism, there developed a school of thought called 'supply-side' economics which placed great emphasis on the role of tax rates in individual decision-making about whether to work, save, and invest. The American economy, these theorists suggested, could be revived by a major tax cut which would effectively pay for itself by generating additional production. Although supply-side economics did not achieve an academic reputation comparable with that of the Chicago school, it did acquire a popular following — in part because many of its tenets were popularized in books such as George Gilder's *Wealth and Poverty*, and because its ideas were given prominence in the pages of the *Wall Street Journal*.[15] The optimistic prescriptions of the supply-siders did not combine at all well with the doctrines of the monetarists, and indeed it was not long before observers of the influence which both schools seemed to be having within Republican policy circles suggested that these ideas seemed set on a collision course. The solutions of the supply-siders also offered the Republicans an attractive and apparently cost-free way both of assuaging middle-class dissatisfaction with the burdens of taxation and of reversing the country's economic recession. And even if supply-side theories seemed to lack empirical validation, they contributed to a quickening of interest in policies associated with the Republicans and the right rather than with Democrats.

Indeed, part of the demoralization of the Democratic Party after the 1980 elections was the result not so much of its basic political losses but rather of the failure to find a new intellectual rationale for its policies and of the realization that much of the coherence of the liberalism which it had espoused during the 1970s had disappeared.

The neo-conservatives, free-marketeers, and supply-siders — and indeed other critics of the existing pattern of government policies such as the increasingly influential public-choice theorists — obviously operated to a large extent in the somewhat rarified atmosphere of the universities, research centers, and think-tanks. Developments in conservative circles at a more routine level of political organization produced in addition a movement which will here be labeled the 'new right'. The range of single-issue groups, institutions, and individuals to whom this label was applied proved increasingly successful during the 1970s in getting their chosen issues on to the political agenda and in creating the impression that the questions which mattered to the American people were conservative ones. The promotion of conservative themes by technically sophisticated methods (especially computerized direct mail) enabled pressure-groups which carefully built up their lists of donors and sympathizers to amass a healthy income and to reach those sections of the electorate that were most likely to be sympathetic to their propaganda. Changes in the electoral laws designed to regulate campaign finance encouraged the direct participation of these groups not merely in the policy process but also in the election campaigns.

Much debate has occurred about the impact of new-right intervention in a number of electoral races in 1980 (and especially on the defeats of such well-known liberal Senators as George McGovern, Gaylord Nelson, Birch Bayh, and Frank Church). There is little doubt that the National Conservative Political Action Committee (NCPAC) exaggerated its own importance in 1980; but, whatever their influence on the vote, many of these groups injected a viciousness into some electoral contests in a manner which may ultimately have proved counter-productive.[16]

American politics in the 1970s has generally been discussed in terms of declining party appeal, a rise in ticket-splitting, and increasing voter apathy, although the 1982 mid-term elections saw an unusual improvement in turnout level.[17] The federal nature of the American political system automatically decentralizes the country's politics; but those politics were further fractured by the changes in the campaign finance laws which encouraged candidates to seek support from Political Action Committees and to adjust their strategies to whatever nexus of issue groups was operating in their state or district.[18] And whereas routine party activity on a regular basis seemed to have lost some of its appeal in the 1960s and 1970s, campaign strategists discovered that the incentive to participate in politics when a moral issue (such as abortion) was involved was still strong.[19] The 'correct' stand on the abortion controversy might therefore yield dividends to the candidate both in terms of votes and of campaign volunteers; and the pressure-groups themselves were quick to encourage their activists to get into a campaign and develop credit with a candidate which would later need to be repaid.

The phrase 'single-issue politics' is perhaps somewhat misleading in terms of the dynamics of the American right in the 1970s. For, while many of the interest groups did organize on the basis of a single issue or a closely connected set of issues, many of the groups themselves co-operated extensively. All interest groups recognize the value of working with other groups with similar objectives.[20] Such a rational strategy accounts in part for the success of the various civil rights groups in the late 1960s and 1970s, so that by working with sympathetic labor organizations, for example, they were able to achieve objectives which might have been beyond their own political strength. What the period of the late 1970s saw was the appearance of a series of alliances on the right, and the coming together of a range of pressure-groups, think-tanks, and individual politicians which may be designated the 'new right'. To many of its critics this tactical cooperation and political interaction suggested a conspiratorial ideological underworld.[21] In fact, what the new right was doing was in many ways simply refining the strategies and tactics of liberal pressure-groups of previous years. Certainly, many of the single-issue groups had overlapping memberships, took their funds from similar sources, and enjoyed overlapping leadership. This was partly because the

'single issues' themselves often appealed to similar constituencies, so that an opponent of the Equal Rights Amendment,
for example, might, if his or her objection was based on the
belief that the ERA threatened the conventional role of the
American woman and the American family, be an easy
(though not inevitable) recruit to the Right to Life movement. Some of these groups would be less than reliable allies
in the new-right movement; but when they did participate
their combined strength could be formidable.[22]

The élites who ran many of these groups largely shared a
common outlook, a common social milieu, and a common
dedication to changing the structure of American political life
and redirecting it towards a pattern which, it was imagined,
had been destroyed by some kind of subversion. Clinton
Rossiter commented on the dilemma of the conservative who
is overwhelmed by the pace of change. He suggested that
when 'a conservative once decides, as many articulate conservatives seem to have decided in explosive America, that his
best of all possible worlds was here yesterday and gone
today, he begins the fateful move toward reaction and
ratiocination that turns him from a prudent traditionalist
into an angry ideologue'.[23] The strand of American political
life which will be referred to as the 'new right' throughout
this book displayed without doubt an angry style which
marked it off from the intellectual theorists of the right on
the one hand and the regular Republicans on the other. For
much of the 'new-right', politics was analogous to a crusade
which demanded the energy and conviction of a zealot. It was
hardly surprising, therefore, if this element in the make-up
of the 'new right' both reinforced its sense of a unified subculture and caused a reaction from those who saw its zealotry
as bigotry and intolerance.

Perhaps the most dramatic development of all in the
politics of the American right in the 1970s was one closely
connected to the style of the 'new right', and, although the
groundwork for it had been laid much earlier, it caused
great controversy during the 1980 election campaign. That
development was the entry into right-wing politics of a
number of individual pastors and clerics who had the professed aim of mobilizing their congregations on behalf of

what were claimed to be religious causes and Christian
candidates. Religion has long been one of the factors shaping
American political culture (especially in the South) and it has
frequently injected a moral element into the country's policies.
Sometimes — as with the prohibition issue — the causes that
have brought the Churches into politics have seemed, if not
eccentric, at least backward-looking; sometimes — as with the
civil rights movement or the nuclear issue — they have seemed
radical. Whether or not Clinton Rossiter is correct in thinking
that the 'grave, godly rulers of early Massachusetts' were the
'first sizeable company to occupy the American right', few
would deny that America's Puritan heritage has provided an
important component of the country's political culture
and that for white Americans at least the teachings of the
Churches and conservative political attitudes have not proved
difficult to reconcile.[24]

In the 1970s the religious revivals (which America intermittently experiences) seemed to benefit the more conservative
evangelical and fundamentalist Churches, although whether
this was a result of demographic change rather than conversion remains unclear.[25] It was hardly surprising if right-wing
tacticians saw in that revival a new and important force for
achieving a 'cleansing of America' and a turning away from
the evils of the 1960s' counter-culture and all its works as
well as a reservoir of votes for conservative candidates. The
formation of groups such as Moral Majority and Christian
Voice as well as the activities of individuals such as Jerry
Falwell and James Robison were directed towards the election
of a Congress purged of the politicians who were lenient towards homosexuals, tolerated abortion and pornography, and
approved of such developments as women's liberation and
sex education in schools. If this was not quite the reassertion
of spiritual values which the earlier critics of secular liberalism
such as Leo Strauss and Richard Weaver had in mind in the
period immediately after the Second World War, it did
represent a self-conscious attempt to revive the idea of
America as a country founded on values other than secular
humanism.[26]

The long-term significance of the bringing together of the
religious right and the new right in the form which occurred

in the 1970s is still a highly debatable issue in American politics. The obsession of the religious right and the new right with the general theme of sexual morality, and especially the issues of homosexuality and abortion, has generated a substantial amount of polemical literature dealing with both the likely impact of renewed right-wing activity on civil liberties and the underlying reasons for the degree of concern with such issues.[27] Gusfield in his analysis of the prohibition movement has pointed to the sense in which moral issues can be interpreted as 'one way through which a cultural group acts to preserve, defend or enhance the dominance and prestige of its own style of living within the total society'.[28] Social or family issues, as defined by the new right and the religious right and publicized by such devices as the Family Protection Bill, may be similarly interpreted as a reflection of the desire by sections of American society to defend their life-style and values against the onslaughts of a secular humanism which had seemed to acquire establishment status in the 1960s.[29] In the case of the fundamentalists and conservative evangelicals — and perhaps in the case of the Roman Catholics — some of those sections were indeed distinctive subcultures. But there was a sense in which this resort to moral issues transcended sectarian positions and represented the concerns of a wide spectrum of American opinion. And while it might be true that much of its concern with such issues as evolution and abortion stemmed from a genuine and spontaneous expression of cultural and moral values, it is also true that the issues were easy to exploit for broad political ends. Ronald Reagan was the product of a cultural reaction against developments which most Americans neither liked nor understood; but he was also aware of the political mileage to be made from exploiting the fears and resentments of Main Street.[30]

In addition to books and essays which have attempted to relate the union of right-wing religion and right-wing politics to tensions within American society, there has also developed a literature about what should be the Christian response to the call for greater political involvement.[31] The writings from the theologians and reflective students of religion are of course an indication of the extent to which the style of the religious right and its concerns have opened a wider debate about the relationship between Church and State in America and the extent to which the moral concerns of a section of society can be extended to a whole nation.

The growth of a well-organized religious right with developed contacts into what has been termed the new right quite naturally prompted those who were opposed to the goals of the religious and new right to mobilize themselves. The major spurt of such activity came in the aftermath of the 1980 elections and brought together the more liberal Churches and a range of politicians through such organizations as People for the American Way, the Committee for American Principles, and Americans for Common Sense. At the same time there developed a new interest in the role of religion in American society, and between the two extremes of the strict separationists and the advocates of imposing biblical morality on American public life there appeared a range of new ventures such as the Institute for Religion and Democracy and the journal *This World*.[32] It also seemed that the activities of some religious groups on the right of American politics legitimized the activities of other Churches that wished to intervene on a range of issues quite different from the ones that excited men like Jerry Falwell and James Robison. Thus, the National Council of Catholic Bishops in early 1983 issued a pastoral letter which appeared to condemn the use of nuclear weapons and which in the words of one commentator reinforced 'the impassioned pacifist and neutralist movements' that had been growing in Europe and the United States as well as the 'establishment strategies which helped to generate these protest movements'.[33]

These separate waves of activity on the right of American politics contributed to the tide which carried Reagan and the Republican Party to electoral success in 1980. But, as Republican Party managers were well aware, there were cross-currents which instead of carrying them to shore might cause them to drown. Practicing politicians may genuinely believe in a philosophy, ideology, or moral cause; but they will usually try to temper conviction with pragmatism. For those looking for portents of a popular rejection of the philosophy of the Great Society, Reagan's victory on a platform of substantial tax cuts, a reduction in the role of the federal government, and a return to the virtues of individualism and independence was cause for optimism. Clearly it did owe much to the supply-side theories of Arthur Laffer, Norman Ture, George Gilder, and the politicians Jack Kemp and William Roth. Clearly it did accord with the desire of the Chicago school to restore the market mechanism and to remove impediments to free enterprise in the system. And clearly the doubts expressed about the developments in the field of social welfare chimed well with many neo-conservative criticisms about the efficiency of such job-training schemes as CETA. But the 1980 campaign by the Republican Party was oriented not to the beauties of the free market or the ideas of Milton Friedman, or even to the need to restore traditional American values such as self-reliance. Rather it was geared to the unemployment issue and was predicated upon the assumption that the Republicans could convince large numbers of normally Democratic voters that the remedies advocated by Reagan and the Republicans could pull the United States out of recession. And while it seemed clear to many observers of the President's own political philosophy that he had a deep-rooted dislike of the Welfare State and an equally strong desire to reverse the trend towards growing federal power in the United States, after the achievements of his first year the President had increasingly to compromise with a Congress which thought differently.

Blaming the problems of the economy on a weak President and a Democratic Congress went hand in hand with an emphasis on selected social issues for selected audiences, a call for a tough line against communism, and a robust rhetoric; but it clouded the mandate which Reagan could claim for his policies. And indeed Reagan's package of tax and expenditure cuts when it came in 1981, as well as the subsequent debates about economic policy, revealed both the extent to which the unity on the right in 1980 was a flimsy covering for a variety of theories and panaceas for the American economy, and also the extent to which it would prove difficult to satisfy the various elements in the electoral coalition which had taken Ronald Reagan and the GOP to the White House.

One of the primary inconsistencies in the Reagan program that emerged soon after the President had taken office reflected the tension within the Republican Party about economic policy as well as the limited role which the President and Congress have in the control of the money supply. The philosophy which personally attracted Reagan — supply-side economics — argued that incentives were all-important and that even if tax cuts did not immediately pay for themselves deficits as such did not matter in the short term. Against this view were ranged both the adherents of a strict monetarist persuasion and traditional Republicans who deplored the idea of sizeable deficits.[34] President Reagan had taken into his administration representatives of a variety of economic outlooks, and this inevitably created confusion and tension in the economic policy process. By the end of 1983, although Reagan had managed to maintain cuts in direct personal taxation, opposition to the level of deficits and to cuts in domestic spending had combined to force substantial modifications in his programs. Though some saw these modifications as reasoned returns to reality, they also allowed supply-siders to claim that their ideas had not been given a fair chance.[35]

Nevertheless, the platform on which Ronald Reagan ran for the Presidency and the budget which he presented to Congress in 1981 involved a substantial and explicit change in the role of the federal government in American life. Reagan and the Republican Party, the neo-conservatives, the free-marketeers and the supply-siders, the single-issue groups and the evangelical right were almost at one in rejecting the proposition that the federal government had either the obligation or the capacity to solve the nation's problems. Indeed, the federal government might very well make many of those problems worse by trying to do so. As Reagan himself put it, it was not for the federal government to solve the country's problems, the federal government was the problem.[36]

The call to 'get government off the backs of the people' was hardly novel in the context of American politics. Richard Nixon had run into a series of clashes with Congress because he wanted to dismantle many of the Great Society programs and used the weapon of impoundment towards that end. President Nixon's philosophy of federalism was predicated upon the assumption that a dangerous imbalance between the states and local government on the one hand and Washington on the other had been created during the period after the New Deal and that there had to be some definite effort to reverse the constitutional trend towards greater federal dominance. Democrats also worried about the role of the federal government, and both President Carter and Governor Brown of California recognized that there was a limit to public tolerance of large bureaucracies spending what was seen as a vast amount of the taxpayers' money. Growing scepticism about politicians and government fueled this feeling that much of what public authorities did was self-serving or redundant. The movement towards deregulation — which affected all parties — represented but one strand in the developing consensus that a reduction in the overall level of government activity was desirable.

Another more dramatic indication of popular frustration with government was the series of tax revolts symbolized in 1978 by California's passage of Proposition 13.[37] Reagan's rhetoric reflected this sentiment of hostility to government. But whereas both Carter and Brown had to bear in mind their Democratic constituencies, which were supportive of federal government, the Reagan rhetoric had no need to be tempered in this way. To criticisms of federal waste could be added the populist appeal to the forgotten man subordinated to the requirements of a growing bureaucracy. The forgotten man, according to Reagan, was the one who paid his taxes regularly, worked hard to better his own position and his family, and, it was implied, regarded 'welfare' as something disgraceful.

Scepticism about the role of government is, of course, an emotion which can be traced back to the very foundations of the Republic. The whole edifice of checks and balances and of judicial review reflects the deeply held belief that government should be constructed in a way which recognizes that men are not angels. The size of the United States has added its own problems to the political culture, for while it may be relatively easy to identify with the local units of

church and neighbourhood or region, it is much harder
to identify with a nation as heterogeneous as America.
The problems of poverty and of unemployment may therefore be ones which Americans acknowledge when they
occur close to home; in the abstract they can be ignored or
dismissed as problems created by Washington. Attitudes
towards government are, however, rarely consistent, and one
of the contradictions which pervaded the public opinion
polls in the 1970s was the ability of voters to combine a
general desire for a reduction in the role of government
and a reduction of the tax burden with a desire to see maintained the specific services from which they might benefit.

The contradiction inherent in the demand for a radical
reduction in government activity and popular support for
a wide range of publicly provided services raises the question
of how clear the mandate of the Reagan administration
actually was in this respect. Two broad hypotheses may
be advanced to help interpret the admittedly rather difficult
poll data on this issue. The first suggests that while there
was indeed a demand for a reduction in certain sorts of
public expenditure, the majority of Americans drew a vague
distinction between the universal services which they could
see themselves using and which they applauded — for example education, libraries, defense, and social security —
and those services which they regarded as minority services
for the undeserving poor. The second possibility is that many
of those who wanted to see cut-backs in public expenditure
did not actually believe that this would entail any real
reduction in the level of provision because they believed the
rhetoric about bureaucratic waste. Thus, in California, where
high property taxes and a large surplus coexisted and where
the referendum allowed these issues to be directly tested,
Proposition 13 represented the culmination of a number of campaigns to slash levels of taxation and expenditure, although
it was not clear how far support for the Jarvis–Gann Proposition would have been sustained had the public really
thought that libraries, schools, and other state services would
actually have been affected by the result. Indeed, attempts to
build on the success of Proposition 13 have had very limited

success even in California itself, although it was initiated in other states, such as Michigan and Massachusetts.

Uncertainty about the extent of the change in public attitudes towards government and about how far the perceived shift to the right would endure once the impact of such policies began to be felt was compounded by the problems which the American political system presents to any administration anxious to see the enactment and implementation of a set of radical policies. Not only does the President have to struggle to get his legislation through a Congress which is itself internally divided; but, as in many Western democracies, he must also guard against the erosion of policies by a bureaucracy which has the dual advantages of specialization and knowledge and which may convert political appointees to its own perspectives. If the President does not himself provide clear political direction, and combine that with attention to detail, it is unlikely that the other instruments of executive control — the Cabinet and the personal staff — will be able to do so. Into the vacuum there will then step the variety of other actors with an interest in policy determination — the pressure-groups, the individual Congressmen and their staff, and the permanent bureaucrats. The contrast between what might have been expected from the Reagan administration and the experience of government ought to illuminate the peculiar difficulties of operating the American system of government.

The format of this book has been constructed to reflect the different dimensions of developments on the right of American politics. Chapter I examines the intellectual group known as the neo-conservatives and their particular concerns, while Chapter II explores the very different phenomenon of the new right. Chapter III discusses the relationship between religion and politics in the United States by looking at the religious right, which, as has been suggested, is closely linked with but distinguishable from the new right. Chapter IV draws some distinctions between the different factions of the contemporary Republican Party and attempts to relate some of the developments of the 1970s in the party to the revival of the conservative movement. Chapters V and VI pick up some of the themes of the right in the fields of social and foreign policy and examine some of the policies of the Reagan administration.[38] Assessing the impact which the ideas of the right have actually had on the Reagan administration is obviously not something which is easy to do; but it is possible to give an overview of the spirit of that administration in a number of diverse policy areas.

It should be emphasized that this book is not intended to be a comprehensive study of contemporary American conservatism; much less is it intended to be a history of the Reagan administration, which obviously cannot yet be written — although a number of preliminary assessments can be and have been made.[39] It is rather an attempt to explore a development within the American political tradition which, like some of the recent developments in British politics, suggests that the forces which shape our politics and determine the effectiveness of our government are far less well understood than political scientists, historians, and sociologists sometimes like to imagine.

CHAPTER I
Neo-conservatism

The first strand of the American right which needs to be examined is the body of ideas, impulses, and tendencies that has come to be labeled 'neo-conservatism'. Although there have been other important intellectual influences in the revival of significant political criticism and reflection from a conservative perspective, the themes raised by the neo-conservative movement have been especially powerful because they have seemed to combine theoretical analysis on a number of levels with a practical concern for the details of routine politics. As a result the questions raised by the neo-conservative element of the American right and the contributions of individual neo-conservative thinkers offer the most convenient starting-point in any attempt to understand how the center of gravity in American politics has shifted in the period since 1968. Three general points should, however, be made before any further discussion of either the themes of neo-conservatism or the ideas of its most articulate spokesmen is undertaken:

Initially, it is important to emphasize that the label 'neo-conservative' has been applied as a piece of convenient shorthand and, as mentioned in the Introduction, it was originally applied by a major critic of the sentiments associated with neo-conservatism.[1] Some neo-conservatives, such as Irving Kristol, cheerfully picked up the label; others refused to accept it. It is, moreover, overwhelmingly apparent that discussion of a neo-conservative *movement* is itself rather misplaced, since the individuals who might be considered or even consider themselves as neo-conservatives are all highly distinctive personalities whose arguments about the state of the polity are in harmony only in the most general sense. Since the advent of President Reagan's administration in 1981 many of the leading members of the group — who would have constituted the core of any pre-1980 study —

have become increasingly unwilling to make common cause
with other neo-conservatives, so that differences between
the various standard-bearers of neo-conservatism have been
brought into the open.[2] Thus, in a sense the different members of the clan have largely gone their own ways since 1981,
and this fact — together with the appearance of a younger
generation of neo-conservatives — has made the group altogether less homogeneous than it was prior to 1980.

Secondly, although the neo-conservatives have contributed to the environment within which some of the central
assumptions and issues of American politics have been re-
defined, and although some of them have participated more
directly in the governmental process, many who consider
themselves neo-conservatives have kept their distance from
the other elements in the conservative coalition which took
Ronald Reagan to the Presidency in 1980 and which have
apparently resuscitated Republican Party fortunes. Daniel
Moynihan, for example, would count as an obvious example
of a politician whose ideas, arguments, and style for a period
chimed well with the foreign- and domestic-policy outlook
of his neo-conservative friends from Harvard and New York
and (on foreign policy) with the general perspective of the
Reagan administration. Yet, as an ambitious Democratic
Senator from New York and one whose own thinking is
undergoing constant change, he has been one of the men
who has tried to detach the label 'neo-conservative' from his
politics. Indeed, in 1982 Moynihan was targeted for defeat
by the new-right organization NCPAC — a fact which underlined the divisions between the new right and the neo-
conservatives.

The arguments of the neo-conservatives contributed greatly
towards making the candidacy of Ronald Reagan and the
kind of policies which the Republican Party advocated in
1980 much more acceptable than they would earlier have
been, and ensured that the Reagan assault on the White
House was not dismissed by the media in the way that Barry
Goldwater's was in 1964.[3] The neo-conservative academics
who did so much to remold that climate of opinion, and the
writers and polemicists who forced the powers that be to
take the heir of the Goldwater movement seriously, have

not, however, been committed to supporting his every step
as President.[4] Serious disagreements have emerged over
foreign policy in particular, and there is in any case the natural
tendency of academics and intellectuals to wish to place
themselves in a hostile and critical position *vis-à-vis* an
administration. In discussing the role of neo-conservatism
in recent American politics, it is therefore necessary to
distinguish between the overall intellectual legitimacy which
they have given to the right as a whole and the level of
support for particular policy options or even a particular
administration.

The final point of general importance about neo-
conservatism is that much of what the neo-conservatives have
advocated is, from the perspective of the mid-1980s, much
less novel and controversial than it was when it was first put
forward. As a result, the ideas of the individual thinkers may
now seem commonplace and even banal. For them perhaps
such a comment would be a cheering recognition that their
common-sense perceptions had indeed influenced the American polity. For the student of American politics it is perhaps
further evidence of the speed with which even the fiercest
of ideological battles may be forgotten.[5]

The most immediate key to understanding the political
positions and style of neo-conservatism is of course the
decade of the 1960s. Norman Podhoretz's autobiographical
rehearsal of the various traumas of those years and his later
reopening of the debate about the meaning of the Vietnam
War for America underline the extent to which those years
seemed to be a watershed period for many Americans and
the extent to which the bitter redrawing of political bound-
aries has affected the subsequent course of American life.[6]
However, while the political passions of the 1960s were
undoubtedly important for the neo-conservatives, the controversies of an even earlier period were also crucial to the
formation of the distinctive tone of much of their writing
and thought. The intensity of political argument that marked
the 1960s was for many of the neo-conservatives reminiscent
of the deep divisions of the cold-war period; and behind
those divisions lay the legacies of the 1930s and the conflict

over totalitarianism. Those ideological, political, and personal
struggles have a continuing resonance in the minds of many
of the influential neo-conservatives and are an important
factor contributing to the character of contemporary neo-
conservatism.

For the general public the most controversial issue of the
1930s was the New Deal, which precipitated a partisan
realignment and caused a transformation of the role of the
federal government in American society.[7] For the much more
limited group of intellectuals and academics based largely
in New York, but also in the Bay area of San Francisco, in
Chicago, and in Los Angeles, the issues of America's domestic
politics were compounded by the question of attitudes
towards the Soviet Union. Fellow-traveling sympathy not
merely for communism but even for Stalin himself was
common in the 1930s, as was formal membership of the
Communist Party. Because the USA — even in the depression
— lacked a strong left-wing party, communist influence
was heavily directed towards the penetration of labor
organizations and other pressure-groups rather than towards
direct electoral participation. Thus the ACLU was a special
object of communist interest throughout the inter-war
period, as was the Congress of Industrial Organisations
after its foundation in 1935.[8]

Yet within the ranks of left-of-center intellectuals fundamental divisions appeared even at the height of the popular-
front mentality of the mid-1930s.[9] The Moscow trials of
1936, for example, although they occasioned protest from
men like Waldo Frank and Edmund Wilson, were actually
supported by such literary figures as Dorothy Parker, Dashiell
Hammett, and Nelson Algren.[10]

Another major division — and one which was to have a
profound effect on the intellectual conflicts of subsequent
decades — was the secession from pro-Soviet communism
of a small group of writers associated with *Partisan Review*.
This periodical has occupied a special place in the cultural
milieu from which many of today's leading neo-conservatives
emerged. As a journal it provided an organ in which modernist or avant-garde literary criticism and writing could be
combined with far-left politics. Originally it had been

founded as a magazine of the John Reed Clubs, which were communist societies named after a Soviet sympathizer who was the author of *Ten Days That Shook the World*.[11] In 1937, however, *Partisan Review* dissociated itself from the official American Communist Party (which was dominated by a pro-Stalinist attitude) and proclaimed its independence and a general commitment to the autonomy of art. Politically, the magazine seemed thereafter to espouse a form of Trotskyism, but its real strength lay in the variety of talented authors — such as Sidney Hook, Dwight Macdonald, and Lionel Trilling — who were associated with it. And, although many of the writers associated with *Partisan Review* in its early days of struggle would retain their left-of-center sympathies, others became in the 1950s pillars of anti-communism in American life.[12]

The political debates of what Eugene Lyons later dubbed 'the red decade' remain evident in the styles of the neo-conservative writers themselves and in the responses which they occasion.[13] Because the primary divisions in American intellectual life in the 1930s were *within* the far left, they were conducted on a highly theoretical plane. Arguments about policy choices were subservient to arguments about doctrinal truth as far as this group was concerned — although of course the ideological positions could be pressed where necessary into service on behalf of a wide range of policy options. As many of the adherents of the left rejected first Stalinism and then Trotskyism for simple anti-communism, they carried with them a heritage of ideas and an awareness of disputes within the communist movement which was unusual among scholars and rare among practicing politicians. Thus, the major figures of the contemporary neo-conservative movement emerged in an atmosphere where it was not merely desirable to have read very large amounts of Marx and his commentators, but where it was also natural to see discussions about the interpretation of his doctrines as part of the daily intellectual fare.

It was not only familiarity with Marx and Marxism which characterized the inellectual milieu from which neo-conservatism emerged. The cultural ambience which produced today's neo-conservatives was New York and the

background to the disputes of the 1930s was in part the New
York intellectual subculture, which had a markedly Jewish
character. Not all of those who are important neo-conservative
writers today are Jewish, and one finds Roman Catholics
such as Michael Novak developing original interpretations of
the relationship between religious values and those of American capitalism.[14] Indeed, by no means all the leading intellectual figures of New York in the 1930s were Jewish; Mary
McCarthy, for example, who was intimately involved in its
intellectual circles, was a Roman Catholic.[15] Nevertheless, as
men such as Alfred Kazin and Daniel Bell have underlined
in their writings, the Jewish intellectual world of New York
in the 1930s was a close-knit one which had some of the
characteristics of a family, albeit one which experienced an
unusual degree of internal feuding.[16]

Daniel Bell has argued that the distinctive Jewish intelligentsia no longer exists in modern America and that there
is now 'no coherent intellectual community'.[17] Modern
America's concern with the Jewish novel therefore presents
something of a paradox:

Typically the Owl of Minerva flies at dusk and knowledge is found after
the fact. In the period of the Jewish intellectual community's decline,
American society has discovered the Jewish writer, be he Saul Bellow or
Bernard Malamud or Philip Roth or critics such as Harold Rosenberg,
who write for magazines such as *The New Yorker* or the *New York
Review of Books*. But that no longer reflects any community: these
are only the broken fragments reflecting their own diffuse anxieties
over the precarious character of American society.[18]

Bell does, however, acknowledge the reality of the Jewish
intellectual community within the New York of an earlier
period, and he draws a distinction between the writers of the
generation who came of age in the late 1930s and those who
became active on the political and literary scene in the
immediate post-war period and the 1950s. Among the
generation he calls the 'elders' were such people as Elliott
Cohen, Sidney Hook, Philip Rahv, Meyer Schapiro, William
Phillips, Hannah Arendt, Lionel Trilling, Richard Hofstadter,
and Delmore Schwartz. In the younger generation come
those figures who were active in the continuing ideological
debates of the post-war years — Irving Howe, Leslie Fiedler,

Irving Kristol, Melvin Lasky, Nathan Glazer, Seymour Martin
Lipset, David Bazelon, Steven Marcus, Gertrude Himmelfarb,
Norman Podhoretz, and Bell himself.[19] Moreover, as Bell
has also noted, the New York Jewish intellectual community
had its own distinctive journals. In the inter-war period these
were *Menorah Journal*, *The New Masses*, and, of course,
Partisan Review; later they were *Dissent*, the *New Republic*,
and the London-based *Encounter*, which Irving Kristol and
Stephen Spender founded in 1953. And two journals based
in New York — *Commentary* (which is the official magazine
of the American Jewish Committee) and *The Public Interest*
— have in their very different ways become the journals
where neo-conservatism and the Jewish intelligentsia inter-
sect.

The specifically Jewish intellectual milieu from which
many of the neo-conservatives came had the effect of making
its members especially sensitive to the importance of religion,
while also, of course, ensuring that they would have some
grounding in the teachings of the Old Testament. This
religious background has had an important impact on
the style of thought of modern neo-conservatism, which
insists on the importance to a society of a shared code of
morals even where orthodox religious observance may be
abandoned. Equally, one can trace to the specifically Jewish
background of many leading neo-conservatives the concern
with preserving the institution of the family and the emphasis
on ethnicity.

In tracing the roots of many of today's neo-conservatives
to the culture of New York in the 1930s one is therefore
locating its origin in a rich and unusual American subculture.
It was a subculture concerned with domestic and international issues, with politics, with literature, and with psychology. It was and is, as Kristol has himself acknowledged,
a 'hermetic universe', and it was a subculture which was
crucially affected by communism. Lionel Trilling, in an
essay on the importance of *Partisan Review*, put the matter
succinctly:

After *Partisan Review* had broken with the Communist Party, some
large part of its own intellectual vitality came from its years of conflict
with Communist culture at a time when our educated class, in its

guilt and confusion, was inclined to accept in serious good faith the cultural leadership of the Party.[20]

Mutatis mutandis, it could be said that the recent vitality of the American neo-conservative movement was a product of the members' participation and schooling in a range of intellectual debates which may now appear very remote from the concerns of bread-and-butter politics and which quite naturally by-passed not only the vast body of American voters but also a majority of the educated élite within the United States. (It is also worth noting that the communist issue in America had different dimensions from that in Europe because of the size of the United States' East European community, a factor which resulted both in a greater degree of anti-communism in those groups and in a greater degree of actual espionage than was prevalent in Europe.) The passions roused in those debates have helped to keep the issue of communism at the center of American political life from the 1930s onwards.

The fact that the political battles of the 1930s caused many intellectuals to reassess their communist beliefs and political loyalties had a major effect on the American right generally, and bequeathed its legacy to the neo-conservatism of the 1960s and 1970s. The experience of conversion and disillusionment was traumatic and created a bitterness in the political minds of some who felt themselves to have been betrayed in the service of a god or set of gods who failed. Similarly, there is often a sense that despite the radical change in the content of an ideology the sense of passionate commitment — even the need for it — remains constant.

One final legacy of the controversies of the 1930s is also relevant to the style in which those of the 1970s were conducted by the intellectual right. The experience of many intellectuals in the inter-war period was the feeling that they had been tricked or duped — inveigled into a sympathetic stance towards communism which was later revealed to have been wholly groundless. Today's neo-conservatives are acutely aware of the fellow-traveling temptation and are sensitive to the fact that so many intellectuals whom they admired fell prey to it.[21] Hence one finds throughout the writings of the neo-conservatives an emphasis on realism and a rejection of sentimentality and emotion. This realism appears far stronger than the normal preference on the right for the solutions suggested by common-sense practicality as opposed to those suggested by abstract theory. The toughness of the neo-conservative thus springs not from the paradoxical position of the intellectual in politics and his sensitivity to the charge of Utopianism, but from the historical memory of how easily the idealism of the intellectual can be exploited.

In emphasizing the importance of the ideological controversies of the 1930s in shaping the outlook of contemporary neo-conservatism, it must of course be stressed that that influence was an indirect one. Today's neo-conservatives did not participate directly in the debates of the 1930s, for they were — as Daniel Bell's distinction between the generations of Jewish intellectuals makes clear — generally too young to have done so. However, their teachers and mentors, such as Lionel Trilling, were directly involved in those controversies so that they remained salient long after the close of the Second World War.

If the 1930s were highly charged ideologically for some Americans, so too were the early 1950s, although in a quite different way; and in the debates of the 1950s neo-conservatives such as Irving Kristol did take an active part. The phenomenon of the cold war and the attitudes associated with McCarthyism transformed the American political landscape for both the intellectual community and the wider community of practicing politicians.[22]

The cold war itself changed both American conservatism and American liberalism and, as the Chambers–Hiss trial at the beginning of the 1950s underlined, created new divisions in American society. Like the Dreyfus trial, that of Alger Hiss did not itself create the ideological and political divisions in the country which it polarized; those divisions and cleavages had been long in the making and were not the result of a single event. The Hiss trial and all the subsequent polemical controversy simply illuminated the extent to which the United States, in its own view a classless society, harbored a range of deep-seated and bitter conflicts. (The continuing potency of the Hiss affair to divide Americans remained strong in the 1980s when Hiss again had one of his petitions for a retrial rejected; and the issue of espionage in America in the early 1950s resurfaced in early 1983 when the House of Representatives once more raised the validity of the Rosenberg trial and execution.[23])

What the Hiss trial also did was to throw the divisions of class and ideology, of partisan preference and regional background, into dramatic relief and to provide a concrete issue by which an aroused and even fearful public opinion could identify the 'enemy'.

The transformation of conservatism itself by the cold war involved two developments. First, there was the purging of American right-wing and Republican politics — at least at the Congressional level — of its immediate isolationist impulse, although the isolationist stream of American opinion did not completely disappear from American life. Indeed, isolationist sentiment — whether relabeled as unilateralism or nationalism — retained distinctive features which became apparent in the foreign-policy debates of the 1970s and 1980s. (Unilateralism is a term with slightly different connotations in the United States from those associated with it in Europe: in the United States it tends to mean a policy of 'fortress America' — a strong defense without overseas entanglements — whereas in Europe the idea has a somewhat more pacifist connotation.)

Secondly, the cold war put conservative critics of totalitarianism into a broad church — that of militant anticommunism — in which the majority of American Democrats also worshiped. Although the backlash against McCarthyism was to some extent to reverse the process, conservative publicists came closer to the mainstream of American political debate than had been the case in the 1930s; the right in consequence no longer seemed confined to the fringes of the country's political life.

Liberalism was itself transformed by the division which foreign policy effectively introduced into its ranks. Those who were soft on communism or unwilling to commit America to an international position of confrontation with the Soviet Union were ranged starkly against those who were eager and willing to shoulder the military and political responsibilities of international leadership of the free world. The division between what was called anti-communist liberalism and what was pejoratively labeled 'fellow-traveling liberalism' split the intellectual community even before Senator McCarthy began his notorious campaign to oust alleged communist sympathizers from government.[24]

The McCarthy period is still a sensitive one for the neo-conservatives and, as has been seen, it is subject to continuing academic reassessment. For the neo-conservatives there was the unpleasant dilemma involved in having to choose between defending those who might threaten America's national security and defending the methods of McCarthyism. The tactics of the 'great fear' might reassure liberals that all was being done to protect the United States from internal subversion; they could hardly be reconciled easily with the values of intellectual freedom which organs like *Partisan Review* held dear — much less with the constitutional principles of due process.

In 1976 Lillian Hellman accused 'the good magazines' of having done nothing to defend civil liberties at the time of McCarthy, and she clearly wanted to underline the ambiguous attitude of men like Irving Kristol, Norman Podhoretz, and indeed Lionel Trilling:

Partisan Review, although through the years it has published many pieces protesting the punishment of dissidents in Eastern Europe made no protest when people in this country were jailed or ruined. In fact, it never took an editorial position against McCarthy himself, although it did publish the results of anti-McCarthy symposiums and at least one distinguished piece by Irving Howe. *Commentary* didn't do anything. No editor or contributor ever protested against McCarthy. Indeed, Irving Kristol in that magazine wrote about McCarthy's critics, Henry Steele Commager among others, as if they were naughty children who needed Kristol to correct their innocence.[25]

The level of sentiment which such a charge could create was evident both from the reply to *Scoundrel Time*'s charge that *Commentary* felt obliged to make in the form of an article by Nathan Glazer and from the tone of Norman Podhoretz's own comments in his second autobiographical book, *Breaking Ranks*. For Glazer, who had been an early academic analyst of McCarthyism and had linked it with the populist tradition, Hellman's charges of supineness were unfounded because the magazines and literary journals generally adopted an attitude of distaste for McCarthyism itself and felt it more important to concentrate on the questions raised by McCarthyism's success.[26] For Podhoretz, however, the central point was still that Lillian Hellman was 'unwilling to recognise that Stalinism could exert no legitimate claims on the sympathies of anyone like herself who professed to believe and value freedom and democracy'.[27] The true scoundrels, according to Podhoretz, 'were not the ex-Communists who had repented of their support for Stalin and his monstrous crimes but the Communists and fellow-travelers who had persisted in defending Stalin and apologising for those crimes'. Not only did Podhoretz pour scorn on Hellman's prose style ('an imitation of Hammett's imitation of Hemingway and already so corrupted by affectation and falsity in the original that only a miracle could have rendered it capable of anything genuine in this third remove'), but he also mocked her claim to have suffered some sort of martyrdom as a result of the McCarthy enquiry:

. . . it seemed nothing short of blasphemous to compare the fate of 'dissidents in Eastern Europe' whose 'punishment' consisted of execution, torture or long years of imprisonment under conditions of hardship scarcely imaginable to Lillian Hellman with, say, the six months Dashiell Hammett spent in jail cleaning bathrooms, let alone the luxury in which she herself lived on the East Side of Manhattan or Martha's Vineyard even when she could no longer command million-dollar contracts for writing Hollywood films.[28]

Such exchanges are important because they show just how bitter the divisions created by the cold war and McCarthyism continued to be in liberalism's ranks (especially when compared to the attitudes then prevalent in Britain); and they explain why the feuds of the 1950s could still be so violent in the late 1970s. Thus, in attempting to understand why the neo-conservative writers of the contemporary period excite what may seem inordinate controversy, given the moderate substance of many of their policy preferences, it is vital to bear this background of the 1950s in mind. It may be that the participants in the cold war controversies deliberately used provocative language to make their points; but for those who felt sensitive about McCarthyism the attitude of the hard-line anti-communist liberals to the niceties of the distinctions between themselves and communists was hardly likely to be reassuring. The tone of much of the rhetoric is perhaps neatly captured by Irving Kristol's blunt assertion:

There is one thing that the American people know about Senator McCarthy; he, like them, is unequivocally anti-Communist. About the spokesmen for American liberalism, they feel they know no such thing.[29]

This statement has now acquired a certain notorious immortality on the American left and, along with Kristol's involvement in partially CIA-funded organizations and magazines like the American Committee for Cultural Freedom and *Encounter*, has enabled his critics to depict his role in that era as being somewhat suspicious. (Kristol himself has denied that he ever knowingly took CIA money.) Yet given the passions of the period it is not perhaps surprising that the insensitiveness to issues of civil liberties which Kristol and others undoubtedly seemed to have exhibited should have been manifested in that way, nor that there should have been a number of efforts to subsidize organs of thought and opinion hostile to communism. What is perhaps more suprising is the embarrassment and indignation which these episodes can generate some twenty years later.

For the American intellectual community, then, the years of the 1930s and the 1950s were ones which split it into two polarized camps. Attitudes to the issues of the 1960s — Vietnam and the rise of the new left — were to some extent built on those older divisions between liberals and the right (though they also eroded such differences) and created new cleavages in the political system. Those cleavages were not, however, confined to the tightly knit intellectual community of New York writers, though they undoubtedly had a substantial impact there; the divisions also polarized the Democratic Party itself and its electorate, in a way which was to weaken the Democrats profoundly.[30]

The events of the 1960s had a substantial impact on

American universities. Direct action taken to resist the war in
Vietnam involved both students and faculty and constituted
a radical challenge to the authority of the government and the
professors. Tactics devised to resist the draft and experiments
with alternative life-styles did not prove conducive to an
atmosphere of tranquility on the campus — much less to a
sense of deference towards the faculty. Academics of a
traditional disposition therefore found that the politicization
of the campus in the 1960s had threatened some of their
deepest cultural values as well as often making their personal
positions deeply uncomfortable. Outside the universities
debate about the disturbances was extended to a wide range
of newspapers, journals, and periodicals and so reached the
general educated public; and because of the vital position
of the participants in those debates in the educational institutions of the United States, the controversies have without
doubt continued to affect the very large number of Americans who experience some kind of college education. (It is
of course a point often made by neo-conservative writers
that the 'explosion' of higher education has had a significant
effect on American politics.) Thus, while critics of neo-
conservatism such as Dennis Wrong and Michael Walzer like
to suggest that the neo-conservatives exaggerate the significance of the 1960s, there is little doubt that the experience
left its mark on a wide range of students and scholars, and
will perhaps continue to affect the operation of America's
universities.[31]

As with the challenge posed to the traditional values of
academic freedom and university autonomy, the other
themes which emerge in the writings of the neo-conservatives
must be set against the background of the disillusionment and
turbulence that characterized the 1960s. Although it does
some disservice to the rich variety of the topics which they
have tackled, five broad neo-conservative interests will be
examined in the remainder of this chapter in order to shed
further light both on the arguments which have come to
qualify as neo-conservative and on the contributions made to
political debate in the United States by individual neo-
conservatives. The themes are the defense of democratic
capitalism; the role which the federal government can properly

play in the American policy process; the topics of ethnicity, desegregation, and affirmative action; the related questions of moral values and religion; the general question of what should be America's approach to foreign policy. Some of these questions would obviously form an integral part of any political discussion in contemporary America; others reflect the special concerns of the neo-conservatives and the very real sense of despondency which many of them have expressed about the fragility of American civilization.

The Defense of Capitalism

The need to produce a theoretical justification of capitalism became apparent to many neo-conservative thinkers in the period of the 1960s, when the American political system seemed to have lost its moral basis and the appeal of varieties of Marxist and revolutionary ideologies was clearly evident in American universities. Irving Kristol acknowledged that a change had come over America when he wrote that in previous generations democratic capitalism 'felt no acute need for a theory about itself' because it could take its spiritual inheritance for granted. Kristol himself set out to remedy the evident deficiency by writing *Two Cheers for Capitalism*, which made the case for capitalism as a system which, despite obvious faults, nevertheless had succeeded infinitely better than any other feasible system in providing a combination of material wealth and personal liberty.

More recently, two authors younger than Kristol — Michael Novak and George Gilder — have produced their own distinctive defenses of democratic capitalism and attempted to fill the gap which they perceived in the writings of modern political analysts. Gilder's arguments are well set out in *Wealth and Poverty*, which as well as being a defense of capitalism has also become a part of the literature on supply-side economic thought. The arguments of Kristol and the neo-conservatives are criticized by Gilder for being too apologetic about the capitalist system:

It is a curious fact that the celebrated group of neo-conservative intellectuals, heralded as saviours of business, discuss the nature and future of capitalism in the same dolorous idiom used by some of the chastened but still assured advocates of 'socialism'.[32]

Capitalism, so far from being an unheroic bourgeois civilization, is celebrated by Gilder for its creativity and the capacity of entrepreneurs to engender wealth. And Gilder seeks to show that capitalism is not anomic but social in the way that its benefits improve the lot of everyone, and that it creates a self-sustaining culture.

Michael Novak's perspective is rather different. His book *The Spirit of Democratic Capitalism* is of major interest as a piece of neo-conservative writing because he seeks to link arguments about the desirability of capitalism with a wide range of moral and political concerns.[33] Primarily he was anxious to provide an account of democratic capitalism from a Roman Catholic perspective; the Roman Catholic Church predated capitalism and as a result had developed a set of attitudes about society which were difficult to reconcile with the reality of modern America. The Roman Catholic Church's social philosophy thus emphasized the distribution rather than the creation of wealth; it reflected a set of pre-modern attitudes to money and, in its yearning for the restoration of a sense of community, seemed suffused with the values of the medieval and feudal past rather than the present.

Democratic capitalism as described by Novak constitutes very much more than an economic system. It has in fact to be understood as a way of life. And it has to be examined as a set of institutions that operate on three planes. At the economic level democratic capitalism is characterized by a predominantly market economy; at the level of the political system it can be said to exist where the structures of government exhibit a substantial degree of respect for the individual; and on the cultural level it is reinforced by a system of institutions moved by what Novak terms the ideals of liberty and justice for all.

Clearly Novak's ambition to go beyond what he sees as Max Weber's definition of capitalism and to produce a more rounded account of the ethos of capitalism owes much to his own background as a Christian socialist with early leanings towards the Catholic priesthood. His justification of capitalism as something other than crass materialism — as an inherent part of a system which maximizes opportunities for individuals to develop their personal talents and callings — is an imaginative attempt to provide a defense of the American free-enterprise system which can both satisfy the demand for a spiritually appealing philosophy and recognize that much of the practice of modern capitalism (and government for that matter) in the West is less than inspiring.

The theory of pluralism which Novak has advanced is unambiguously incompatible with any single vision of the social order and, while as a Christian he recognizes the existence of sin in the world, he does not wish the State to try to impose virtue on its citizens. Certainly, there is a core of common, indispensable morality which must be insisted on; and Novak also believes that the political system can 'under suitable checks and balances wrest a reasonable degree of goodness, decency and compassion from less than perfect materials'.[34] What is unacceptable is any attempt to legislate either for a Utopian society or for the perfect man; and the democratic capitalism which Novak describes is 'not a system aimed at defining the whole of life'. The distinction between what it is proper for the government to do and what trespasses on the realm of the individual's private concerns is clearly an acute one for Novak. Faced with the choice between the tradition of American pluralism and any possibility that American institutions could be refashioned to reflect religious values, he firmly opts for the former and says categorically that 'Christian symbols ought not to be placed in the centre of a pluralist society'.[35]

Thus, both George Gilder and Michael Novak seek to link capitalism to the moral and political system which capitalism generates, although in Novak's case the nuances of interest are firmly rooted in the spiritual quality of society, whereas Gilder's interest seems to be in the material opportunity which dynamic capitalism provides for all citizens.

Much more could be said about the effect both of Irving Kristol's defense of capitalism and of Gilder's and Novak's writings. Suffice it to say here that these men have succeeded in producing forceful statements of the case for the Anglo-American system of democratic capitalism. While Kristol's basic defense of capitalism is somewhat pessimistic, since he acknowledges that the structure of capitalist societies is unlikely to command philosophical enthusiasm, he too lauds its ability to minimize the dangers inherent in all polities and to maximize the spiritual, economic, and personal opportunities available to all. And he is also anxious to place stress on the necessity of capitalism for a free society and its compatibility with ethical values.[36]

The Role of Government

Scepticism about the role which the federal government should play in the political system stemmed directly from the frustrating experiences of the Great Society years.[37] Even if many of the criticisms of Great Society programs were unfair or arose from unreasonable expectations about what could be achieved within so short a space of time, for many people these initiatives seemed to have resulted in the expenditure of large amounts of public money without any corresponding reduction of the ills they were designed to ameliorate. In addition, the consequent expansion of the federal bureaucracy inevitably worried those who wished to maintain a balance in the constitutional system. The questioning of whether such problems as poverty, crime, or the crisis of the inner cities could ever be solved coincided with a degree of self-doubt on the part of the social scientists who had earlier rushed to assure the federal government that their expertise could be harnessed to eliminate the social evils of modern America. The particular contribution of the neo-conservatives to the more general appraisal of the deficiencies of American social policy in the 1960s combined the use of social science data with a willingness to challenge many of the liberal assumptions of the 1960s and to approach familiar topics with what might seem at first sight a cold-hearted lack of emotional commitment. According to Irving Kristol, whose various academic and journalistic contacts make him in many ways the prime example of a neo-conservative author and who is indeed acknowledged as the 'godfather' of neo-conservatism, the problem with the Welfare State was its paternalism. Kristol, however, does not wish to allow the free market complete sovereignty in this field, since he believes in the priority of politics over economics and would presumably not wish to rule out the possibility of selective governmental intervention in welfare. For Kristol, as for many neo-conservative critics, the primary issue is the degree of governmental intervention and the efficiency with which services are provided.

From the point of view of public policy issues, Kristol's most important venture occurred in 1965 when together with Daniel Bell he founded *The Public Interest*. This was one of the first public policy journals in the field and, although it has since had many imitators — even perhaps to the point where its own role is no longer as clear as it was initially — its early quality did a great deal to set in motion a more sophisticated approach to public policy questions than had informed the 1960s. In this respect the magazine has helped to create a new consensus and a new set of concerns within the policy sciences. For some critics, of course, the scepticism about such 'problems' as poverty and inequality is destructively negative and may seem to confuse an appreciation that such matters have many dimensions and a complex causality with a preference for limited intervention and pessimism about the policy-makers' ability ever to be able to ameliorate these conditions. For others it has added a much-needed realism to the study of society and caused legislators and academics to focus not so much on the problems of framing social legislation as on the problems associated with its implementation.

Ethnicity, Desegregation, and Affirmative Action

The themes of ethnicity, desegregation, and affirmative action have been of particular concern to the neo-conservatives, and examinations of various aspects of public policy associated with this area occur throughout the pages of *The Public Interest* and *Commentary*. Nathan Glazer, one of Kristol's co-editors of *The Public Interest* and a Professor in the Department of Education at Harvard, has made a number

of important academic contributions to the understanding
of ethnicity within the United States as well as a passionate
attack on the practice of reverse discrimination.[38]

Interest in issues related to ethnic identity and racial
equality occurs in the neo-conservatives' writings for a number of reasons. First, at the most general level, the neo-
conservatives are united in believing that the categories of
race and ethnicity are at least as important as those of
class, if not more so. Thus, Daniel Bell wrote in a recent
essay:

> . . . the emphasis on class has until recently overshadowed the under-
> standing of what is today loosely called ethnicity — national, cultural,
> linguistic, religious, communal, tribal, or primordial attachments. . . .
> Today that emphasis on class is diminished.[39]

According to Bell, the reasons for the diminution in the
importance of class as a category and the resurgence of
ethnicity as a salient factor in modern politics reflect both
the changed structure of Western societies and the development of a situation in which a number of groups compete for
scarce resources in the political market-place. Moreover,
as Bell points out,

> the striking fact is that ethnicity, and historical and traditional power
> rivalries have a larger explanatory range than Marxism and class in
> understanding the bewildering conflicts between the Soviet Union
> and China, between China and Vietnam, and between Vietnam and
> Cambodia. The paradox is that Marxism, as a conceptual set of ideas,
> is of least use in explaining the internal structures and the national
> conflicts of the Communist states themselves.[40]

As analysts who wish to understand the dynamics of
contemporary society, the neo-conservatives must inevitably
pay attention to the character of ethnicity and nationalism,
although it would be hard to believe that their own ethnic
background would not in any event have alerted them to
its significance.

A second reason for the general neo-conservative interest
in ethnicity is closely related to the first one. For many
neo-conservatives a major problem of modern Western
society is its atomization. The alienated and anomic individual does not in the eyes of the neo-conservative make good

material from which to build a responsible citizenry. In order, therefore, to try to restore the sense of community, neo-conservative sociologists such as Daniel Bell and Nathan Glazer — echoing Tocqueville's arguments — want to strengthen the range of intermediate institutions and identities which may be interposed between the individual and the State, whether those identities be linguistic, ethnic, or religious. The ethnic pluralism which Bell sees an an inevitable feature of many Western societies and which is, of course, especially evident in the United States is thus turned into a force for stability. Like the doctrine of pluralism itself, the concept of ethnicity may thus acquire a normative as well as an analytic and descriptive content.

A third reason for the neo-conservative concern with race and ethnicity is the much more immediate one that racial issues have long divided American society and that, even though *de jure* segregation has largely disappeared from American life, debate continues about how best to produce greater social and economic equality between different ethnic groups. Particular controversy has raged around the demand for policies of affirmative action or positive dis-crimination in favor of disadvantaged minorities as a way of redressing the injustices caused by preexisting patterns of inequality.[41] Such policies trouble the neo-conservatives on a number of grounds, but principally because they appear to mark a dangerous movement away from equality of opportunity towards some kind of equality of outcome. Those policies also concern them because they affect the country's schools, universities, and professional training, and therefore seem to threaten academic autonomy. In addition, the fact that many neo-conservatives are Jewish makes them frequently unsympathetic to the use of quotas.

The question of affirmative action has been the subject of considerable litigation in the last decade, and the cele-brated cases of *De Funis, Bakke*, and *Weber*, so far from settling the issues, have simply underlined the problems surrounding the application of the policy of desegregation.[42] By 1983, however, Nathan Glazer, one of affirmative action's major neo-conservative critics, had to some extent mellowed on the topic, although it was not clear whether this was primarily because he believed that it had in any case run its course as a specific policy.[43]

Busing — the practice of integrating schools by transferring pupils from one school catchment area to another — has also excited considerable controversy, both among intellectuals who are sceptical about the extent to which schools contribute to or can mitigate inequality and among the general public, where the issue has often divided natural Democratic supporters from their own party.[44] In the 1980s the technique of busing remains a real option only in certain areas, such as Boston and Los Angeles, where integration within the metropolitan area is possible. However, the general topic — like that of affirmative action — raises in an acute form the clash of values between, for example, concern for locality and neighborhood control on the one hand and the more abstract goal of racial integration on the other.

It is not perhaps surprising that the neo-conservatives have been quick to point out the weaknesses of a policy which appears to run counter to the general public's view of fairness and which also appears increasingly unlikely to produce either greater equality or an improved racial climate.

One aspect of the debate about the role of minorities and the appropriate policies to be adopted in relation to them which has excited considerable passion is the question of intelligence tests and their use in education and employment. Behind the issue there obviously lurks the sensitive topic of whether some groups are inherently more 'intelligent' than others — an issue which is inevitably bedevilled by accusations of racialism whenever it is mentioned.

The trend of liberal thinking — as is evident in Supreme Court decisions and elsewhere — has been to try to reduce the role of intelligence tests as having a disproportionate impact on certain groups, but to avoid the abstract question of the relationship between race and IQ. For many neo-conservatives, on the other hand, such an approach is intellectually unacceptable and they wish to continue debating the relationship between intelligence, the environment, and group achievement in intelligence tests. As it was put in 1979, in a review of a work by Thomas Sowell (an eminent black neo-conservative economist) in *The Public Interest*:

When Sowell explains that three-quarters of all black males who fail Army mental standards come from families of four or more children, or that 52% of National Merit Scholarship finalists from five child families were first born and 6% were fifth born, he demonstrates that test scores can be a useful tool of analysis, and their politicization has meant a significant loss of useful data.[45]

Neo-conservatives would like to think that the dispassionate collection and deployment of data — regardless of their ideological implications or political sensitivity — are one of their characteristic traits and that their advocacy of objectivity in the public policy process has been one of their major contributions to American administration. Yet they are not themselves always free from ideological bias. Equally, much of their own experience suggests that, while it might in theory be desirable if all major issues of public policy were subjected to dispassionate and objective scrutiny, in reality there are some issues in the United States which are so sensitive that such a situation would be virtually impossible. And policy topics which raise questions related to race are obviously in a category which will be politically delicate whatever the academic merits or demerits of an issue — as Daniel Moynihan found when he attempted to tackle the problem of black poverty in America.[46]

Apart from the fact that Daniel Moynihan is a New Yorker of Irish extraction rather than Jewish, he does underline how wrong it is to identify neo-conservative orientations in politics with simple Republicanism. (Moynihan was, for example, a fierce critic of President Reagan's handling of the issue of social security reform.)

Moynihan, who had been educated at New York's City College (an educational institution with a special place in the intellectual history of the 1930s and 1940s), also did graduate work at Tufts and the London School of Economics. He came into contact with Irving Kristol when the latter was editor of the *Reporter* and Moynihan was contemplating a book on the political life of Governor Harriman. In 1960 Moynihan joined the Kennedy administration as an assistant to Arthur Goldberg, the Secretary of Labor, and in 1963 he was appointed Assistant Secretary of Labor in charge of the Office of Policy Planning and Research. Moynihan was

retained by Lyndon Johnson after the assassination of
President Kennedy and it was from within the Johnson
administration that he began to develop his critical perspective on the Great Society programs and especially on their
approach to the problems of poverty and the family.

Moynihan was catapulted into the center of political
controversy in 1965 when he wrote — originally, it seems,
for consumption by only a few senior officials rather than
the general public — a report on the problems faced by
blacks in the United States. He argued that those problems were extremely complex and that the nature of the
black's position within American society meant that discrimination could not be removed simply by legislative
initiatives any more than equality before the law would
produce real equality. Interestingly, by contrast with many
neo-conservatives, Moynihan at this point seemed to advocate
some form of preferential treatment for blacks in an attempt
to produce greater equality of outcome. Certainly he seemed
to feel that equality of opportunity was a rather hollow
equality, given the inability of many blacks to take advantage
of the so-called opportunities:

> . . . the evolution of American politics, with the distinct persistence of
> ethnic and religious groups, has added a profoundly significant new
> dimension to that egalitarian ideal. It is increasingly demanded that
> the distribution of success and failure within one group be roughly
> comparable to that within other groups.[47]

One indicator of black disadvantage and a contributory
cause of the syndrome in which blacks suffered dispropor-
tionately from low income, unemployment, disease, crime,
and drug addiction was family instability. Moynihan's analysis argued that 'at the heart of the deterioration of the fabric
of negro society is the deterioration of the negro family'.
Unless something were done about this situation there was,
the report argued, little hope of blacks actually taking
advantage of the opportunities made available as a result
of the civil rights movement. As commentators on the report
have noted, the document was a curious hybrid which sought
to present certain facts derived from the social sciences and
an unusual policy position which combined misgivings about

the effectiveness of legal intervention in producing racial justice with an assumption that black America's morality might be different from that of white America. What in a sense made the report controversial was the willingness of its author to discuss such sensitive issues publicly.

Moynihan's career and his approach to politics are illuminating in the attempt to understand the common concerns of the neo-conservatives and their attitudes to contemporary issues. His background gave him the belief (which is certainly shared by men like Norman Podhoretz and perhaps by all successful men of recent immigrant extraction) in the opportunities for mobility in American society and in the promise of American democracy as a system conducive to individual fulfilment. Thus, Moynihan would be unlikely to accept the criticism of the new left that American institutions were fundamentally flawed by inequality and injustice, though of course Moynihan's sensitivity to the racial problem has suggested to him the need for some substantial reforms within the system.

The Significance of Religion

A fourth theme which interests the neo-conservatives and which — as will be explored in more depth later — has come to form an important part of the ideology of the American right as a whole is the importance of religious affiliations and what, for want of a better phrase, might be called orthodox moral standards. In the Roman Catholic Church the importance of family and community loyalty, and suspicion of the over-arching State, produce a conservative disposition which may be reinforced by that Church's emphasis on authority, although in the United States, at least, the degree of authority which the Church of Rome has been able to exert has proved limited. And because of the Jewish heritage of many of the neo-conservatives, there is an inevitable interest on the part of neo-conservatives in the interrelationship between religion and politics.

It is perhaps worth stressing, however, that the way in which intellectuals such as Norman Podhoretz, Nathan Glazer, and Daniel Bell tackle the questions associated with

religion in America is very different from the approach of
what will be examined later under the headings of the 'new
right' and the 'religious right'. In these two cases there is a
desire to maximize the votes of right-of-center candidates
combined with an almost paranoid concern with certain
issues of sexual morality such as abortion and homosexuality.
In the writings of neo-conservatives (as defined in this chapter), while there is often a strong personal religious commitment, there is also a desire to expound the contribution
which religious values make to the overall health of a society.

Daniel Bell, for example, has argued that the United
States has long been affected by two contradictory impulses.
On the one hand there is the notion of self-control, which
he sees as a product of puritanism and associates with the
work ethic which is so vital to capitalism. On the other
hand, however, there is the impulse of individualism. In
the past the notion of self-control meant that profits from
industry would be invested rather than consumed. With the
decay of puritanism, however, the ethic of abstinence has
been eclipsed by the ethic of individual self-realization.
According to Bell, individualism — which might formerly
have been restrained by traditional and ascriptive ties — can
therefore no longer provide both the urge to produce profits
and the urge for self-fulfilment. It will, on his argument,
degenerate into simple hedonism and lead to a world in
which people are 'straight by day' and 'swingers by night'.[48]
Thus, there emerges in Bell's writing a concern to retain
religion as a force which can provide unity in the culture and
keep the two contradictory impulses of the post-Reformation
era in uneasy alliance. His analysis may be somewhat exaggerated and it is never clear how inevitable he believes the
erosion of religion as a major cultural force to be, or whether,
in his view, all religions will serve the purpose of cultural
solidifiers or only some of them will do so.

Bell himself has a rather unusual perception of politics and
on a number of issues he is probably not in harmony with
his fellow neo-conservatives. For while he describes himself as
a conservative with respect to culture, he says that he is a
socialist with respect to the economy and a liberal — in
American terms left of center — with respect to politics.

The centrality of culture in Bell's writings and the rejection of economic determinism offer another example of how far the neo-conservatives' approach to policy differs from that of the Chicago school. For, while Irving Kristol (for example) is adamant that no societies have been able to maintain a democratic polity while abolishing free enterprise, that in theory — if not in practice — ought to allow ample room for varieties of mixed economies. (In fact, Kristol's utterances sometimes come close to taking the unreconstructed Hayekian line that substantial amounts of planning inevitably eliminate freedom and that communism, socialism, and social democracy are sufficiently similar to make it not worth while drawing fundamental distinctions between them.) The almost exclusive emphasis on the role of the market which can be found in the writings of Milton Friedman would be quite alien to Bell, who has suggested that so far from the structure of the economy shaping the culture, it is the culture which shapes the economy. This process occurs when, for example, the culture of hedonism generates new wants and the economic order responds to them. Unfortunately, as Bell argues, the unrestrained hedonism which has been unleashed from its religious constraints has in a sense become the justification for capitalism; however regrettable the wants of the masses may be, capitalism has come to rest its claim to moral superiority on its capacity to deliver those 'goods'.

Although the tone of much neo-conservative analysis of morality and religion suggests that on some issues it is indeed censorious about the permissiveness of contemporary American society, there is a concern for tolerance and a dislike of extremism which differentiate the academic neo-conservatives from the advocates of a return to biblical morality and the virtues of American family life. Certainly, the neo-conservatives remain hostile to the counter-culture (or the counterfeit culture, as Bell called it) and there is a sense in which for all neo-conservatives the permissive society cannot be reconciled with personal responsibility. Bell, indeed — in one of the major characterizations of epochs in American society which make him both provocative to read and liable to be mocked — has commented on the significance of the counter-culture as a historic turning-point in the United States:

the rise of a hip–drug–rock culture on the popular level (and the 'new sensibility' of black mass humour and violence in the arena of culture) undermines the social structure itself by striking at the motivational and psychic reward system which has sustained it.[49]

In this sense, according to Bell, the culture of the 1960s had a new and perhaps distinctive historic meaning as an end and as a beginning. Clearly Bell found the destructive synthesis of art and politics in the 1960s disturbing, but it must not be automatically assumed from that that he would share the views of those who, for example, wish to limit the availability of books in America's schools and public libraries, although Kristol for one has made a strong case *for* the censorship of pornography.[50]

The American Role in the World

The final theme which is common to neo-conservative writing is a straightforward defense of the American role in the world and a hostility to communism in international politics.

Neo-conservatism in relation to American foreign policy contains a number of inherent contradictions of its own, and like so much else in American politics has been heavily influenced by the experience of the Vietnam War. Many of the neo-conservatives had reservations about the way successive governments handled the war, but what divided them from the more radical critics within and without the Democratic Party was their basic patriotism and loyalty to the United States even in the circumstances of a war which seemed difficult to justify. Thus, Norman Podhoretz has commented on the extent to which he was shocked by the realization that the forces of what he called the 'Movement' — the liberals and radicals who combined opposition to Vietnam with a range of adherence to the counter-culture — actually thought the United States was evil:

Not only did I reject the view that the United States was as evil in its way as Nazi Germany had been; I even objected to the idea that it was evil in any degree. That there were many things wrong with the country

I had been saying for a long time now. But *evil*? Beyond redemption? In need of and deserving to be overthrown by force and violence? I could not believe that the condition of the blacks, let alone of the young, justified any such apocalyptic verdict.[51]

Thus, for Podhoretz (as for many neo-conservatives) Vietnam was an issue which identified those who were basically anti-American both within the United States itself and in the wider international arena. Podhoretz himself is a prime example of someone whose political outlook had been shaped by the group of anti-Stalinists who wrote for *Partisan Review* in the immediate post-war period. As he himself has put it, he then acquired their contemptuous attitude towards 'liberals who were willing to apologise for the crimes of Stalin's regime, and were accustomed to falling back on a double standard of judgement in discussing the Soviet–American conflict'.[52]

The anger at the double standards used when discussing the foreign policies of the United States as opposed to those of other countries has also affected neo-conservative thinking about human rights policies and the United Nations. Daniel Moynihan's period as American Ambassador to the United Nations was important not merely because it witnessed the growing impatience of the American public with the rhetoric of anti-imperialism which Third World countries had grown accustomed to use against the United States on every possible occasion; it was also important because it saw the official American representative there making plain the adminis-tration's unwillingness to tolerate the manipulation of the institution of the United Nations against the interest either of the United States itself or of her friends, such as Israel.

This harsher and more sceptical attitude towards the United Nations and the demand for a realistic assessment of American interests in the world — as well as a desire to cut through what was seen as the cant inherent in much of the rhetoric of liberals on the subject of imperialism and the developing countries — was also expressed in the writings of Jeane Kirkpatrick. She became especially concerned with the problem of naïveté in foreign policy as a result of study-ing the results of the Carter administration's human rights policies, which in her view had brought about the downfall of regimes friendly to the United States without any tangible benefits in return. The United States, she argued, needed to wake up to the fact that democracy was a fragile plant and that truly democratic societies had been rare in the history of the world. To refuse to deal with dictators and to apply unrealistic moral standards to them was therefore misguided if the only consequence was the replacement of a dictatorship by a communist-oriented totalitarian State. For while autocracies might develop into democracies (although the process was a slow one), it was rarely the case that a country, once it had undergone a communist revolution, progressed to democracy.

Mrs Kirkpatrick's attitude towards human rights and her vigorous rejection of the notion that America need feel any sense of moral guilt about its role in the world led President Reagan, who had read her essay 'Dictatorships and Double Standards', to appoint her as Ambassador to the United Nations. Yet after Reagan took office she was not promoted, as some suggested she should have been, to be National Security Adviser when William Clark was transferred from that post in 1983; and the failure to promote her underlines the extent to which even a belligerent President will be affected by traditional foreign-policy élites.

The general neo-conservative recognition of the fact that foreign policy must be based on a realistic appraisal of the country's national interest does not answer the question of where America's self-interest lies. Neo-conservatives such as Irving Kristol have been keen to emphasize the extent to which they believe that the United States must recognize the importance of resisting the Soviet Union wherever possible, and, of course, anti-communism is a central part of the neo-conservative intellectual and ideological make-up. Yet it is never entirely clear whether the United States, in the view of the neo-conservatives, has a duty to resist communism everywhere, or whether its opposition to any expansion of Soviet influence ought to be on grounds of immediate strategic or ideological interest. Thus, from time to time even in neo-conservative circles it is argued that a realistic approach to American foreign policy makes it necessary to contemplate removing the American nuclear umbrella from Europe and removing the American troops stationed there, because America has no direct interest in the security of Europe. Such arguments are, rather confusingly, frequently combined both with exhortations to defend freedom everywhere, with force of arms if necessary, and also with a pronounced feeling of apprehension that the Vietnam experience may have signaled to America's allies and enemies alike an inability to become involved in a military engagement outside the United States itself.[53]

Realism in foreign policy also produces a peculiar problem for some neo-conservatives with respect to Israel. The justification of continued American financial, political, and military support is not simply one of American national self-interest; but writers such as Kristol and Podhoretz quite naturally do not want to question the American commitment to Israel as they do the American commitment to Western Europe.

What should be our overall assessment of the neo-conservative contribution to American political debate? The American political tradition, as has been frequently noted, has been dominated by liberalism and its attendant concepts of individualism, progress, and the pursuit of happiness. Founded on the basis of a revolution, the American political scene has therefore had little room for the variety of pessimistic conservatism which has stressed the need to order the political system so as to constrain man's evil nature. The neo-conservatives are not themselves immune from this basic American optimism, and Irving Kristol at least is well aware of the limited appeal of any conservatism which yearns for the past or celebrates a static social order. What he and his fellow neo-conservatives have sought to produce is a conservatism shorn of pessimism and a synthesis which Kristol has claimed is absolutely 'free of nostalgia'.[54] Indeed, according to Kristol it is precisely because the neo-conservatives can claim to have produced a forward-looking conservatism that its left-wing critics are driven to a 'frenzy of denunciation'.[55]

Whether or not the achievement of the neo-conservatives will be any more than the presentation of the more conservative side of the American liberal tradition remains to be seen. The combination of being able to write with the disposition of conservative theorists and yet to remain within the mainstream of American political life has made the neo-conservatives distinctive. While wishing to conserve the American way, they recognize that *laissez-faire* capitalism is not a perfect structure but a system which has adapted reasonably well to the demands made upon it; and they believe that in an unromantic and prosaic manner the bourgeois-capitalist system is likely to continue to provide a better option than any of the other systems which might be canvassed as alternatives. They realize that society's interest is sometimes going to be in conflict with that of the individual and wish to bolster the sense of civic responsibility against the rights of the individual — which they do not regard as unqualified even if such sentiments are sometimes unpopular in a constitutional system which has increasingly stressed individual rights. The neo-conservatives' marked orientation towards *American* politics has meant that they have been able to influence the intellectual climate, unlike earlier generations of conservative publicists, who so often seemed and were lonely voices crying in the wilderness. The price to be paid for that success may, alas, be that what is distinctive about them today may well be forgotten in the formulation of tomorrow's consensus.

CHAPTER II
The New Right

The neo-conservatives operate at the level of intellectual debate and policy research, rather than at the level of day-to-day political organization. Of a very different character within the coalition of the American right is a tendency which will be defined here as the 'new right'. Although the phrase 'new right' is one which has perhaps now passed into popular parlance — having first been used by Kevin Phillips in 1975 — its meaning can still give rise to confusion.[1] It is therefore essential to try to define as far as possible what is meant by the term, while bearing in mind that no single definition will be uncontentious. Clearly the term 'new right' designates a self-conscious strand within American conservative politics; but the questions of how it differs from the old right and how it relates to the neo-conservative movement and to the religious right need to be examined further.

The new right is not, of course, a party or formal organizational grouping; and in attempting to distinguish between the new right and other streams of the conservative movement one must realize that, although there are some organizational links, one is seeking to identify a distinctive style as much as an organizational base or even a coherent ideology. There are a number of groups, individuals, and foundations which would not merely be seen by most observers to constitute important parts of the new right, but which would so identify themselves. Unlike the label 'neo-conservative', which many have sought to shed, the label 'new right' has not appeared to those who wear it to be such an unfashionable badge. Moreover, it is worth noticing that there is a very important set of links between the groups and individuals of the new right — both at the individual and the organizational level — which maximizes the scope of the personalities and interests involved. In addition, the new right has deliberately sought to penetrate existing voluntary organizations and institutions in order to expand its influence.[2]

The new right can be defined as a loose movement of conservative politicians and a collection of general-purpose political organizations which have developed independently of the political parties. Such groups as Howard Phillips's Conservative Caucus, Terry Dolan's National Conservative Political Action Committee, and Paul Weyrich's Committee for the Survival of a Free Congress would obviously count as part of the new right. Also of considerable importance is the American Legislative Exchange Council, which operates primarily at the state level. Although the vast majority of elected politicians associated with the new right are Republicans, the new right and the Republican Party have a somewhat uneasy relationship, and many of the organizations which train candidates — such as the Committee for the Survival of a Free Congress — are willing to support conservative Democrats as well as Republicans.

Alongside these groups, and working in tandem with them on many projects, are a host of single-issue groups which have become more prominent in American politics in recent years.[3] Examples of single-issue groups clearly sympathetic to the new right would be the militant anti-abortion group Life Amendment Political Action Committee (LAPAC) and California state Congressman H. L. Richardson's Gun Owners of America. Interest groups have always played an important role in the American political process; what distinguishes the subspecies of new-right single-issue groups is the aims of the groups themselves and the methods which they employ.

In between the general political committees and the narrower single-issue groups are multi-purpose pressure-groups whose concerns are wider than a single issue but not as all-embracing as CSFC or NCPAC. Thus, a group such as Moral Majority would count as a new-right pressure-group with a range of concerns focused within the area of family and social issues, although some authors see it more as a distinctly American form of religious expression.[4] Because it could be seen as part of both the new right and the religious right some aspects of the Moral Majority's structure and organization are included in this chapter.

In addition to pressure-groups such as those already

mentioned, there exists a range of research institutes and think-tanks, some of them long-established, which are sometimes labeled 'new right' and have strong connections with leaders of the conservative movement and the new right. Care must be taken, however, not to over-simplify the style of these bodies. Thus, the Heritage Foundation, a Washington-based institution providing background briefs and research with a right-of-center bias, could most comfortably be placed within the new-right movement. But the American Enterprise Institute, which is rather more academic and removed from practical politics, operates in a manner akin to the Brookings Institution — i.e. predominantly as a public policy research institute. It too has close links with the Reagan administration and shares also some of Heritage's concerns and interests.

Outside Washington, the Hoover Institution for the Study of War, Peace, and Revolution (at Stanford) and the Institute for Contemporary Studies (in San Francisco) have made important intellectual contributions to the conservative movement, although neither would be counted as belonging unambiguously to the new right.

The Heritage Foundation was founded with tax-exempt status in 1973, using money from Richard Scaife (of the Mellon family) and Joseph Coors, the Colorado brewing magnate. Coors had already been involved in financing two other right-of-center research enterprises with which Paul Weyrich was associated, the Schuchman Foundation and Research and Analysis.

The Schuchman Foundation (which was named after one of the founders of Young Americans for Freedom) had apparently not developed a role for itself until Paul Weyrich, who was later to found the Committee for the Survival of a Free Congress, suggested that it be transformed into a conservative legal counterpart of Ralph Nader's public-interest group. Research and Analysis, by contrast, was the first attempt by Weyrich and Coors to found a conservative-oriented think-tank, but it failed because at that time (the early 1970s) business had not yet been drawn into political activity on a large scale.

Richard Scaife, who gave substantially more money to

establish the Heritage Foundation than Joseph Coors did, now has a long history of donations to right-wing organizations. Among other projects and institutions which he has supported since 1973 are the Hoover Institution, the Center for Strategic and International Studies at Georgetown, the Institute for Contemporary Studies, the American Legislative Exchange Council, Accuracy in Media, and the Committee on the Present Danger.[5]

The Heritage Foundation was not, it should be noticed, a comfortable ally of the Reagan administration after the victory of 1980. In addition to its provision of background briefs for Congressional staff and for Congressmen themselves, the Foundation issued a number of policy critiques of the various departments and expressed disappointment at some of the appointments of the Reagan administration.

Much debate occurred over whether the new right was really all that new or whether, in fact, it simply consisted of the personalities of an earlier generation of right-wing activists (especially those who had been active in the 1964 Goldwater campaign and in Young Americans for Freedom) dressed up in more modern and appealing clothing. Although there were elements of continuity between the new right and the old, some features of the new right made it qualitatively different from earlier manifestations of conservative activity.

In attempting to draw out what is distinctive about the new right of the 1970s, one may identify five features distinguishing it from the orthodox Republican Party (with whom relations have often been stormy), the older conservative movement, and the neo-conservatives. These are its aggressive mood of determination; its attention to organizational detail; its hostility to the existing party structure; its special agenda of issues; its populism.

The New Mood of the Right

The first characteristic of the new right which deserves to be mentioned is its determination to succeed. It is this quality which separates the younger breed of conservative activists — such as Howard Phillips and Paul Weyrich — from the older conservatism of Robert Taft or even Barry Goldwater.[6] And it also to some extent separates the new generation on the right from the more aloof and intellectual conservatism of William Buckley. The wish to transform American conservatism from what Clinton Rossiter dubbed 'the thankless persuasion' and to fashion it into a powerful ingredient in American political life at all levels of the political system has revived a number of issues — such as the teaching of evolution — and organizations once thought to be moribund.[7]

The extent to which it is possible for the right to sustain its ability to seize the intellectual and organizational initiative and to put liberalism on the defensive is a matter for speculation. Here it is necessary to note only that some of the intellectual pessimism associated with the old right has disappeared and that the change of mood has been a factor in improving its ability to recruit members, to raise funds, and to win support in elections. As Charles Moser put it in relation to conservatives within Congress (although the point is equally valid in relation to the right outside Congress), 'the chief distinction between Old Right and New Right is one of temperament and political strategy'.[8] Old-line conservatives, he argued, had been reluctant to band together, displayed 'an ingrained minority psychology of defeatism', and tended to think of themselves as 'lonely warriors fighting the liberal onslaught alone'.[9] Thus, although it seemed to many observers that the right in general and the new right in particular had lost much of its advantage in the 1982 mid-term elections, nevertheless even then the climate in which Republican candidates operated and the general mood of political debate were vastly different from those of the early 1970s.

Political Organization

A second feature of the new right which makes it distinctive is its emphasis on the details and techniques of campaigning and fund-raising. Obviously, all parties and pressure-groups must pay some attention to this, but the new right has flourished in the more fluid political atmosphere of the

1970s and 1980s. This attention to what might be called the marketing side of politics has been clearly reflected in the activities of Richard Viguerie, the direct-mail entrepreneur whose role in the new right has been central both as a specialist in direct mail and as a publisher of right-wing magazines like *New Right Report*, *Conservative Digest*, and *Political Gun News*.[10]

Richard Viguerie commented on how he determined to become the most successful direct-mail fund-raiser in the United States and how he perceived that organizational improvement, not ideas, was what the new right needed:

We had outstanding writers, debaters and public speakers like Bill Buckley, Bill Rusher, Russell Kirk. I could have tried to go that route. And I probably wouldn't have amounted to a hill of beans. I didn't have the educational background, and I was starting too late to catch up with the others who had a twenty year head start. But I realized that what we didn't have was someone who could take ideas, the writings and the books and market them to the people.[11]

Viguerie's remarks underline the perception which many young right-of-center politicians had at the time of Goldwater's defeat in 1964 — that having the correct values and policies was useless without the power to sell them to the electorate. The power to sell these ideas was, it was believed, severely limited by the liberal and Democratic bias of the media, as well as by the paucity of right-of-center journalists of the top rank and the ignorance of politicians who attempted the task.

By the use of direct mail the impediments of media distortion of conservative views and the problem of fund-raising itself could be overcome in a single shot: the message went straight to the political consumer and the money came back directly to the organization without being funneled through party sources. Direct mail as a method of political communication was not, of course, invented by the new right. Many politicians, including Henry Cabot Lodge, George McGovern, and even, at an earlier period, Woodrow Wilson, had tried mailing campaigns; but the new right has perfected it in a way which has inspired imitation in both the major parties.

Direct mail is a technique adapted from the wider world of

marketing and has several distinct advantages as well as a few disadvantages.[12] As a medium it is extremely flexible, in that it can accommodate a range of messages and slogans so that the characteristics of a particular constituency can be taken into account and exploited relatively easily. It is a medium which allows for precise measurement of impact, since the rate of return on a mailing can be counted and no other surveys have to be done to try to assess the effectiveness of an advertisement. Its major advantage, however, is that it enables the promoter of a product to reach that segment of the market in which he is interested with the maximum amount of efficiency. In order to achieve this, successful segmentation of the population must occur so that the 'constituency' to be targeted by a mailing can be isolated. Where the issues are age- or income-related, this preselection is very important because it is neither economic nor politically sensible to send mail on social security issues, for example, to those in their twenties; and the identification of likely respondents on specific topics forms an important part both of the major parties' activities in this field and, of course, of the various pressure-groups who solicit membership and money in this way.

Direct mail also allows effective saturation of a specific geographic area, which can be very useful in preparation for an election or referendum campaign. And it is possible to create an image of personal contact and communication which the more anonymous forms of advertising — 'telethons', for example — cannot do.

In addition to the advantages which the commercial world has known for some time, direct mail has special advantages for the new right and perhaps for the right in general, including the Republican Party.[13] The technique of direct mail came to seem a natural tool for new-right causes and organizations because it provided a simple way of reaching the group which the extreme right and many conservatives regard as their special constituency — the so-called 'silent majority'. It is a way of mobilizing and activating sections of society which might not normally be joiners of pressure-groups, parties, or voluntary organizations (other than their local churches, perhaps).[14] Although some research has suggested that individuals who subscribe to organizations via direct mail, as opposed to joining groups through ordinary social intercourse, do not differ greatly from individuals who participate directly in those organizations, it seems clear that the new right believed that there was a potential constituency of citizens whose resentments, fears, and concerns could be tapped by direct mail but who would probably not engage in more active politics.[15]

On one level of democratic theory a method of mobilization such as direct mail does have the benefit of spreading participation and ensuring that voices which might otherwise go unheard are taken into account by the political élites. On another level, however, it is obvious that the way in which this process occurs involves the simplification of political debates and divisions, frequently to the point of distortion. And it has been suggested that the creation of single-issue constituencies by direct mail without the need for the normal accommodation demanded by personal encounters within a voluntary association may make politics in the United States less amenable to bargaining and compromise.[16] (It is also a very different medium from television, which tends to soften and dilute political arguments because it can only be directed at a heterogeneous audience.) Certainly, much of the material used in direct mail can seem crude because the message has to be conveyed quickly; and on the right it often combines a degree of sensationalism and a message which may appear negative. Thus, for example, it was much easier to get the arguments of the anti-abortion movement across by direct mail than it was for its opponents to put their case. The anti-abortionists can shock by the use of gory pictures of aborted fetuses whereas the proponents of choice have to convey the more complex images of social problems emanating from an unwanted pregnancy.[17] And while occasionally this technique can be counterproductive — as it was in Robin Beard's 1982 race for the Senate seat in Tennessee — this aspect of the medium is sufficiently pronounced to cause concern among those who would like to raise the level of political debate in the United States.[18]

The fact that Richard Viguerie's name has become the

most famous in connection with the use of direct mail by the new right does not mean that he handles all direct mail for conservative causes. Many organizations find him too expensive, and he has been widely criticized for the share of the receipts which he is believed to take and for the fact that he may make it a condition of his contract with a candidate or organization that he keeps the copyright of the lists which he constructs for a campaign or mailing.[19] Some organizations prefer to shop around the various firms which now specialize in this field, and others experiment with their own in-house lists and packages — a practice which may become more common as the cost of the software necessary for a mailing declines.[20] One authority has pointed also to the strikingly different tactics of PACs with respect to direct-mail strategy. Some — such as the Committee for the Survival of a Free Congress — prefer a higher response from a small loyal list. Others — such as the National Committee for an Effective Congress — prefer to keep a much larger list. And not all PACs rely to the same extent on direct mail for their funding and publicity.[21] Until 1983 Stephen Winchell Associates handled much of the direct mail of the Republican National Committee and also acted as direct-mail consultant for new-right groups such as Gun Owners of America and the California Law and Order Committee.[22] Another important direct-mail consultant on the right is Bruce Eberle, whose firm (Bruce Eberle and Associates) did the mailings for the 1976 Citizens for Reagan Committee, for Jeffrey Bell's new-right challenge in the 1978 New Jersey Senatorial primary, and for a range of conservative-oriented groups, including those opposed to SALT II.[23]

The use of direct mail has particular significance in states, such as California, where it takes a great deal of organization to get propositions on to the ballot and where referendums, initiatives, and recalls are frequent. There the firm of Butcher–Forde, which specializes in direct mail but is not exclusively Democratic or Republican in orientation, handled the direct-mail solicitations for both Howard Jarvis's Proposition 13 and the later attempt by Jarvis to broaden the initiative into a major tax reform movement.[24]

The significance which direct mail has acquired has

depended upon the development of a number of sophisticated computer and word-processing facilities. This technology became readily available only in the 1970s, but the impact would not have been as great had it not been for the reforms of the election laws and campaign procedures following Watergate.[25]

It is not necessary here to describe in detail the changes which were brought about by the Federal Election Campaign Act of 1971 and its subsequent amendments (especially the 1974 amendments); but it is necessary to provide some idea of their provisions because they have shaped the environment in which the political parties operate and have to a large extent determined the tactics of the new right. Without a basic appreciation of this aspect of the American electoral scene it would be difficult to understand quite why the techniques of direct mail and organizations such as NCPAC have enjoyed such success — at least in 1978 and 1980.

The legislation of the early 1970s was designed to control both the extent to which rich individuals could influence the political process by funding candidates or parties and the way in which money was spent.[26] Although the legislation has not worked in quite the way envisaged by the drafters of the electoral reforms, it has introduced greater openness into the system and made candidates, pressure-groups, and parties more conscious of the politics of fund-raising.

The Federal Election Campaign Act made a crucial distinction between contributions and expenditures and strictly regulated contributions to candidates and their authorized committees. Individual contributions to candidates were limited to $1,000, which had the immediate effect of excluding many of the old-fashioned 'fat cats' from a large part of the political scene and making it imperative especially for the parties, but also for individual candidates, to find ways of raising money in smaller amounts. The technique of direct mail was perfect for this task.

Direct mail has been used both by individual candidates and pressure-groups to broaden the base of the Republican Party so that the number of financial donors to the GOP has risen from some 34,000 in the early 1970s to over a million in 1980, if the contributions to the Republican

National Committee, the Senatorial Campaign Committee, and the Congressional Campaign Committee are added together.[27] Moreover, for 1980 the average individual contribution was \$26 — a figure which makes it easier for the Republican Party to present itself as the people's party rather than the tool of entrenched interests.

The features of direct mail which make it an odd and often suspect method of political campaigning may have more to do with the success of the right in using it than with its intrinsic defects. Nevertheless, it demands very little contact between the candidate and the direct-mail consultant. Larry Sabato has reckoned that it is not 'too unusual for the consultant never to meet the candidate at all'.[28] As a result some material must go out in the candidate's name which is either not tailor-made to his appeal or over which he has little control. Secondly, direct mail is unusual because 'a good financial balance sheet counts for more than winning'.[29] Therefore direct-mail consultants have no embarrassment as a result of advising losing candidates or being associated with challengers rather than incumbents or with hitherto novel or obscure organizations.

This aspect of the industry has inevitably made it well suited to the challenges mounted by the new right in the late 1970s. Thus, the National Right to Work Committee (which was founded in 1954–5 to oppose the legalization of the closed shop and has substantial links with an earlier generation of conservative activists) used direct mail to promote anti-union causes; and the American Security Council (which was organized to promote a more assertive defense policy) used it to promote its views on SALT and American defense policy.[30]

The ability to cope with candidates who may lose sorts well with the somewhat shrill, negative messages of much of the new right — or the anger of the neglected majority, depending on one's perspective. Larry Sabato, who has written one of the most illuminating books on political consultants, quotes William Lacy of Eberle Associates in support of the theory that many direct-mail consultants may actually *prefer* working for challengers as opposed to incumbents, and that consequently the medium has a built-in negative message:

In most cases in conservative direct mail, the strategy must be a negative one directed at the incumbent. We like to go with challengers . . .
With challengers you can really take out after an incumbent.[31]

The debate about the merits and demerits of direct mail
will doubtless continue, but at this point it is necessary only
to note its usefulness to the new right in the recent past and
the fact that it has produced (albeit sometimes against the
candidate's interests or wishes) a degree of nationalization
in political contests because it facilitates out-of-state contributions. The recognition of the right's advantage in relation
to direct-mail fund-raising and solicitation led to changes in
the Democratic National Committee, which under Charles
Manatt started to restructure the direct-mail facilities available to Democratic candidates at all levels.[32]

Direct mail is not, of course, the only development in the
field of election technology which has aided the new right,
nor the only product of the new political landscape created
by the reforms in electoral law which had unintended consequences. The whole importance of political consultants
and pollsters has been enhanced by the decentralization of
candidacies and elections which occurred in the early
1970s; and, while there may have been a slight shift back
to a more centralized party system (which may become even
more necessary if the costs of fighting an election become
prohibitive), the general trend over the last fifteen years
has certainly been towards a fragmentation of elections.

From the perspective of the new right the most significant
change has perhaps been the increase in the role of PACs,
which have been transformed from being primarily an instrument whereby organized labor entered the political process
into one by which corporations and single-issue groups can
play a decisive part in the political arena.

A Political Action Committee is either a connected PAC
with a 'separate segregated fund' into which a corporation,
labor union, or trade association can transfer money for
political purposes; or it is an independent 'self-sustaining
organization'. The ideological and single-issue PACs of the
new right are mostly independent and cannot use the funds
of other bodies for their administrative costs, whereas the

'separate segregated funds' may be supported by their parent organizations.[33] (Before the Federal Election Campaign Act of 1971 it was theoretically illegal for corporations to give money to candidates under the Corrupt Practices Act of 1925, although of course business did use its wealth to influence political matters.) Connected PACs may solicit only from their own membership lists; the non-connected PACs (which are the ideological single-issue or multi-issue groups) can go beyond those lists for financial support.

Political Action Committees may support candidates, and while, as has been mentioned, an individual may give only $1,000 to a candidate, he may give $5,000 to a multi-candidate PAC. Corporate PACs — for example, those formed by businesses or large law firms — tend to distribute their campaign money primarily to incumbents on the assumption that they will thereby achieve access to decision-makers. Although the Heritage Foundation's President, Edwin Feulner, has suggested that business has gradually become more willing than previously to put its money where its ideological heart lies, even if that means giving to Republican *challengers*, it may be difficult to justify this use of money to share-holders.[34]

One important aspect of the role of the PACs which was not envisaged by the framers of FECA has been the use of the so-called 'independent expenditure loophole'. It was foreseen that many PACs might want to spend money on their own account to promote or defeat particular candidates or causes without necessarily coordinating that expenditure with a candidate, his authorized committee, or a political party. However, the original legislation set limits on the amount which could be spent in this way. But in 1976, in a major constitutional case — *Buckley* v. *Valeo* — the Supreme Court struck down such limits, so that where money is spent with no direct linkage between the candidate and the PAC no effective spending limits apply.[35]

The independent expenditure provision obviously gives a very great advantage to candidates whose positions on certain issues might mobilize a range of wealthy PACs in their election races; and it has proved extremely important to the new right because many of the wealthy non-connected

PACs fall firmly within its ambit. Indeed, in 1982 five out of the top ten PAC spenders were acknowledged elements of the new right. However, in some of the most notorious recent examples of out-of-state intervention by PACs the candidates who were allegedly being helped by PAC activity did in fact try to reduce or remove it.[36]

The figure for the amount of money received and distributed by PACs varies from election to election. But there is also a marked imbalance between incumbent and challenger. In 1978 the average Congressman got 27 per cent of his money from PACs, whereas the average challenger received only 13 per cent of his cash from this source.[37]

The new right proved adept at developing new skills to fit the new environment of politics of the 1970s and at exploiting loopholes in laws designed to prevent electoral unfairness and to ameliorate some of the worst excesses caused by the role of money in American politics. The attention which the new right devoted to these matters was also mirrored in the ability of entrepreneurs such as Paul Weyrich and Terry Dolan to manipulate the various tax laws which determine whether or not a group qualifies for tax-exempt status and whether donations are tax-deductible. Undoubtedly some of the ways in which these groups treated the laws and some of their activities bordered on the illegal, just as there were claims that contacts between independent PACs and candidates in fact occurred. (People for the American Way in 1983 suggested that at the time of spending money in an election PACs should have to reveal to the FEC against whom the effort was directed.[38]) Certainly, the loophole in the election law made possible the extensive expenditure by NCPAC in 1980 in a number of Senate races, which in effect helped the Republican challengers. Theoretically, independent expenditure could be used to promote or to oppose a candidate; the important point is that it must not be tied to a candidate's organization. In practice the greatest political controversy was generated by *negative* expenditures — money spent to blacken a candidate's reputation. Intervention by groups prepared to use this tactic became increasingly unwelcome to the candidates who stood to benefit. Dan Quayle of Indiana, James Abdnor of

South Dakota, Charles Grassley of Iowa, and Steve Symms
of Idaho in 1980 all repudiated NCPAC tactics, although
with varying degrees of anger; and none found the new
right's presence as counter-productive as Laurence Hogan
did in Maryland in 1982.[39]

Attitudes to the Two-party System

A third feature of the new right which must be borne in
mind in trying to distinguish it from its predecessors is that
it is hostile to existing parties and to the established party
system. Quite clearly, a majority of the candidates whom
the new right supports are Republicans but the new-right
leaders owe no loyalty to the Republican Party as such.
Richard Viguerie revealed his feelings about the GOP in
1976 when he remarked that the Republican Party was
going to be as difficult to sell as the Edsel or Typhoid Mary:

> The Republican Party is like a disabled tank on the bridge impeding
> the troops from crossing to the other side. You've got to take that
> tank and throw it in the river.[40]

It is thus their own brand of populist conservatism and
their own agenda of causes which the new right wished to
promote, and its tactic was to try to build coalitions across
existing party lines and around salient single issues and
causes. Obviously party loyalty — much less party cohesion
within Congress — has never been as strong a factor in American politics as it has been in Britain. And the recent explosion of PACs, political consultants, direct mail, and
single-issue groups has to some extent weakened the role
of the two major parties even further, although in the period
since 1976 there has been some evidence of a recrudescence
of party activity. The new right's initial emphasis on putting
together coalitions of like-minded single-issue groups and on
providing all manner of electoral services for ideologically
compatible candidates was a rational and pragmatic response
to a new political environment in which the national party
committees were not fulfilling the needs of individual candidates. Equally it was a result of dissatisfaction that occurred
within the Democratic Party in particular because of the

trend towards greater internal party democracy and the 'new politics', and because of those whom Jeane Kirkpatrick called the 'anti-war, anti-growth, anti-business, anti-labor activists'. These developments had left some formerly stalwart Democrats without a comfortable party base.[41]

The element of distrust of the established parties which is to be found within the new right does, however, go even deeper than a simple perception that in conditions of party dealignment there might be room for a new conservative movement. For there is in the outlook of the new right a certain degree of paranoia and a resentment of existing political élites. The belief — perfectly illustrated in Paul Weyrich's attitudes — is that the regular Republican Party will always try to play down ideological issues in the interests of pragmatism, and this belief pervades much of the new right. Paul Weyrich himself has commented on the difficulty which he experienced when as an aide to Senator Allott of Colorado he tried to persuade the Senator to make busing an issue in his campaign.[42] According to Weyrich, he wanted Allott to 'get out front' in opposing the use of busing but Allott ignored the advice and ultimately lost. Similarly, at an earlier date, when the Supreme Court was handing down its decisions on school prayer, Weyrich (who was then a young reporter in Wisconsin) telephoned Claude Jasper, the State Chairman of the Republican Party, to see whether any partisan mileage could be made from the issue. The reaction of Jasper was apparently one of stunned surprise, since in his view the Republican Party did not get involved in such issues. The explanation of why the Republican Party shuns such themes as school prayer and busing is, for a man with Weyrich's background, heavily dependent on the party's social composition. In Weyrich's opinion the Republican Party is still too much under the domination of the groups and interests whose primary motivation in politics is economic; 'value-related' issues, he would argue, appeal above all to the ordinary man, the individual who feels that his neighborhood school and his community are threatened by the federal bureaucracy and who believes in the preservation of local control of governmental activities wherever possible.

Distrust of the regular Republican Party has on occasion prompted some members of the new right to flirt with the idea of an independent third party. In 1976 Richard Viguerie actually pronounced that the Republican Party was dead and threw his weight behind the American Independent Party — even going so far as to seek the vice-presidential nomination on the American Independent Party ticket. Shortly after the 1976 presidential election, however, he admitted that such ventures were unlikely to succeed in the context of a United States in which the two major parties wrote much of the states' election law. And although subsequent disappointments with the Reagan administration kept the idea afloat, it may generally be assumed that the new right will for all practical purposes be working through the established parties even if it is not entirely of them.

The appearance of Ronald Reagan as a real contender for the Presidency in 1980 gave the new right (initially, at least) a highly acceptable candidate. Although the new right had preferred other standard-bearers of their cause, Reagan seemed to espouse many of their values; and he did not come from the Eastern Establishment breed of Republican politicians epitomized by George Bush (who was loathed for his social style) and, in an earlier generation, Nelson Rockefeller (who was loathed for his political liberalism). In terms of Kirkpatrick Sale's rather pithy nomenclature, Reagan was very much the cowboy pitted against the patricians and yankees who had dominated the GOP for so long.[43] And, as the *National Journal* noted, Ronald Reagan was willing to acknowledge the movement behind him as a conservative and principled one when he became the first President to address a conference of conservatives and talked of their common cause as 'truth-seekers'.[44]

The enthusiasm for Reagan was not, however, total. Other right-wing Republicans had greater appeal — for example, Philip Crane and John Connally; but it was recognized that in Reagan the new right had a candidate who came nearer than most of the others to their positions and who could win. After his election, however, the new right showed an element of self-destructiveness and sectarianism which has perpetually marked much of the thinking and testimony of the American conservative movement. It was thus not long before the claim was heard that the Reagan administration (and the President's own true political values) were being undermined and betrayed by his personal staff — most notably James Baker and Pendleton James, who had special responsibilities in the White House for personnel and appointments. By 1982 it was clear to many in the conservative movement that, while they could expect rhetoric from the President, they could not necessarily expect support for their pet projects, especially action on the divisive social issues which they thought so important.

The cause of the disillusionment was explained differently by different critics. The initial selection of members of the administration had itself been a matter of considerable controversy. In order to assist the formation of a right-oriented administration, carefully constructed lists of reliable conservatives (including a resource bank of a thousand right-of-center academics) had been prepared by the Heritage Foundation, but were soon ignored by the transition team and the staff close to the center of the new Administration. (There were also some very public fights of political significance between what looked like the ideological and the pragmatic sides of the Reagan team — for example, between William van Cleave and Caspar Weinberger.[45]) The administration itself included in key posts a number of individuals whose ideological credentials were either unknown or suspect. As it was put at the end of 1981 by Richard Holwill, the compiler of the Heritage Foundation's series of reviews of the administration's accomplishments:

The reason for the Administration's failure to accomplish more in the first year is surprisingly consistent from department to department and from agency to agency — personnel.[46]

And Willa Johnson noted in the same volume:

Political sensitivity was also a major element lacking in the personnel staff. Early consultation with members of Congress could have avoided many problems and 'holds' placed on nominees in the Senate. The individual assigned to provide political guidance and alert the personnel staff to potential confirmation problems in the Senate was circumvented during the transition and did not go to P.P.O. (Planning and Personnel Office).[47]

Yet other commentators have noted the extent to which the Reagan administration used the appointments at its disposal to inculcate a new philosophy throughout the administration.[48]

The first year of the Reagan administration was inevitably dominated by economic strategy and foreign policy, and the desire to support the new President seemed for a while to produce an unusual cohesion among Senate Republicans. Much of this cohesion, it is true, was on the economic issues and depended on the skill of Senate leader Howard Baker in keeping the more divisive social issues off the agenda. The occasionally difficult legislative maneuver — for example, the sale of AWACS to Saudi Arabia — was a useful reminder to the White House that even in a honeymoon period the President could not count on an automatic party vote for his proposals.

However, as the second and third years of the administration approached, a number of factions both in and out of Congress became suspicious that their special concerns and interests were again to be ignored and the conservative quality of the administration had been lost. So concerned did some of them become about the fear of betrayal that on 1 February 1982 six representatives of the new right and the conservative movement insisted on a meeting with President Reagan at the White House.

The groups which came together at the White House that month represented a number of different strands in American right-wing and conservative politics; what was common to all was the suspicion — so marked a feature of the new right — that the interests of the regular Republican Party would take precedence over their own causes. John Lofton was present as the editor of *Conservative Digest*, a glossy magazine published by Richard Viguerie which has become in some ways the house organ of the new right. John O'Sullivan and Edwin Feulner were there from the Heritage Foundation to put their criticisms of the administration's policies (Feulner, prior to becoming President of the Heritage Foundation, had worked for the Republican Study Committee, a pressure-group within the House of Representatives which was formed to promote right-of-center policies among

Congressmen and to organize the right wing of the party there; John O'Sullivan, before becoming editor of Heritage's *Policy Review*, had been a leader-writer for the British *Daily Telegraph*; in 1983 he returned to Britain to become that paper's Deputy Editor.)

In addition to these personalities of the new right there were present men who reflected a somewhat older style of conservatism. Tom Winter and Alan Ryskind were respectively the editor and political correspondent of *Human Events*, a small-circulation newspaper which had presented a critique of liberal policies and attitudes since long before the conservative revival associated with the new right and Reaganism. *Human Events* had been founded by Frank Hanighen, Felix Morley, and William Henry Chamberlin in 1944, when conservative politics were very much a minority intellectual position; and although it still has a very small circulation its influence within the tightly knit world of Washington conservatives has grown steadily, so that at one point it was described by President Reagan as his favorite reading. Also at the White House meeting was M. Stanton Evans — another link with an earlier generation of conservatives and a man who as a prolific writer had sought to organize conservative schools of journalism to counter the influence of the liberal media.

The primary complaint of these representatives of the new and less-than-new right was the extent to which Reagan's appointments had been biased against what they saw as 'real' conservatives. Of special cause for concern was the apparent vetoing of William van Cleave as head of the Arms Control and Disarmament Agency and the alleged failure to eliminate elements of what was termed 'Kissinger-style détentist thinking' from the State Department. True to the suspicion of betrayal from within, the source of these failures was once again seen as the White House staff, and in particular James Baker.

A New Issue Agenda

The fourth feature which characterizes the new right, exhibiting a different quality from older right-wing organizations and causes, is its concern with a highly charged set of domestic issues, which are different in kind from those which used to excite the indignation of American conservatives. This is not to say that the New American right does not still become anxious about the threat of communism, whether at home or abroad; nor does it mean that it no longer believes in capitalism and the free market. What is important is the extent to which the new right has expanded the agenda of its concerns to include a number of moral and social issues — 'family issues', as they are sometimes called — which have not usually been explicit themes in conservative political argument in America. Much of the history of American conservatism has been the history of reaction to dislocative social change or the perception of a threat to existing ways of life; but during the period 1945–74 the right had seemed preoccupied with the more pressing concerns of economic and foreign policy and had appeared to accept a degree of change in the climate with respect to issues of personal morality.[49]

The clearest possible indication of the divisions which exist between the new and the old right was given under the Reagan administration when in 1981 Barry Goldwater (a long-time hero of both the new and the old right) and Sam Hayakawa opposed Jesse Helms's social agenda because it contained items which they regarded as intrusions by the State into the private affairs of the individual citizen. Yet Paul Weyrich, among others, has emphasized the extent to which the new right believes that it is a mistake for any party — especially the Republican Party — to become the prisoner of economic issues. For on this argument, while an administration must clearly take a stand on economic policy and will be greatly affected by the course of economic recovery, if it stakes its reputation on economic achievement it may fail electorally and will certainly be vulnerable, whereas a more broadly based one might succeed in riding out the storms of a recession.

The emphasis on family or social issues which characterized the new right in the 1970s was in part a response to the perceived permissiveness of an earlier decade. But it has also had the effect of involving religious leaders much more directly in

American political life and of opening arguments about the
extent to which the United States is a society whose social
norms should rest on biblical precepts as opposed to being
a pluralist society based on the constitutional separation of
Church and State.

For the leaders of the new right, the social issues fitted
perfectly into their strategies for mobilizing new groups and
realigning older constituencies in a number of different
ways. Sensitive social issues such as abortion or the right
of homosexuals to teach in schools can be used to mount
direct-mail campaigns which both raise money and produce
excellent publicity. Hard-hitting negative campaigns can
be conducted around such issues in races at the federal
and state levels of politics. The more familiar themes of
foreign policy and the economy are not so easy to exploit
in the search for funds or the attempt to oust an incumbent
— except perhaps when an issue like the return of the Panama
Canal presents itself. But almost all Americans will react
to campaigns which mention the 'destruction of innocent
life', the control of pornography, the defense of the family,
and, in a slightly different sphere, the issues of law and
order and busing. And indeed it was in the very reluctance
of the two regular parties to use these issues that the new
right found a vacuum to be filled, because new-right spokesmen have argued that it is precisely on these issues that the
legislative élite and the mass public are at odds and that the
public most needs to make its voice heard.

Equally, the concentration on family and social issues
had the advantage of encouraging mobilization at the grass-
roots level. Indeed, this aspect of the new right's agenda
and tactics is perhaps in the long term the most significant,
although in some ways the easiest for the student of American politics to overlook — focused as he often is on the
developments within Congress and Washington. For while
it is relatively easy to see a reversal of Republican Party
fortunes at the national level and to envisage the loss of the
White House to a resurgent Democratic Party, the conservative tide at the grass roots may be much more difficult to
stem. Nor is it merely a question of gains which conservatives
have made at the state legislative level — important though

these are, especially in a climate where the balance of constitutional power is likely to move back towards the states
and where issues such as reapportionment are concerned.
There has been a change of style in many of the state parties
as a result of a harder and more ideological input into the
Republican Party. In California, for example, some saw a
change of character in the state GOP in the late 1970s,
reflecting in part the impression made on Republicans by
the passage of Proposition 13 and the rise of law-and-order
issues. In Alabama and Alaska state Republican parties found
themselves infiltrated by the Moral Majority. School boards
have found themselves the target of new-right organizations
throughout the United States, especially where issues such
as busing, textbook selection, creationism, and the imposition of sex education in the schools were concerned. The
issues associated with the control of textbooks and the
removal from public libraries of books deemed offensive
by some pressure-groups have also become inflammatory.
Indeed, one case about textbook censorship actually reached
the Supreme Court.

The reasons for banning and burning books vary, as do
the organizations concerned with cleansing American class-
rooms of suspect literature. Explicit sexual material attracts
opposition, as does any book which seems to undermine
parental authority or religious beliefs. Particularly vulnerable
are works which seek to promote questioning of values,
whether they be political or moral. Homosexual writers are
deemed a source of impurity, and one organization called
Save Our Children invited parents to fight to remove from
the classroom such authors as Tennessee Williams, Hans
Christian Andersen, Emily Dickinson, Willa Cather, and,
somewhat bizarrely, John Milton.[50] Although many of
these attempts at mobilization seem to be at a relatively
low level, they have several advantages for the new right.
They appear to organize the community on behalf of its
own values rather than those of either an alien bureaucracy
or a suspect secular humanism.[51] They attract less opposition
than that aroused by the more visible national campaigns on
abortion and school prayer, and can sometimes succeed before
the 'enemy' even realizes that a campaign is in progress. They

have the advantage of politicizing groups in the community and identifying conservatives who, once integrated into the political process, will be available for action on behalf of other conservative causes. And they provide further names of potential donors via direct mail for the whole range of issues on which the right wishes to campaign.

One organization in the new-right spectrum deserves special mention because of its concentration on state-level politics — namely, the American Legislative Exchange Council. It was originally established by familiar figures in the conservative movement, especially M. Stanton Evans of the American Conservative Union, Edwin J. Feulner of the Republican Study Committee and later the Heritage Foundation, and Paul Weyrich. Just before the 1980 presidential elections the executive director was Kathy Teague, who was also chairman of Paul Weyrich's Free Congress Research and Education Foundation. Among its activists there are prominent members of the new right with a range of links into other groups. H. L. (Bill) Richardson, who had attempted to beat Alan Cranston in the 1974 California Senate race, was director of ALEC for a period, and has founded Gun Owners of America — a more extreme version of the NRA defending the right to possess hand-guns and other firearms — as well as the Gun Owners of California and the California Law and Order Committee. Morton Blackwell, who became President Reagan's religious liaison officer, has long been associated with Weyrich's weekly luncheons to discuss foreign policy. And many other leading ALEC figures have been associated at the state level with the campaigns to defeat ERA and to alter the philosophy and practice of public education.[52]

The way in which ALEC has raised its money and its general strategy illustrate many of the points already made about the devotion to organizational detail and its ability to capitalize on social issues. Much of ALEC's fund-raising has been done by Mike Thompson of Thompson and Associates, who — apart from being an early activist in Young Americans for Freedom, like Richard Viguerie — has handled the direct mail for many of the groups opposing SALT II and for the campaigns on the right-to-work issue. ALEC's supporters include donors to other new-right causes — among them Joseph Coors, the Scaife Foundation, and the Eli Lilly Foundation.

An interesting feature of ALEC is its tactic of suggesting bills to state legislatures; details of suggested state bills are contained in a regular publication, *Suggested States Legislation*. In 1977–8 bills were apparently selected and drafted by a special ALEC committee and covered such topics as abortion, a requirement for free-enterprise education in schools, and the testing of public-school teachers for basic competence. Other proposals were resolutions by which state legislatures could condemn the Panama Canal Treaties (although of course these legislatures have no jurisdiction in the matter) and constitutional amendments on issues such as the level of state taxation.[53]

These 'suggested state legislation books' were sent free to every state legislator in the country, as was H. L. Richardson's briefing book on a proposed amendment to make Washington, DC, a full state. Apparently, while the new-right connections of ALEC might have been obvious to many commentators, some legislators were then sufficiently innocent to think that it was a neutral organization analogous to the Council of State Governments and the National Conference of State Legislatures. Indeed, a group of Democratic–Farmer–Labor Party representatives from Minnesota were apparently sent by their legislature in 1978 to an ALEC session in Carmel, California, to look for new ways to administer welfare programs more cheaply without reducing the benefits. Needless to say, they were surprised and shocked to discover the true character of ALEC, which, as one study put it, turned out on this occasion to be running 'nothing more than a campaign school for far right political candidates' and was graced by the presence, *inter alios*, of Philip Crane and Lyn Nofziger.[54] The tapping of the issues which are important at the American grass roots and among the American silent majority echoes an earlier Republican interest in exploiting the latent divisions within the ranks of traditional Democratic voters.

In addition to the work of the American Legislative Exchange Council, the Free Congress's *Initiative and Referendum*

Report provides further evidence of the importance attached
to state- and local-level politics. By 1979 ALEC was reckoned
to have some 10 per cent of the nation's state legislators as
members, although, as has already been suggested, many
more are bombarded with its literature.

Interestingly, the Moral Majority has proved far less
successful in establishing strong state and local organizations.
When it was first formed the intention was to set up a viable
organization in every state, but the effort seems to have had
mixed results. By the middle of 1981 it claimed the affiliation of 100,000 clergy of various denominations and a
membership of 4 million. But studies of local Moral Majority
activity reveal an overwhelming dependence at local and
state level on Baptist pastors and very little evidence of
professional full-time political organization. In 1981 Charles
Cade, the field director of Moral Majority, suggested that
sixteen states had effective Moral Majority branches, but he
seemed to concede that elsewhere the impact of the group
was marginal.

One aspect of the Moral Majority's organizational structure
which seems to cause it difficulty in the development of
effective political organization is precisely this reliance on
highly independent Baptist pastors who offer the opportunity of access to local communities, but who can resist
any attempt at national control. Daniel Fore in New York
caused embarrassment because his views seemed to verge
on anti-Semitism, and the Maryland state organization had
to be repudiated when its leaders undertook a campaign to
prosecute a local baker whose major offense was the sale of
lewd biscuits and cakes. As the Executive Director of Moral
Majority put it in 1982, the problem of organizational
'incontinence' (*sic*) was one which the group had not completely solved.[55]

The issues which state and local Moral Majority organizations have taken up vary with local circumstances. Moral
Majority members and organizations have been in the forefront of book-banning campaigns and of anti-abortion
efforts focused on the state legislatures. In California and
New York the state groups have been energetic in their
efforts to repel the drive for homosexual rights. And in

Indiana, where Birch Bayh was defeated in 1980 after a long tenure in the Senate (during which he was associated with the drive to amend the constitution to give equal rights to women), the state Moral Majority has been pressing a long legislative agenda including the repeal of the state's child abuse laws and the reinstatement of its laws against sodomy. (Indiana — described by two recent authors as a microcosm of what America once was — repealed its laws against inter-racial marriage only in 1964.[56])

Populism

Linked to the emphasis on grass-roots issues is the final feature of the new right which distinguishes it from other elements of the American political spectrum, namely, the element of populism which so clearly colors new-right thinking and activity. The term 'populist' is notoriously difficult to define, and in American politics it has frequently been pointed out that there is a populism of the left — associated with the progressive era — as well as a populism of the right, which could be associated with the politics of Senator Joe McCarthy as well as with the tradition of southern demagogues exemplified by Huey Long and George Wallace.

Richard Hofstadter highlighted what he called the paranoid style in American politics, and mention has already been made of the fear of betrayal which exists in some sections of the new right. There is little doubt that on the new right there is indeed both a suspicion of existing established insti-tutions — including the two major parties — and an element of hatred of those tendencies in modern society which appear both threatening and different to the new right, be they intellectuals, foreigners, homosexuals, or communists. Politics is seen in absolute terms, not as a pragmatic activity about which reasonable men may differ. Conspiracy is never very far away and will usually involve plots between the 'Eastern Establishment', the Council on Foreign Relations, the Trilateral Commission, and the Rockefellers.

Both Richard Viguerie and Paul Weyrich make a certain amount of capital out of their relatively humble origins and lack of attainment in higher education; and Weyrich constantly reiterates the point that the Republican Party is still too responsive to the 'values of the country club' rather than to the values of the 'man who lives at the end of the subway line'. Thomas McIntyre, himself a victim of new-right tactics in New Hampshire, has highlighted the extent to which 'home town America' embodies the culture which the new right wishes to restore, but even he cannot entirely condemn that culture.[57] Certainly, the new right sees its appeal as being potentially very strong among the lower-middle-class Americans, whose status and ethnic origins frequently seem to demand a reassertion of their authenticity by explicit rejection of anything which could be classed as 'un-American'.

The populist sentiments and background of many new-right leaders differentiate them even from the cosmopolitan conservatism of figures on the right such as William Buckley (who founded the Young Americans for Freedom, which gave so many new-right leaders their entry into right-wing politics), and clearly divide them from the old established Republican families such as the Scrantons and the Tafts.

The populism which characterizes new-right politics is also to be found in the style of many of the Churches and religious groups which have integrated a fundamentalist or conservative evangelical form of Christianity with a right-wing political message. Indeed, a recent study of the so-called electronic Church (the pastors who use television and radio to communicate their political message) found that all the major television preachers, with the exception of Robert Schuller, drew a disproportionate percentage of their audience from the South and that the next most hospitable region for these preachers was the mid-West. These areas are, of course, the traditional home of American populism, and the appeal in such places of men like Jerry Falwell, Oral Roberts, and Rex Humbard is not perhaps surprising. This continuing strand of the American political tradition has long troubled observers. Thus, for example, David Danzig drew attention in 1962 to the 'inherently conservative bent' of fundamentalism and argued that it had been reinforced by local factors:

In Bryan [William Jennings], as later in Huey Long, the hatred of finance capitalism or 'Wall Street' by a rural population could produce the reforming spirit of Populism without apparently liberalizing the impacted prejudices of fundamentalist social attitudes.[58]

The important point is the congruence of religious and political fundamentalism in the creation of an outlook which characterizes both the new right and the religious right. As two authors have recently said about media religion (although it could as easily apply to the new right across the board):

To fundamentalists, the world is one giant battleground for the struggle between good and evil, which rages in all realms: moral, religious, social, spiritual and political. There is no room in fundamentalism for differing social perspectives or political systems. *Compromise is sin.*[59]

The new right in politics has the veneer of modernity because it has taken advantage of the new election technology and has no difficulty with either the operation or the fruits of modern American capitalism. Beneath the surface, however, there are ideas and attitudes with a very long pedigree in United States history.

CHAPTER III

The Religious Right

Prominent among the concerns of the group of neo-conservative intellectuals and new-right groups as discussed in the previous chapters have been the interlocking themes of religion, morality, and culture. However, the treatment which is accorded to these issues by men such as Daniel Bell, Irving Kristol, and Michael Novak is different from the kind of consideration accorded them by groups such as Moral Majority, National Christian Action Coalition, Religious Roundtable, and Christian Voice. The growing political involvement of religious sects and Churches with right-of-center political pressure-groups, candidates, and causes in the United States has attracted a good deal of journalistic coverage and some short polemical studies.[1] As yet, however, it has been the subject of relatively little scholarly investigation; and such writing as there has been in the area by political scientists has tended to concentrate on the electoral impact which religion and religious groups might have had — especially in relation to Ronald Reagan's 1980 presidential victory and the defeat of certain liberal Senators in that year.[2]

The electoral significance of religious affiliation is important and the perception that the new right might be able to mobilize conservative evangelicals and fundamentalists on behalf of its campaigns has been a powerful factor in drawing certain Churches and church leaders more directly into the political arena. But the development of organizational, financial, and personal links between political and religious leaders and their followers has a significance for the American system of government far beyond the simple question of delivering the vote. The legitimacy of active religious involvement in politics and the nature of that involvement raise basic questions about the character of American society and politics, and may of course have direct and indirect effects on policy.

In one sense the current debate about the extent to which it is proper for the Churches to be involved in politics simply highlights an ambiguity and contradiction which have been a feature of the American constitution since its inception. Although most Americans assume that theirs is a secular State, it is secular only in the sense that the Constitution was initially interpreted as clearly prohibiting the existence of an established Church at the national level, as forbidding legal privileges for one Church as against another, and as precluding the administration of religious tests. The extension of the Bill of Rights to the states via the Fourteenth Amendment inevitably had implications for religious issues at the state level; but various views can be taken about the degree to which government may extend aid and assistance to all religious bodies within the United States and about the original intentions of the Founding Fathers with respect to religion.[3]

The early settlers were motivated by a desire to escape from the impositions of religious orthodoxy in Europe but, as Roger Williams's experience in Massachusetts underlined, they were by no means committed to the idea of freedom of religion. If immigration made the ideal of a puritan theocracy unattainable, it could not eliminate from American life the yearning for a society where biblical precepts and saintly men would govern the society as a whole.[4] Nor has the rapid social change which America has experienced in the last century mitigated the conflicts produced by clashes of cultural values. The reassertion of hostility to the teaching of evolution in some parts of the United States in the 1970s and early 1980s (which led to major court cases in Arkansas and Louisiana) also bears testimony to the continuing strength of fundamentalist values in the wider society and culture even in the late twentieth century.[5]

In the post-1945 period it seemed to many observers that the Supreme Court was attempting to eliminate some of the controversy and ambiguity surrounding the relationship between religion and other aspects of American life. Just how systematically it was in fact developing a coherent theory of Church and State based on the 'no establishment' and the 'free exercise' clauses of the First Amendment remains open to debate; but in a series of cases dealing with such disparate issues as school prayer and the constitutionality of parochial schools receiving public funding, the Supreme Court struggled with the problems associated with reconciling religious pluralism with a secular polity.[6]

Yet in the late 1970s it was evident that not only were some of these decisions — particularly the ones related to school prayer — extremely contentious but in addition a range of new religious issues had appeared on the agenda of the constitutional decision-makers. Thus, the case of Bob Jones University, which unsuccessfully fought to keep its charitable status because it implemented a policy of forbidding interracial dating and marriage on the campus, became a *cause célèbre* in which all the different theories of separation of Church and State were raised in legal argument.[7]

Some commentators had seen the development of Church–State relationships progressing naturally through a series of stages going from greater involvement to less.[8] In the first stage the United States experienced a range of practice at the state level, so that while establishment of religion was forbidden at the federal level, some states (e.g. Massachusetts and South Carolina) did have their own established Churches. When the last state Church was disestablished — a distinction enjoyed by Massachusetts in 1833 — it could be said that one element of uncertainty about the role of the Church in American life was over. It should be remembered, of course, that although there had been Churches which were originally offshoots of the Anglican Church in England, by no means all of these state-established Churches were in fact Anglican or Episcopalian, as they came to be called after the Revolution. In New England, as opposed to Virginia and the Carolinas, the dominant influence was Congregationalism. The fact that the primary influence in New England was a radical theology which looked towards the authority of the Bible, and especially the Old Testament, was to have profound consequences for the development of the United States' political culture as a whole.[9] As James Madison put it, 'If the Church of England had been the established and general religion in all the northern colonies . . . it is clear to me that slavery and subjection would have been gradually insinuated among us.'[10] Instead there developed an ideology of resistance to absolutism and conformity to the moral law which directly derived from puritanism and which not only gave New England a distinctive outlook but, after independence, affected the development of the American understanding of the proper relationship between Church and State.

If the first stage of American religious history could be said to be bounded by the Massachusetts disestablishment, the second stage was one in which Protestants as a cultural and political group dominated American society. Although the Congregational and Episcopalian Churches had had to give way in the face of competition from a variety of other Churches and sects, nineteenth-century America was still overwhelmingly Protestant, and that dominance remained effective until well into the twentieth century.

In the third period of American religious history — and a case could be made for seeing 1945 as the watershed rather than 1914 — the religious composition of the United States was such that Protestant Churches could no longer claim preeminence. The legitimacy of the Roman Catholic Church, which was flourishing, had to be acknowledged as well as the national importance of more modern sects such as the Church of Jesus Christ of the Latter Day Saints (or Mormons), the Jehovah's Witnesses, and the Seventh Day Adventists. The changing significance of Roman Catholicism was underlined by the election to the Presidency in 1960 of John F. Kennedy, a Roman Catholic from a well-known Boston Catholic family.

Although Kennedy's nomination did generate some controversy about the extent to which he was likely to be influenced by the Roman Catholic hierarchy, the fact that as a candidate he was able to deal with the issue so decisively suggests that another Roman Catholic nominee would have virtually no problems as a result of his religious adherence.[11] It also shows how far the United States had traveled since 1928, when Al Smith's defeat was greeted with the flaming crosses of the Klu Klux Klan throughout the land because of his Catholicism. It is perhaps one of the ironies of contemporary American politics that the activity of right-of-center groups in the mobilization of the Churches has in a

very real sense legitimized activities by a number of other religious groups and Churches both on the right and the left of
American politics. Thus, the role of the Catholic bishops in
the nuclear freeze debates of 1983 was not merely important
in itself but interesting for the extent to which it represented
a renewed Roman Catholic presence in active politics.[12]

Perhaps equally significant from the point of view of the
development of cultural and religious pluralism in the United
States has been the role of Judaism, which grew to be a major
force in American life with the successive waves of late
nineteenth- and early twentieth-century immigration from
Eastern Europe.[13] In addition — and it is this that is seen as
most threatening by many Christians in America today — it was
impossible by the middle of the twentieth century to ignore
the existence of substantial minorities in the American population who were either outside the Judaeo-Christian tradition
altogether (for example, Americans of Japanese and Chinese
descent) or who were entirely secular in outlook.[14]

In such circumstances it might have been assumed that
the majority of religious organizations would have seen the
merits of the federal government adopting a position of strict
neutrality not merely between denominations but also
between the cause of religion itself and secularism — a
neutrality which would have entailed the gradual reduction
of areas of overlap between Church and State. Yet three
broad developments proved such an assumption to be fal-
lacious, and ushered in a new period of controversy about
the role of the American Churches by catapulting them into
the mainstream of political debate and constitutional discussion. These three developments were a changing pattern
of church membership; the appearance of issues capable
of being used to mobilize hitherto apolitical Christians;
the emergence of new styles of church leadership and organization and the perception of a mutual interest on the part of
new-right and religious leaders in common activities and
campaigns.

Changing Patterns of Church Membership

The first feature of American society which led to a new

relationship between religion and politics in the United States in the 1970s and 1980s was the growth of those Churches which may be termed 'conservative', 'fundamentalist', or 'strict' — a growth that was only in part the result of demographic change. Problems inevitably arise with the use of these terms, since words like 'fundamentalism' have a number of different connotations and, to make matters more complex, the concept has slightly different nuances on each side of the Atlantic.[15] One scholar of evangelicalism in American life has described the fundamentalism which emerged in the 1920s in America, and which will probably be best remembered for its adamant rejection of evolution, as a 'loose, diverse and changing federation of co-belligerents united by their fierce opposition to modernist attempts to bring Christianity into line with modern thought'.[16]

As Marsden notes, the twin opposition to modernism and the theory of evolution stemmed from the fundamentalists' assessment that the crisis of early twentieth-century America existed because the biblical foundations of American civilization had been undermined.[17]

Although the most recent attempt by the right to integrate the Churches into a political coalition of conservative forces constitutes a substantially novel development in American politics, it should never be forgotten that it draws on a tradition of mobilization which has been a feature of American political and social life for a much longer period. As Marsden's analysis makes clear, the fundamentalists of the 1920s and their successors had much in common with other religious traditions in America in the early years of the twentieth century. Evangelicalism, revivalism, pietism, the holiness movements, millenarianism, Reformed confessionalism, Baptist traditionalism, and other 'denominational orthodoxies' — all these shared some of the spirit of fundamentalism. What distinguished fundamentalism, in Marsden's view, was its stark opposition to modernism.[18] Other scholars have emphasized the extent to which American fundamentalism and conservative evangelicalism have been shaped by and in reaction to the symbolic and structural constraints of modernity.[19] And, although most writers have seen it as a distinctly North American phenomenon, there have been disagreements about the centrality of fundamentalism to that continent's religious history. Thus, while some have seen it as a marginal aspect of American life, others have located it firmly in the mainstream of nineteenth-century Protestant experience.[20]

Nineteenth-century American Protestantism was a complex entity which by the turn of the century had become deeply split at the élite level by the efforts of some theologians to synthesize the teachings of Christianity with new scientific findings, especially Darwinism. As a result of these developments a number of organizations were formed to keep alive the conservative views of the Bible and its teachings. What is important to remember in the American context is that although there are such organizational aspects to the divisions over doctrine, many of the major denominations in the United States have both conservative and liberal factions, so that the battles often rage within rather than between Churches.

The fact that it is difficult to translate conservative and evangelical views into simple organizational loyalty does not mean that all organizational ties are politically irrelevant. One politically relevant way of distinguishing between Protestant Churches in the United States is to divide those which are ecumenical in outlook from those which are not; or, more formally, one can divide those which adhere to the National Council of Churches of Christ in the United States from those which do not. The Churches which do adhere to the National Council are generally regarded as being on the liberal end of the theological spectrum, as opposed to the more conservative non-affiliated Churches. In 1981 the *Yearbook of the American and Canadian Churches* listed thirty-two constituent Churches of the National Council, and of this number there were twenty-eight which were further affiliated to the World Council of Churches. The World Council has itself become a special object of criticism for conservative Americans because of its association with the transmission of aid to revolutionary regimes in the Third World and its criticisms of American policy towards South Africa and Central America.[21] The distinction made on the basis of organizational affiliation is a crude one, but it has been used by at least one scholar to chart the decline in terms of membership of Churches judged to be theologically 'liberal' by comparison with those judged to be theologically 'conservative'. Dean Kelley, in a book which acquired some prominence in the United States, suggested that during the 1960s each of the Churches which he designated the five 'wheel-horses' of the ecumenical movement in the United States — the Episcopal Church, the United Methodist Church, the United Presbyterian Church, the Lutheran Church, and the United Church of Christ — declined in membership.[22]

By contrast, other denominations seemed to be 'overflowing with vitality'.[23] Churches with increased membership over the period 1960–70 included the Southern Baptist Convention, the Assemblies of God, the Churches of God, the Pentecostal and Holiness Groups, the evangelicals, the Mormons, the Jehovah's Witnesses, the Seventh Day Adventists, and the Church of the Nazarene. Moreover, Dean Kelley detected a correlation between the decline in Roman Catholic membership which was first reported in 1970 and the transformation of the Roman Catholic Church following Vatican II from a relatively authoritarian one to a more liberal one.[24]

Statistics about church membership are notoriously unreliable since Churches may return figures of nominal rather than active members, and some Churches — especially the small conservative ones — emphasize their autonomy and the lack of organizational ties between their congregations. Nevertheless, the figures are important because they show why new-right leaders in the 1970s became convinced that there was a massive and untapped constituency which could be mobilized if only the correct techniques and issues could be found. Table 1 sets out the statistics of a selection of American Churches for the period 1950–79 and underlines the differential growth-rate between the various kinds of Churches. Of particular interest, given the volatility of the area, is the rise of the Southern Baptist Convention, which almost doubled its membership over the period.[25] Clearly there is a great deal of diversity among these Churches; and conservatism in theology, even if established, does not automatically translate into political conservatism, much

TABLE 1

Membership of Selected United States Churches 1950–1979

	1950	1960	1970	1979	% change 1950–79
American Lutheran Church	1,587,152	2,242,259	2,543,293	2,362,685	+ 48.9
Assemblies of God*	318,478	508,602	625,027	958,418	+ 201.0
Church of God (Cleveland, Tennessee)†	121,706	170,261	272,278	411,385	+ 238.0
Church of Jesus Christ of Latter-day Saints [Mormons]	1,111,314	1,486,887	2,073,146	2,706,000	+ 143.5
Episcopal Church	2,417,464	3,269,325	3,285,826	2,841,350	+ 17.5
Jehovah's Witnesses‡	not available	250,000	388,920	526,961	+ 110.8
Lutheran Church in America §	[2,395,356]	[3,053,243]	3,106,844	2,921,090	+ 21.9
North American Baptist Conference	41,560	50,646	55,080	42,779	+ 2.9
Roman Catholic Church	28,634,878	42,104,900	48,214,729	49,812,178	+ 74.0
Southern Baptist Convention	7,079,889	9,731,591	11,628,032	13,372,757	+ 88.9
United Methodist Church¶	[9,653,178]	[10,641,310]	10,671,774	9,653,711	+ 0.0
United Presbyterian Church in USA	[2,532,429]	3,259,011	3,087,213	2,477,364	− 2.2

* The total for 1950 is a composite one, following a merger of several component bodies.
† This is one of America's oldest Pentecostal Churches. Founded in 1886, it took this name in 1907.
‡ The figures for 1950 are not available. Calculations are therefore based on 1960–79.
§ The figures for 1950 and 1960 are composite totals following mergers.
¶ The figure for 1950 is a composite figure following a merger.

Source: C. H. Jacquet (ed.), *Yearbook of American and Canadian Churches* (1981), 238–9. Calculations have been rounded to the first place of decimals.

less into votes for specific parties, candidates, or causes. Nevertheless, the Churches which Dean Kelley identified as being of a conservative theological disposition do seem to have certain common features which are politically relevant.

The social gospel is less important to most of these Churches than it is to the mainstream ecumenical Churches. The expiation of sin in the individual is the primary concern of the majority of conservative Churches, and, in the rejection of the social gospel, *laissez-faire* capitalism and fundamentalism can unite with ease, given the social gospel's implied support of an enhanced role for government. Critics of both fundamentalist and conservative attitudes have long noted the association between the two casts of mind and the correlation of their beliefs. As *Christian Century* commented in 1921:

When the capitalist discovers a brand of religion which has not the slightest interest in the 'social gospel', but on the contrary intends to pass up all reforms to the Messiah who will return on clouds of heaven, he has found just the thing he has been looking for.[26]

The publication of the *Fundamentals* over the period 1910–15 was made possible by two rich Los Angeles businessmen, Lyman and Milton Stewart, and there is a sense in which American religious values have been used to support a business-oriented culture. Certainly, today's conservative evangelicals see no contradiction between capitalism and the Gospel. As Jerry Falwell put it in *Listen America*:

The free enterprise system is clearly outlined in the Book of Proverbs in the Bible. Jesus Christ made it clear that the work ethic was a part of His plan for man. Ownership of property is biblical. Competition in business is biblical. Ambitious and successful business management is clearly outlined as a part of God's plan for His people.[27]

Tension between the affairs of this world and those of the next thus does not threaten the theology of America's conservative Churches; still less does it challenge the alliance of fundamentalists and the political right. Indeed, biblical doctrine can be invoked to back the work ethic which men such as Daniel Bell fear may be disappearing from American society. As well as a lack of emphasis on the social gospel, the conservative Churches and sects share other characteristics. There is an insistence on the literal truth of the Bible and on its 'inerrance', as well as an egalitarian and anti-élitist approach to its interpretation. Above all, perhaps, there is a quality of particularism about these Churches which both attracts and reflects their middle-American constituency.

Historians of religion in the United States have noticed how all of its Churches have developed features which reflect the democratic environment of the country and which make American denominations more like each other than like their European counterparts.

The tension produced by America's liberal and democratic environment was especially marked in relation to Roman Catholicism in the late nineteenth century, although it has been noted that the liberal tendencies within the Roman Catholic Church in America at the time were more practical than doctrinal.[28] Two papal encyclicals — *Longinqua Oceani* (1895) and *Testem Benevolentiae* (1899) — attempted to deal with the peculiar problems faced by Roman Catholics in a polity with a strong doctrine of the constitutional separation of Church and State and with the 'heresy' of Americanism.[29] The international and domestic sources of the controversies of the period and their links with attitudes towards modernism in theology were varied; but there can be little doubt that the considerations and circumstances which existed in North America were different from those which obtained in Europe and that the Roman Catholic Church in the United States felt itself to be in an especially awkward situation.

The fact that American religion has a distinctive flavor has been evident in the country's more recent religious history. Many of the Churches which have been experiencing a major expansion are very evidently stamped by the American character, and date from revivals at the turn of the nineteenth century (this would be true, for example, of a variety of holiness sects). The Mormon Church is grounded on the belief of a second coming in the New World and has a quintessentially American element in its theology. Other Churches in the United States simply draw analogies between the experience of the original chosen people and the experience of the American settlers, so that their language is suffused with Old Testament imagery and their arguments make explicit the parallels between ancient Israel and modern America. In some cases such beliefs go hand in hand with support for the modern State of Israel; in other cases they are completely remote from the politics of the contemporary Middle East and can even be combined with anti-Semitism.[30]

A Changing Agenda of Religious Issues

The second development which has had the effect of bringing together the American religious and political right has been the appearance of a set of issues on the national agenda of interest to conservative Christians. Much has already been said about this development, but such themes were necessary to mobilize evangelicals and fundamentalists, who traditionally had a high propensity not to vote and to eschew political activity. This cluster of issues has come to be known as 'family issues' or 'social issues', and they are central to the activity of both the new right and the religious right.[31]

Such family issues could of course be divisive in a society with a divorce rate as high as that in the United States. There was accordingly some reluctance on the part of the Republican Party prior to the 1980 election to become too identified at the national level with such questions as abortion or school prayer, as opposed to the bread-and-butter issues of inflation, unemployment, and the economy. There is little doubt that the former set of issues was one of the most important instruments for bringing together fundamentalist Christians concentrated in the Bible Belt, and political tacticians saw them as one method of building new political coalitions in specific regional subcultures of the United States.

Discussion of 'family issues' in the politics of the 1960s and 1970s clearly involves the discussion of specific single issues (notably abortion) and the whole theme of sexual morality and behavior. It also involves basic philosophies of government, since conservatives and liberals divide over the role to be ascribed to the family and the preferred means for strengthening that role within the political system.

Interest in the role of the family in contemporary America was heightened when Jimmy Carter, towards the end of his 1976 election campaign, announced the proposal for a White House Conference on Families. In the course of the Carter administration Joseph Califano, the Secretary for Health, Education, and Welfare, emphasized the extent to which the federal government desired to strengthen families and 'restore them to their rightful place as the corner stone of national well being'.[32] This was to be achieved in part by the elaborately designed White House Conference on Families, which Congress endorsed by Joint Resolution in August 1977.

The thinking behind this proposal was that there was a need for a complete review of the modern family and the way it was affected by federal government policies, since families — however defined — had clearly to adapt to a range of outside pressures and social changes. In Washington a coalition of some twenty-eight organizations was formed to plan the Conference and ensure that the idea was followed through successfully. The coalition wished to ensure that the diversity of life-styles in modern America was taken into account by the Conference and that the focus of the Conference was the impact of federal public policy on the family. It also wished the Conference to consider the extent to which private organizations and informal systems of support could be strengthened by government policies.[33] Included in the coalition were orthodox church bodies such as the National Council of Churches and the National Council of Catholic Charities; but alongside them there were bodies such as the National Gay Task Force and Parents without Partners, which suggested a more radical approach to the whole subject.

The right had in any event a different vision of how the American family could be strengthened. Rather than emphasize the opportunities open to federal government to support families, it preferred to emphasize strategies to keep government out of family life and to reassert traditional moral values. The presence of suspect groups with radical claims in the planning stages of the Conference turned the whole process into one which the right could exploit for publicity;

and in the course of the Carter Presidency it developed a series of programs to implement *its* vision of the American family.[34]

Thus, if family policy for liberals entailed programs designed to provide safety-nets and support when the free-enterprise system failed to function efficiently (and also therefore suggested an enhanced role for the federal government), the right's understanding of family policy was very different. Conservatives wanted programs designed to strengthen traditional family relationships and to bolster parental authority. Family issues as defined by the right involved an orthodox definition of the family (to exclude homosexual unions, for example) and a rejection of governmental initiatives which might undermine the decision-making power of the family; and conservatives emphasized moral rather than economic concerns. Such an approach was on one level perfectly compatible with the ideals of the Republican Party and its platform of reduced governmental functions and greater scope for free enterprise; but on another level it implied a desire to reverse social change and even, in questions of moralty, to intervene in the private lives of American citizens.

Of the controversial issues of the 1970s which are included in the cluster of family issues few were as potent as that of abortion in bringing the Churches into political life. Following the Supreme Court's decision in the cases of *Roe* v. *Wade* and *Doe* v. *Bolton*, in 1973 a range of groups mobilized at the national and state level to modify and oppose the impact of the decisions. The court had decided that, *inter alia*, a mother had an unconditional constitutional right to an abortion during the first trimester (i.e. three months) of pregnancy and that, while thereafter the State might intervene to place conditions on the performance of an abortion, the initial decision was a private one between the woman and her medical adviser.[35] Subsequent moves by the anti-abortion lobby to restrict the availability of federal funding for abortions were largely successful (in part by the device of attaching riders to appropriations bills); but other initiatives — especially those to introduce a constitutional amendment on the subject and attempts to place direct legislative restrictions on the courts' jurisdiction in this matter — were less successful, although Senator Hatch's motion to restrict abortions in 1982 was voted out of the Judiciary Committee.[36] And throughout the 1970s and 1980s the courts were forced to adjudicate on the legality of abortion-related issues. These include whether the parents of a minor needed to give their consent before an abortion could be performed, whether abortions after the first trimester had to be performed in a hospital, whether a state or city could impose a delay between the consent to and the performance of an abortion, and the extent to which the person desiring the abortion should be given information about the nature of the procedure.[37] What is important to note here, however, is the effect this question had on the relationships between active church-goers and political leaders. The theme of 'protecting innocent life' drew religious leaders and their followers into politics in a way which was more analogous to a crusade than to ordinary politics. It encouraged religious groups who felt strongly on the topic to learn the techniques of effective organization in politics and brought them into contact with potential political allies whom they might otherwise not have met. Those contacts, once gained, became a resource at the disposal of both the Churches and the political right, and could of course be used for mobilization on other issues.

The abortion question also reminded American politicians and the electorate of the recurrent power of moral questions in American politics. In a period of declining party activism (in which the impetus to participate in political campaigns or to perform any voluntary party activity is weak) emotive moral issues like abortion may provide a powerful stimulus both to the recruitment of campaign helpers and to the revenues from political donations, and ultimately affect the voting.[38]

The centrality of the abortion issue in American political life after 1973 was also significant because it brought together the Roman Catholic Church with the Protestant fundamentalists and evangelicals in a single political cause. While Roman Catholic bishops have frequently intervened in American politics, Roman Catholic politicians have recently been anxious to assert their independence of ecclesiastical influence. Indeed, until the abortion and then the nuclear freeze issue the Church itself had appeared to want to keep a low political profile. Abortion is, however, seen by most Roman Catholic theologians as murder, and it is not surprising that both priests and laity should be in the forefront of the anti-abortion debate. The disruptive power of the issue was seen in the 1980 election campaign, when Cardinal Humberto Madeiros published a pastoral letter on the subject to his diocese of Boston. The letter was, according to the press, clearly timed to influence the Massachusetts primaries and was especially aimed at Barney Frank, a liberal Democrat, who was running in the Fourth District, and James Shannon, who was running in the Fifth. Frank's district had previously been occupied by a Roman Catholic priest, Robert Drinan, whose liberal sympathies had caused the Vatican to order his withdrawal from active political life.[39]

The controversy over the pastoral letter and the rapidity with which new-right organizations such as the National Conservative Political Action Committee and Conservative Caucus intervened in the politics of Massachusetts highlighted the extent to which the new right saw moral issues such as abortion as ones which could be exploited in the search for conservative votes. In the event, Frank in particular refused to modify his position on the sensitive issues of morality. He won narrowly in 1980 but with a more generous margin in 1982, when he was coping with redistricting and having to run against Margaret Heckler, a well-known Massachusetts Republican.[40]

In contrast to the controversy over the Frank seat in Massachusetts, where liberal sentiment constrained the impact of the Right to Life issue, it seemed that the abortion question did influence the unexpected results of some other races in 1978, 1980, and 1982. For example, Christopher Smith, a conspicuous Right to Life activist, won election in 1980 as a Republican in New Jersey's Fourth District following the defeat of the Democrat Frank Thompson, who had been tainted by the Abscam scandal.[41] Moreover, he held on to the seat in 1982 when he might have been expected to lose. Similarly, although Republican Mick Staton in West Virginia subsequently lost to a Democrat, he made some political mileage in 1980 out of the range of social issues, especially the theme of textbook censorship, which had become important in the area.[42] And the abortion issue figured prominently in the defeats of a number of liberal Senators in 1978 and 1980.

Second in importance only to the abortion issue has been that of tax-exempt status and federal control of church schools, and the possibility of public finance of parochial schools. Because of the disciplinary and pedagogic problems associated with public (i.e. state-financed) schools in America, the 1970s and 1980s have seen a remarkable growth in the number of private — largely religious — schools. Of particular interest from the point of view of this survey has been the growth in the number of parochial and church schools and the extension of such private education from the Roman Catholic to the Protestant Churches. By contrast with the Roman Catholic schools, which were always in need of federal assistance, the Protestant schools have made it clear that they have no wish for financial aid, since they abhor the idea of any governmental intervention in their affairs. The phrase 'Christian schools' has thus come to signify not so much the traditional Catholic schools of the big cities — which have always been a feature of the American educational scene — but the range of often very small private schools attached to fundamentalist and Baptist congregations throughout the United States. Jerry Falwell indicated the perceived importance of these schools when he claimed in 1980 that there were 14,000 'conservative Christian schools in America' and that they were then growing in numbers at the rate of three per day.[43] These schools, though they seek to avoid government regulation, so that little information is available on them, are indirectly affected by government policy because they enjoy charitable status, which means that they are exempt from taxation. However, in 1978, under the Carter administration, the Internal Revenue Service tried to implement a policy which would have required all schools founded after 1953 to abide by public policy guidelines on matters of racial integration. Unless schools were willing to do so the tax-exempt status of a school would be removed. The legal source and the precise meaning of this initiative were unclear, but the campaign against it brought into political alliance a large number of Baptist pastors and new-right pressure-groups. Bob Billings, who became the Executive Director of the Moral Majority and later joined the Reagan campaign as its liaison officer with the Christian right, had been an early activist in this sphere. In the direct-mail campaign against the Internal Revenue Service it was possible to see the potential power of the fundamentalist and conservative evangelical Christian constituency in issues which aroused it.

The cause of the Internal Revenue Service action was not an arbitrary desire to extend its jurisdiction. It arose in part from the belief that many, if not most, of the Protestant Christian schools existed to circumvent the desegregation process that the courts had imposed on the public schools, especially in the South. Such a view may over-simplify some of the motives of the founders of the schools and of the parents who opt to send their children to them, since the curriculum in these establishments is also very different from that of the public schools; but certainly the notion that these schools are 'segregation academies' is a belief widely held by civil liberties groups and one that is hardly dispelled by the reluctance of the schools to allow oversight and monitoring of their activities.[44]

The appearance of these fundamentalist schools on the contemporary American educational scene and the political controversy which they have generated have thus been both rapid and recent, for until the end of the 1960s most commentators would have seen the Roman Catholic parochial schools as the only serious cause of constitutional controversy.[45] As late as the 1964 revised edition of Anson Phelps Stokes's and Leo Pfeffer's classic study of the relationship between Church and State in America this view held sway. 'The only serious problem in Church–State relations as far as Church schools are concerned', they wrote, 'is provided by the efficient parochial school system of the Roman Catholic Church.'

One reason why religious Americans had become dissatisfied with the public schools was their increasingly secular character.[46] From a position where non-denominational prayer was acceptable along with such practices as carol-singing, Bible instruction, and Scripture study, the public schools of America seemed increasingly to have taken a stance which suggested outright hostility to religion. Such a position — combined with the poor educational standards of many schools and in some cities the threat of violence — has convinced increasing numbers of parents that modest parochial schools or conservative Christian schools would inculcate Christian values along with basic skills of literacy and numeracy better than the larger and more progressive schools of the public system.[47] At the same time there has been a concerted move from some politicians on the right to reintroduce voluntary non-denominational school prayer — a proposal which, unlike the other 'social issues', seems to have widespread support amongst the general public.[48]

Historically, there is a certain oddity about the character of the coalition which has been formed to fight on behalf of such issues as school prayer, abortion, and aid to church schools. One of the major litigants in the series of cases which led to the crucial Church and State decisions after 1945 was a group called 'Americans United'.[49] This group had formerly been called 'Protestants and Others United for the Separation of Church and State', a title which clearly indicated the initial anti-Catholic bias of the organization. The major constituency of 'Americans United' was indeed Protestant fundamentalism, and its litigation was inspired by the fear that Protestants might find themselves subsidizing Catholic schools. Certainly Southern Baptists — the group now most enthusiastically experimenting with religious schools of their own — initially espoused a strong theory of the separation of Church and State. And it would have been difficult to imagine them entering into any coalition with Roman Catholics for whatever reason.

While it would be premature to proclaim the death of anti-Catholicism in conservative circles in America, the appearance of a new enemy — secular humanism — has had the dual effect of transforming attitudes towards that religion and of altering the fundamentalist perception of the proper constitutional relationship between Church and State. It is perhaps interesting in this context that some of the leading figures in the new right's organization — for example, Richard Viguerie and Paul Weyrich — are Roman Catholics, as are many of the younger generation of neo-conservative activists. And one of the more remarkable achievements of the new right has been its ability to get Roman Catholics elected in unlikely territory, as occurred in 1980 when Jeremiah Denton was elected to the Senate from Alabama and Don Nickles was elected as Oklahoma's Senator.[50] Although Viguerie admits that achieving cooperation between Roman Catholics and Protestants is not always easy, there is clearly a determination to build bridges between conservatives of different faiths in the hope that it will pay political dividends.[51]

In addition to the two issues of abortion and support for church schools, there is of course the plethora of moral questions which have provided the material for new-right activists. It is difficult to draw a sharp line between these issues, but what is perhaps germane to the manner in which the religious right has been activated in the United States is the way in which the appearance of these issues has acquired a symbolic value in the characterization of modern American history. Many people have argued that there is a correlation between moral decadence, exemplified by the rise in the number of abortions, and the failure to inculcate Christian values in schools; and they would relate both to the changing role of the United States in the world and its inability to exercise moral influence. The perceived decline in American power and prosperity that occurred during the 1970s and which came to a climax during the Carter years is seen as a judgement on America. It was quite understandable that many Christian and conservative Americans would find the sexual permissiveness of the 1960s difficult to reconcile with their religious beliefs; what was less predictable was the way some Church leaders linked the so-called counter-culture and its inherent moral degeneracy with the material and spiritual erosion that followed Vietnam.[52] The close identification of American Protestants with the ancient Israelites and the puritan conviction that Americans are the new chosen people continue to influence contemporary religious and political rhetoric. Testimony before the House Judiciary Committee on the subject of school prayer in 1980 underlined both the perceived connection between America's political and moral decline and the analogies between the current experience of sinful Americans and the historical experience of ancient Israel. James Robison, one of the fiery evangelists of the fundamentalist movement and a leading figure in 'Campus Crusade', argued before the Committee that the events of the previous fifteen years — specifically Watergate and Vietnam — were the direct results of the collective sin of the United States.[53] God had turned his face against his chosen people, and the plagues then being visited upon the United States were a sign of the Almighty's anger at the national refusal to obey the tenets of the Bible and the exclusion of prayer from the schools. The process of returning America to the path of righteousness involved not merely a recognition that the State might be subject to biblical morality and that secular humanism could not serve as a philosophy; it also suggested that an active determination to reverse the process of secularization would be materially beneficial and was a patriotic duty.

Robison's denunciation of contemporary ethics and his call to Christians to 'come out of the closet' and become active in American politics represent one strand of the reaction against certain trends in American society and are important as an illustration of the thinking of the new religious right. However, it is important to bear in mind that reaction against those cultural changes so abhorred by religious conservatives spread beyond the religious communities. As has been seen in relation to the neo-conservatives, journals such as the Jewish *Commentary* attempted to preserve a sense of cultural traditionalism and to prevent the triumph of cultural nihilism in realms as diverse as literary criticism and sexual behavior.

The mobilization of religious leaders and Churches around some of the controversial issues of the period did not meet with an entirely enthusiastic response from all religiously inclined Americans. Indeed, such is the variety of American religious opinion that the problems of homosexual rights, abortion, and women's liberation divided them deeply.

The stark terms employed by the fundamentalists, suffused as they were with the prohibitions of the Old Testament, frequently repelled the leaders of the liberal Churches, who had no enthusiasm for a crusade to bring the United States back to the *mores* either of Leviticus or of the early settlers of Massachusetts. The backlash within the Churches developed both over specific issues and over the attempt to put together a coalition of the kind typified by the Moral Majority. Thus, on the abortion question a religious alliance was formed, the Religious Coalition for Abortion Rights. This group consisted of more than twenty religious organizations — Protestant, Catholic, and Jewish — and some fourteen denominations dedicated to the preservation of freedom of choice with respect to abortion.[54] The organizations People for the American Way and Americans for Common Sense were also active in opposing new-right and new Christian right activities, and included on their boards several prominent churchmen.[55]

A New Style of Leadership

One of the factors which hastened the mobilization of the religious right was the emergence of a new generation of religious leaders and political activists who were willing to adopt new techniques to promote their causes and who were much more politically aware than their predecessors. As with the success of the new right described earlier, the availability of the techniques themselves encouraged the exploitation of issues and the development of a style which itself had profound consequences for the ideology of the right.

The importance of direct mail to the new right has been outlined in an earlier chapter; in conjunction with other marketing techniques it was also central to the evangelizing and fund-raising techniques of many of the individuals who sprang to prominence within the religious world.[56] Here it is necessary to mention another factor on the American scene which has shaped the ability of Churches to exert political influence, namely broadcasting.

Radio and television have, of course, long been used by

evangelists, but the style and professionalism of these preachers changed radically during the 1970s. Father Coughlin
might recognize the genre of a Jerry Falwell or a James
Robison, but technology has clearly brought an immense
change in the ability of preachers to reach large audiences.
Even the style of Billy Graham looks somewhat antiquated
by comparison with the slick productions offered by Pat
Robertson and Jerry Falwell himself. Television programs
turned pastors of independent local congregations into national
personalities and brought in vast amounts of money, although
after 1980 many commentators began to notice that the
temptation to expand a broadcasting empire had exceeded
the market and that the financial base of some of the organizations was very fragile. Indeed, one religious broadcasting
network was forced to sell satellite time to the owners of
Playboy magazine in a frantic attempt to avert financial
disaster. And while some of the appeals for money on religious programs do not indicate impending bankruptcy, there
is an element of truth in the constant reminders that the
ministry depends upon individual donations.

Some idea of the style of these television evangelists'
offerings can be gleaned from the names of the shows. Jerry
Falwell, who is the head of Moral Majority, runs a program called the *Old-time Gospel Hour*, a title which echoes
Charles E. Fuller's *Old Fashioned Revival Hour*. Falwell
broadcasts services directly from his well-attended church
in Lynchburg, Virginia, and he has founded an institute
of higher education called the Liberty Baptist College, whose
graduates are frequently to be found as legislative aides to
right-of-center Congressmen and as assistants to like-minded
pressure-groups such as Christian Voice.

Falwell, like other television evangelists, combines in his
programs fundamentalist theology with a distinctly conservative political message, which emphasizes the link between
Americanism, the Bible, and support for conservative causes.
For example, in 1980 viewers were encouraged to telephone
pledges of support as a sign of their conversion to Christ and
were also offered a range of special kits, such as an 'Old
Glory' flag to enable them to demonstrate their support of
the United States. Implicitly, this entailed advocacy of the

candidacy of Ronald Reagan and opposition to President Carter. The blend of religion and politics has a justification beyond the personal preferences of the preachers themselves, however. As the television audience for religious programs has reached what is considered saturation point, many preachers have been advised to vary the format of their shows either by making them more obviously entertaining or by including a greater social and political content.

The impression which is given is of a highly professional production, and as a result some theologians have criticized the religious value of the finished goods. Certainly, the consumer is not likely to be unduly troubled by the output of many of these shows and their intellectual content is variable. Yet whatever the reservations about the effect and content of religious broadcasts — and even if one believes they have passed their peak — there is little doubt that they have become a major factor in the politics of the right and in the broadcasting industry. An example of the growth and potential of religious broadcasting is Pat Robertson's *700 Club*. The *700 Club* takes the form of a nightly interview program or 'chat show' in which Robertson, a Southern Baptist preacher, is the compère. Robertson has constructed a varied and extensive media empire for himself. It was estimated that by 1979 Christian Broadcasting Network had a ninety-minute program on 150 television stations, both domestic and foreign; it had access to 1,800 cable television systems; and it had an announced income for that year of $54m.[57] In addition it was estimated that Robertson had 800 employees, as well as a $20m. headquarters which was constructed in the shape of a cross at Virginia Beach.

Religion and politics are mixed in Robertson's programs in a manner which has emphasized the need for resistance to secular humanism and moral perversion. After 1980, however, Robertson tried to distance himself from the new Christian right. In 1976 he gave support to born-again candidate Jimmy Carter, but during the Carter Presidency he became disappointed with the administration and switched support to other candidates and causes — usually further to the right. Robertson's emphasis in the program is on the relevance of the Gospel to the solution of personal problems, but his magazine, *The Perspective*, deals with a wide range of issues, including foreign policy, arms negotiations, and the economy. Not surprisingly, it was against SALT II and the Equal Rights Amendment; it has also apparently derived from the Gospel clear views on wage and price controls, the size of the federal budget, and the desirability of national health insurance.

Another prominent religious broadcaster is Jim Bakker, who used to work for Pat Robertson but now runs his own program called *The PTL Club*. Bakker's activities caused him to be investigated by the Federal Communications Commission, the independent regulatory commision which controls broadcasting in the United States.

Although the size of the religious broadcasting networks is clearly substantial and their financial turnover is large, the general consensus seems to be that their audience figures have leveled off and may even be declining.[58] Arbitron and Nielson, who conduct independent estimates of viewing size, put Pat Robertson's weekly viewing audience at 380,000, James Robison's at 460,000, Jerry Falwell's at 1,400,000, and Jim Bakker's at 670,000. Of course, the television preachers themselves have tended to inflate the size of their audience. Ben Armstrong, then the Executive Director of the National Religious Broadcasters' Association, estimated that in September 1981 airwave preachers owned and ran approximately 1,400 radio stations out of an approximate total of 8,000 in the United States. More than 75 per cent of the time of these stations is devoted to presenting religious programs; but there are other programs which can be distributed through the ordinary secular stations, which can then broadcast them in order to produce a token amount of religious material. In addition, according to Armstrong's estimates there were in September 1980 thirty-five completely religious television stations — a figure which had risen to fifty by the end of 1981.

The electronic Church was not, however, the only novelty on the religious scene. New organizational developments occurred to link fundamentalist and conservative Christians to the political right in a more formal way which was seen as presenting a greater threat to customary patterns in American political life.

A range of organizations has been formed to get Christians more actively involved in politics and cause them to use the polling booths on the right's behalf. Before examining some of them, it is important to bear two points in mind. First, there is a very high turnover of organizational leadership and structure. It is difficult to keep track of the movements between the élites of the new and the religious right, whether these occur for tactical political reasons or as a result of personality conflicts. (Sometimes, of course, a group may change its name to avoid the wrath of the Federal Election Commission or the Internal Revenue Service.) And where a group has attempted to organize itself into state and local chapters, there may be massive variations between areas in the degree to which any real state organization exists. But if some groups seem to be here today and gone tomorrow, it is possible to establish a degree of continuity between their leading personalities. The second point to notice is that there is a very large overlap between the organizations which exist to promote causes of interest to both the new right and the religious right. The various groups of the new right and new religious right have access to the same Congressional adherents, and many of their advisory committees are near-duplicates of each other. Inevitably, the funding is also sometimes drawn from the same sources — whether these be large donors or the smaller givers who are tapped by direct mail. After all, the philosophy of direct mail entre-preneurs such as Richard Viguerie is based on the assumption that once one has given to a cause one has a stake in it and will therefore give again to the same cause; and direct-mail fund-raisers also assume that those who give to one cause will be likely to give to related causes. From the perspective of the critic of both the new right and the religious right, the overlap of personalities and organizations can appear to be a conspiracy, and monitoring groups such as Group Research are anxious to make public the links between some of the newer think-tanks (such as the Heritage Foun-dation), business and industry, and individual politicians or lobbyists. In reality, though, the connection between pressure-groups, industry, and politics is so pervasive in American life that there is little that the right does which can be distinguished in this respect from the activities of the Democrats.

It is perhaps somewhat ironic that the first extensive public discussion of the relationship between religion and politics in the 1970s was with respect to Jimmy Carter's claim to be a 'born-again' Christian.[59] His emphasis on his personal religious commitment as a candidate in 1976 could conceivably have won him votes, and it certainly reasserted his cultural ties with the South, which for the first time in many years voted solidly on a state-wide basis for the Democratic presidential candidate.[60] After the 1976 campaign, however, the performance of President Carter received increasingly poor ratings from the evangelical and fundamentalist communities. During his Presidency efforts to integrate those communities with the more politically motivated organizations of the right proceeded apace.

The origins of the association between the new right and the Christian fundamentalist community go back to the early 1970s at least. There had been a series of attempts to bring together pastors of mainly Southern Baptist backgrounds and the isolated spokesmen of the right, many of whom had been associated with Young Americans for Freedom, the organization which was pressing the Republican Party for clear conservative policies in line with the philosophy of Barry Goldwater.

Prominent among the organizations which came to link the religious and political right in the later 1970s were the National Christian Action Coalition, Moral Majority (although, as has been seen in the last chapter, this moved after its formation to become more a political than a religious group), Christian Voice, and Religious Roundtable (which later changed its name simply to Roundtable). All these groups were founded with slightly different emphases and have slightly different tactics and constituencies. One key figure in the formation of one of these groups was Ed McAteer, a former salesman for Colgate–Palmolive. McAteer had firsthand knowledge of the evangelical community and its leaders as a result of his service on the Tennessee Baptist Foundation and some other Christian foundations, and his marketing expertise and contacts made him extremely useful in organizing Christian political activity. In particular, he had worked with an organization called the Christian Freedom Foundation. John Conlan, an ultra-conservative Congressman from Arizona's Fourth District, had asked McAteer to become national organizer for the Foundation in 1974 and, although the Foundation could not be rated a great success, the job did bring him into intimate contact both with the evangelical community and with the political right. (Conlan himself made an unsuccessful bid for the Senate seat in 1976, but lost after a primary campaign which was marked by anti-Semitism and bigotry.) McAteer's acceptance of the job with the Christian Freedom Foundation enabled him to develop his links between the right and the world of conservative Christians, especially since at that time the Christian Freedom Foundation was specializing in promoting free-market economic views among its evangelical and fundamentalist constituents.

McAteer's connection with the Christian Freedom Foundation was important for two reasons in addition to the obvious access to the political networks which his job gave him. (These contacts were of especial interest to the new right because they were in the south and south-west of the country.) First, it underlines the extent to which new-right leaders who came to prominence in the late 1970s — Richard Viguerie and Paul Weyrich, for example — were exaggerating when they claimed that theirs was a wholly new synthesis of religion and politics and a new movement in conservative politics. For, as McAteer's personal career shows, there were some links with the older right-wing causes and personalities as well as with older organizations of the right. The technology of the new right — especially the use of direct mail and television — has changed the style; but there already existed a right-wing community in various states which could be drawn on for support in the late 1970s. Secondly, McAteer's experience with the Christian Freedom Foundation shows how think-tanks and foundations which have been established for one purpose can be radically altered

by the appointment of new organizers or by the receipt
of new money. In the case of the Christian Freedom Foundation the link with older right-of-center tendencies is very
clear, in the person of J. Howard Pew, who between 1958
and 1962 had given over a million dollars to the Christian
Freedom Foundation and had served on the advisory committee of the John Birch Society's monthly magazine,
Monthly Opinion.

Another key figure in the attempt to unite the theo-
logically and politically conservative of America has been
Revd Robert (Bob) Billings. He had been instrumental in
founding a fundamentalist Bible College in Indiana called
Hyles–Anderson College, and he held a doctorate from Bob
Jones University – the university which, because of its
racially discriminatory policies, in 1983 was judged by the
Supreme Court not to be exempt from income taxes. Billings
had been an early enthusiast for establishing Christian schools.
The fight against the Internal Revenue Service's attempt to
deny tax-exempt status to fundamentalist schools had been
conducted by Billings as head of the National Christian
Action Coalition in conjunction with the American Conservative Union. Billings himself had only once attempted
to enter electoral politics, when in 1976 he ran for a House
seat in Indiana. Although defeated in the primary, even
in that short space of time he had come into contact
with a range of politicians on the right and had met Paul
Weyrich.[61] Weyrich's major interest in 1976 was the growth
of his Committee for the Survival of a Free Congress but
he apparently encouraged Billings to move to Washington,
where he became an active figure in the world of right-wing
Christian politics. When the Moral Majority was founded
in 1979 he became its executive director; and in the summer
of 1980 he left the Moral Majority to work for Ronald
Reagan's election as liaison officer with conservative Christians. The latter move was not popular with everyone on the
Reagan campaign staff, and there was a brief period in 1980
when Billings did not know whether the appointment was in
fact going to be vetoed. After the 1980 election – and
despite the claim that the Department of Education ought to
be abolished – Billings moved into the administration.

Initially, he had wanted to head the Department of Education's private school office; but he was opposed as too extreme by the Council for American Private Education and was ultimately given a job running the Department's regional offices — a post in which he appears to have had little impact.[62]

Between 1976 and 1978 the worlds of men who were primarily political entrepreneurs (such as Weyrich, Phillips, and Viguerie) were thus being integrated with the world of the evangelical right. When Howard Phillips founded Conservative Caucus in 1977 he persuaded Ed McAteer to become one of its principal organizers. The dominant strategy of Conservative Caucus at this time was to build up support for conservative candidates at the grass-roots level of politics (at the state level and below), to ensure that where possible conservatives should be nominated in primaries, and to create publicity for conservative themes in the various elections. The quiet methodological organization of Conservative Caucus reflects the new right's concern with effective organization and mobilization rather than education. The perceived decline of regular party organization and activity at the grass roots, which was such a feature of American party politics in the 1970s, thus appeared to constitute an opportunity for the conservative movement, and in 1978 the group's methods gained some national attention when the State Chairman of the Conservative Caucus in New Hampshire was elected to the Senate. Gordon Humphrey, as a freshman Senator, rapidly provided evidence that the small but motivated group of new-right politicians at the national level were prepared to pay attention to organization at all levels even if, for example, that meant flouting some of the established conventions of the Senate. From the perspective of local organization, what the Conservative Caucus and groups like it valued, even in New England, the stronghold of liberal Republicanism, was the way small community churches could provide a natural unit for mobilizing voters and offer a basic but highy effective substitute for a precinct organization.

Perhaps the first political organization to test the political responsiveness of evangelical Christians in the climate of the late 1970s was Christian Voice, a group founded in 1978 by Revd Robert Grant and directed by Richard Zone, both of whom were Baptists. Initially, Christian Voice had strong support from the Mormon junior Senator from Utah, Orrin Hatch, who was very much associated with the new right.[63] It also acquired support from Representative Robert Dornan of California. By 1980 it had assembled a board of twenty-seven Congressmen, although it was noticeable that this group was very much weighted towards the Republican Party. Prior to the election of 1980 it had only three Democrats on its Congressional Advisory Board and these — Sonny Montgomery of Mississippi, the late Larry McDonald of Georgia, and Bob Stump of Arizona — were untypical Democrats. Larry McDonald was for long a leading member of the John Birch Society; Sonny Montgomery was a Democrat who regularly voted with the Republicans on domestic issues and was a pronounced hawk on foreign policy (although such a posture did not make him altogether unusual in the politics of the Democratic Party in the late 1970s); and Bob Stump was a Seventh Day Adventist who used the label 'conservative' in his election campaigns and later became a Republican.[64] None of these would presumably have been considered mainstream Democrats by anyone's standards.

One other obvious feature of Christian Voice's Congressional representation prior to the 1980 elections was a bias away from the North-East and towards the West, the South, and the so-called 'Southern Rim'. At the level of demographic change as well as of economic and political importance, the movement towards this part of the United States is well known. Power within the Republican Party has for some time been shifting away from the more liberal areas of the country, and especially away from the New York Establishment Republicans, for so long associated with the Rockefellers and various banking interests. The new areas of Republican dominance are ones where traditionally fundamentalism and conservative Christianity have been strong, and it is hardly surprising, therefore, that this strength should be reflected in political movements such as support for Christian Voice. In the South the Republican strategy has been to try to promote an ideologically and perhaps ethnically based realignment or, failing that, at least to establish a viable system of two-party competition. The results have varied from state to state, with some states (e.g. Louisiana) still exhibiting only the frailest of Republican Parties. In others, such as Tennessee, there is real competition. The important point is that it is by no means impossible to envisage a Republican surge there; in a number of ways the once solid Democratic vote has been fractured.

The electoral strategy of Christian Voice itself was one which was very simple in conception and has become popular with the spread of direct mail. A so-called Report Card on Congress was issued by the Washington organization which in 1982 had already been run for some time by Gary Jarmin. Fourteen crucial issues were selected and each Congressman or Senator was ranked on the basis of his percentage of correct votes. In theory this process was educational and hence perfectly legitimate for an organization whose tax status (technically known as 501. c. 3) made it tax-exempt but prohibited it from engaging in direct *political*, as opposed to educational, activity; in practice its effect and threat were generally perceived as being pro-Republican, especially in the 1980 Senate races, since almost all the Democratic Senators up for reelection at that time were rated poorly by Christian Voice.

The issues selected by Christian Voice for its 1980 scorecard nicely convey the flavor of its concerns and illustrate why for many Americans the intertwining of religious and political issues has proved so abhorrent. Because the technique of targeting a vulnerable Senator in a state-wide race appears to be more effective than targeting an incumbent Congressman in a smaller district, the issues selected for the Senatorial score-card are of especial interest.

Fourteen votes were chosen as tests of a Senator's moral suitability for reelection. The first issue was designed to test opinion and attitudes towards Taiwan and China — a topic which has long divided the Republican Party and continued to do so well into the Reagan administration. Senator Percy, a relatively liberal Republican and a senior GOP spokesman on foreign policy, had offered an amendment to the Taiwan Enabling Act of 1979 with the purpose, according to Christian Voice, of making it unequivocally clear that the United States would defend Taiwan, which it referred to as a 'loyal friend and a Christian ally', against any attack from 'Godless Communist China'. President Carter had opposed the amendment, which was rejected by 50 votes to 42. Another foreign-policy issue included in the Christian Voice list was concerned with Rhodesia. Prior to the Lancaster House agreement of 1979 there had been moves in Congress to end American sanctions against the so-called internal settlement and the Muzorewa regime. Senator Stennis spearheaded an attempt to kill an amendment in favor of sanctions by liberal Democratic Senator Tsongas and liberal Republican Javits. Christian Voice's comment on this vote was that ending United States sanctions would lift an enormous burden from a Christian, pro-American nation under attack by atheistic Marxist forces 'seeking to destroy Christianity and Rhodesia's democratically elected racially integrated government'.[65]

The other issues selected by Christian Voice — with the possible exception of the Kemp–Roth amendment to control government expenditure and to reduce taxes — fell squarely within the gamut of social issues which have become a major theme of the new right and the religious right, and reflected the special concern of conservative Christians. Yet critics were quick to point out the anomalies that resulted from the overall scores in the House and the Senate. Senator Frank Church, who lost his Idaho Senate seat in 1980 and whose votes had been given a 23 per cent correct rating by Christian Voice, pointed out that Richard Kelly, the Republican from Florida who was indicted in the Abscam scandal, had achieved a 100 per cent rating, as had Congressman Bauman, a leading figure of the new right who was forced to resign because of his homosexual activities.[66]

The constituency which Christian Voice sought to tap differed from that of the other religious-right groups founded to bring together morally conservative Americans. Moral Majority, which was founded in 1979, represented an attempt to reach beyond the conservative evangelical and fundamentalist community and to form an organization that could bring together Protestants, Jews, and Roman

Catholics. In fact, although it is clear that Paul Weyrich and Richard Viguerie were involved from an early stage of the organization, and although both are Catholics, the movement at the grass roots is almost exclusively dominated by Baptist pastors. Howard Phillips brought a Jewish presence to the early planning sessions, but the Moral Majority's appeal to Jews was hardly increased when Revd Bailey Smith, who was then President of the Southern Baptist Convention, declared that God Almighty did not hear the prayers of Jews.[67]

It is true that support for Israel is seen as crucial to the Moral Majority, but that could be explained either as a personal commitment of the Moral Majority's president, Jerry Falwell, or by the conviction of some on the religious right that the founding and preservation of the State of Israel has some biblical significance. It may be doubted whether it has completely eradicated a certain strain of anti-Semitism which has long characterized fundamentalist thought in the United States, and which is not seen as incompatible with devotion to the Jews of the Bible. By contrast, some Jewish groups who would have seemed natural opponents of everything for which the Moral Majority stands have been willing to make common cause with the new right and the religious right simply because of their defense of Israel at a time when even within the United States its policies have been subjected to extensive criticism.[68]

Falwell's own role in Moral Majority has been extremely important, and the organization now reflects his personality and priorities to an extent which has perhaps weakened it as a vehicle of new-right coalition-building. Falwell's own account of how he was drawn into the venture has increasingly emphasized the spiritual rather than the political origins of the Moral Majority. In *Listen America* he describes how he was flying home to Lynchburg (where his church and Liberty Baptist College are) when suddenly in the darkness of the cabin he felt that God was calling him and telling him that 'good people of America' must be brought together and made to rise up against the growing tide of permissiveness and moral decay that was apparently crushing in on society from every side.[69]

In a later work, Falwell emphasizes the extent to which the Moral Majority represents a reaction to the 'fruits of liberalism, both in politics and religion' and the extent to which his own decision to form the organization was influenced by fellow-pastors:

Facing the desperate need in the impending crisis of the hour, several concerned pastors began to urge me to put together a political organization that could provide a vehicle to address these crucial issues. Men like James Kennedy (Fort Lauderdale, Florida), Charles Stanley (Atlanta, Georgia), Tim La Haye (San Diego, California), and Greg Dixon (Indianapolis, Indiana) began to share with me a common concern. They urged that we formulate a nonpartisan political organization to promote morality in public life and to combat legislation that favored the legalization of immorality. Together we formulated the Moral Majority, Inc.[70]

The decision to form an organization such as Moral Majority had not, of course, come exclusively from a personal revelation. The links had been made much earlier, and Paul Weyrich and Richard Viguerie had for some time been anxious to recruit Falwell, with his immense personal appeal and television audiences, into their groups. Falwell's own interest had been centered on the saga of tax exemption, and it appears that it was Ed McAteer who introduced Falwell to Weyrich. Indeed, it seems that his involvement in the idea to create an organization of morally conservative Americans had begun as early as March 1979. Responsibility for the actual name 'Moral Majority' is, however, claimed by Weyrich, who says that he mentioned the concept in a meeting with Bob Billings, Jerry Falwell, and Howard Phillips. Certainly, several planning sessions between the gurus of the new right and the religious right occurred between March 1979 and the official birth of the movement in Richmond, Virginia, in September 1979.

The original idea that the Moral Majority would develop state organizations has not been implemented fully. By the summer of 1980 it had skeletal state structures everywhere except in Utah, where it was either thought impractical or unnecessary to organize a state chapter. Optimistic claims about the possible 'outreach' of the group suggested that there might be as many as 85 million Americans with whom to build a 'pro-family Bible believing coalition'. It was suggested in 1979 that Falwell's budget was in excess of $15m., and in January 1980 Moral Majority started to publish a journal, *Moral Majority Report*, whose circulation rose from 77,000 to 482,000 by October.

However, the actual direction of Moral Majority's activities seems to have shifted somewhat. The strategy outlined by Richard Viguerie suggested that much work should be done on the educational and legal front: 'The Moral Majority won't directly help candidates, but it will give politically concerned Christians a way to meet and work with each other.'[71]

One aspect of electoral involvement which it proclaimed as its special task was voter registration, and indeed by July 1980 it claimed to have registered 2.5 million voters. The accuracy of this claim is difficult to assess. Such studies as have been done of grass-roots activity by the Moral Majority suggest that the organization is less than thriving and, as the Executive Director of the Moral Majority admitted in 1982, its organizational structure has given cause for concern.[72] The fact that in 1982 Moral Majority closed down its Political Action Committee, which could back candidates, provides further evidence of a certain lack of direction. (It retained its tax-exempt political form — Moral Majority Inc. — its tax-deductible and tax-exempt Moral Majority Foundation, and its Moral Majority Legal Defense Fund.)

Another organization which was formed to bring together the new-right groups and the religious right has, however, been based on a rather different model from that of Moral Majority. Religious Roundtable (later simply renamed Roundtable) was formed by Ed McAteer with the apparent purpose of providing an umbrella organization for the range of groups which might be interested in fighting on specific moral issues. Because of McAteer's own close ties to Conservative Caucus and his long association with the world of evangelicals, the first planning sessions of Religious Roundtable brought together a wide cross-section of religious leaders and representatives from the major right-of-center pressure-groups. Viguerie, commenting on this development, said that he could think of no better example to indicate the kind of activity now occurring on the right:

It is talented, aggressive leaders meeting and deciding on a course of action in an important area. The Religious Roundtable is just one example of the coordinated, structured conservative activity in a New Right area that didn't happen six years ago.[73]

The thinking behind the umbrella group was that Religious Roundtable could 'reach and activate' tens of millions of other conservatives who, according to Viguerie, 'may play a part when Congress considers legislation affecting abortion, private schools, prayer in schools, sex in the media and a strong national defense'. At the first planning session of the group, which was held in September 1979, the familiar new-right cast of Paul Weyrich, Howard Phillips, Richard Viguerie, Bob Billings, and Senator Gordon Humphrey of New Hampshire was supplemented by Phyllis Schlafly of the anti-Equal Rights Amendment crusade, Clay Claiborne of a group called Black Silent Majority, and Richard Dingman of the Republican Study Committee. Also present was Lance Tarrance, a pollster who had done a good deal of the investigation of social issues for Weyrich's Committee for the Survival of a Free Congress.

Among the religious leaders present were many who had come because of their long associations with Ed McAteer or Bob Billings. These included the founder of the Wycliffe Bible Translators and Ben Armstrong of the National Religious Broadcasters. Also present were Adrian Rogers, the then President of the Southern Baptist Convention, Bob Dugan, the public affairs director of the National Association of Evangelicals, John Talcott of the Plymouth Rock Foundation, and John D. Beckett of Intercessors for America.

Reactions and Impact

The threat posed to liberal causes and to the Democrats specifically by the organization of fundamentalists and conservative evangelicals into the structure of the new right was difficult to measure and difficult to counteract. On the one hand, too obvious an association with the idea of secularism might alienate an electorate which was basically friendly — as the polls seemed to show — to religious causes; on the other hand, the Democrats could hardly emphasize their own religious appeal and risk alienating liberal support. The dilemma of 1979–80 was made all the more acute by President Carter's own proclaimed religious convictions, so that the policy of keeping a strict separation between religious and political convictions was difficult to adopt without inviting ridicule.

In May 1979 President Carter did, however, appoint a liaison officer to foster the Democratic Party's relationship with the religious groups and Churches of America and to try to counter the new right's campaign to equate a vote for God with a vote for conservative candidates. Robert Maddox, the man chosen, was 43 and had the task of trying to reconstruct Democratic support, especially in the South. He had been a Baptist minister in Calhoun, Georgia, before entering the service of the White House. However good his contacts with Southern Baptist churches, it was not until well into the campaign of 1980 that Maddox really went on the offensive and launched a full-scale attack on both the credentials of the Republican presidential candidate and the tactics of the new right. The argument which Maddox used — and it was one which was finding increasing favor among liberal evangelicals of the sort represented by *Sojourners* magazine, as well as among the main-line ecumenical Churches — was that the aims of organizations such as the Moral Majority were incompatible with traditional understanding of the constitutional separation of Church and State. Indeed, Maddox asserted that the conservative Christian movement was bent on 'taking over the country' and 'turning it into a Christian republic by imposing by law their understanding of Christian morality'. Maddox also drew a parallel with McCarthyism, pointing out that instead of finding a Communist under every rock the Christian right was now discovering 'a secular humanist under every rock'.[74]

Later in the campaign more speeches were made denouncing the role of groups like Moral Majority, and bodies such as People for the American Way placed advertisements in newspapers and took television time to point out the dangerous mix of religion and politics that had come on to the American scene.

The precise influence of religion at the 1980 presidential and Congressional elections is difficult to determine. The Michigan data, when broken down by religion, suggest that 'born-again' Christians differed very little from other voters in either their policy attitudes or their partisan preferences.[75]

The integration of the new right and the religious right has been sufficiently controversial to generate fears of a radical transformation of the style of American politics. Certainly, some defeated Senators and Congressmen (e.g. Frank Church and John Buchanan) did blame their defeats upon the influence of groups such as Moral Majority — which in Buchanan's case, in Alabama's primary elections, was especially ironic since he was in fact an ordained minister and a Republican.

It was not only in the arena of electoral politics, however, that the growing political awareness of the fundamentalists and television evangelists was felt. The American political system has a number of points of access and offers many opportunities for the application of political pressure. The growing sensitivity of the new religious right on family issues and the greater activity of the new right generally in this field have caused special attention to be paid to judicial appointments. The nomination by President Carter of Patricia Wald for the Washington Court of Appeals aroused a chorus of protest from new-right and religious-right groups, because she was seen as being anti-family on the basis of articles which she had written suggesting that children ought to be given rights against their parents. Not only are such pressures likely to continue, but the conjunction of a Republican Senate and a Republican President with vacancies to be filled on the Supreme Court makes it probable that the composition of the United States' highest judicial tribunal will reflect the conservative preferences and sensibilities of Reagan's wing of the Republican Party. Surprisingly, however, the first Reagan appointment to the Supreme Court, Sandra Day O'Connor, did cause anger in new-right circles. Mrs O'Connor had been nominated to replace Justice Potter Stewart, and had previously been an Arizona legislator. What annoyed the new- and religious-right groups was that during her time in Arizona politics Mrs O'Connor had voted for a liberal abortion bill. Thus, although the confirmation went through the Senate without a hitch, the August 1981 issue of *Conservative Digest* made plain its feelings about Mrs O'Connor by featuring her on its cover with the caption 'President Reagan's first broken promise'. The promise of a pro-family appointment had been broken, and it is unclear whether the fact that Mrs O'Connor was the first woman to be appointed to the Supreme Court did anything to win back the female vote. Interestingly, in the light of *Conservative Digest*'s attempts to emphasize the significance of the appointment, the journal reprinted an article by two Washington journalists, Rowland Evans and Robert Novak, which suggested that the reason for Mrs O'Connor's elevation in the face of opposition from conservative and religious groups was that the President shared the view of his closest aides, Ed Meese and Jim Baker, that the Moral Majority was of little significance to Reagan's political coalition. One by-product of the controversy, therefore, was to focus attacks on the White House staff and make new-right and religious-right groups press their claims all the more intently for fear of being ignored.

For the immediate future, however, the significance of the revival of religious involvement in the political arena is the extent to which it may have shaped America's political agenda in a negative fashion by discouraging the raising of issues such as public funding of abortions and deflecting candidates from speaking out against the obvious absurdities of the creation-science movement. The development has also sparked off a reconsideration of the role of religion in American life and legitimized an enhanced political role for all the Churches. Whether the religious right will leave any more enduring mark than the new right on the character of politics in twentieth-century America remains to be seen; what is clear is that together both have caused a range of political, intellectual, and religious leaders to question some of the easy assumptions about the country's political and cultural development.

CHAPTER IV

Republicans and the Right

The beneficiary of many of the developments described in the preceding chapters was the regular Republican Party. Over the period since 1976 it had been forced to reassess its policies and to reform its organizational structure, thereby beginning its recovery from the situation it was in immediately after Watergate. In 1978 the Republicans made spectacular gains at both the Congressional level and the state legislative level; in 1980 the GOP captured the White House and the Senate and further improved its position in the House of Representatives and in a number of state legislatures. While the mid-term elections of 1982 cast some doubt on the durability of this Republican trend, it was sufficient to remind observers that the imbalance in the system of party competition which had been so marked a feature of the previous decade could be reversed, and even caused some commentators to suggest that it was no longer accurate to think of the Democratic Party as having a natural majority in the political system.[1] However temporary the Republican revival may yet prove to be, the developments of this period gave the GOP fresh confidence in itself and affected the character and style of the party as an institution.

Although there was clearly considerable change within the GOP in this period, the resurgence of intellectual energy and political activity on the right owed much to forces operating outside the orthodox party channels. Perhaps inevitably, on occasion many of the efforts to promote conservative causes and to inject new life into the Republican Party created tensions between the ideological activists and its older élites.

Even without the explicit differences of outlook in relation to the role of parties which divided regular Republican partisans from the newer 'movers and shakers' of the conservative movement such as Paul Weyrich (some of whom flirted intermittently with the idea of an independent conservative party), there were conflicts of values and outlook within the Republican Party in the 1970s. The increasing organizational sophistication of the conservative faction within the Republican Party began to attract media attention from the mid-1970s. Its growing sense of ideological determination posed problems of party management within Congress and for the Republican National Committee outside it. Such changes suggested a shift in power within the Republican Party and the potential for a new Republican coalition.

In Congress much attention was claimed by the vocal and self-assertive new right. But this element of the GOP was in many ways only one aspect of the transformation which had occurred within the Republican Party. The trend to the right had affected almost the whole of the Congressional party, so that when Ronald Reagan became the party's presidential candidate in 1980 he had no difficulty in conducting a conservative campaign which a united GOP could back. Yet, when the Reagan administration took office it was members of the mainstream Congressional leadership such as Howard Baker, Robert Michel, Robert Dole, and Trent Lott who proved able to deliver legislation. The extreme right, by contrast, was divided and failed to secure the passage of any of its major social legislation.

The general movement towards conservative positions within the Republican ranks did, however, isolate the GOP's liberal and progressive wings. This section of the Republican Party had been based primarily in the North-East and it was increasingly conscious of the extent to which demographic shifts were undermining its political viability.[2] The right of the Republican Party, by contrast, had much of its strength in the expanding areas of the West and Southern Rim. The Goldwater coalition of 1964 had based its campaign strategy on the recruitment of groups from the South and West; and the Reagan effort was heavily predicated upon the candidate's appeal in the same areas.[3] Now these areas were gaining seats through redistribution in the House at the expense of the North-East and mid-West. During the 1970s the right's aggressive tactics — manifested, for example, through two factional organizations called the Republican Study Committee in the House and the somewhat shadowy

Steering Committee in the Senate — also presented problems
for the traditional Republican loyalists who did not necessarily
warm to a new style of intra-party politics.

Although there had been complaints throughout the
1960s and 1970s that Republicans lacked forceful leadership in Congress, the increased visibility of factions was
not entirely welcome to all Republican legislators. Republicans who had spent a considerable amount of time
working with the Democratic majority to craft legislation
on the basis of bipartisan consensus sometimes became
exasperated with attempts to disrupt the timetable of the
legislative process. Congressman Barber Conable, a GOP
mainstream politician and the senior Republican on the
Ways and Means Committee, expressed a clear preference
for helping to govern the country as opposed to taking
partisan postures. In the mid-1970s he charged the Republican right with being the party's most 'negative group'
and cast doubt on its size and influence. Similarly Albert
Quie, who was independent Republican Governor of Minnesota between 1978 and 1982, disagreed with the new
ideological emphasis which could be found in the party
in the latter part of the 1970s; it was, he declared, mere
'tilting at windmills'.[4]

However, the Republican right's enhanced activity over
the 1970s had the effect of changing further the *mores* of
Congress, although it could well be argued that by the late
1970s changes in patterns of behavior with respect to such
issues as seniority and apprenticeship were already far advanced and that the Republican right was reflecting rather
than initiating changes in the internal operations of Congress.[5] Nevertheless, the assumption (to take one example)
that freshmen Senators would not challenge the party leadership seems still to have been sufficiently strong in 1977 to
have caused criticism of Utah Senator Orrin Hatch's activities
during his first term in Washington.[6]

For the Republican National Committee the divisions
within Republican ranks brought problems as party chairmen
sought to preserve the image of unity and as senior party
officials tried to minimize the bitterness of the legacy left
by primary fights in which candidates of the right were pitted

against mainstream Republican incumbents. The experience of John Buchanan's defeat in the 1980 House primary in the Alabama Sixth District and the defeat of the regular Republican Party's preferred candidate for the Senate race in the same state by right-of-center Jeremiah Denton exposed internal divisions, just as New York Senator Jacob Javits's defeat by Alfonse d'Amato (who was backed by a Committee for the Defeat of Jacob Javits) raised the question of whether increased mobilization of conservative forces might debilitate the Republican Party as a whole.[7] Certainly Ronald Reagan, although in many ways a sympathizer with the new right and an outspoken champion of conservative positions, was very conscious of the need to preserve Republican unity wherever possible. Thus, he refrained in 1978 from intervening in the New Jersey Senate primary when new-right candidate Jeffrey Bell challenged the well-established liberal Senator Clifford Case.[8]

The 'hard-ball' tactics of NCPAC proved counter-productive in the 1982 Congressional elections, and even caused some change of strategy by NCPAC during the campaigns. Unlike in 1980, only one of the twenty Senators targeted for defeat by NCPAC in 1982 actually lost, and their top three candidates for defeat in the House were also reelected.[9] Moreover, NCPAC intervention actually seemed to help some Democrats. Thus, for example, Paul Sarbanes, who was running for reelection to the Senate in Maryland, found that being targeted by NCPAC enabled him to raise money early and to turn the role of NCPAC into an election issue. In 1981 William Brock's successor, Richard Richards, indicated party dissatisfaction by joining with Democratic Chairman Charles Manatt to suggest establishing a commission to investigate the electoral role of PACs and by asking them to stay out of races where they were not wanted.[10] (Richards's tenure of the Republican chairmanship was marked by conflicts both with the White House staff and with the various new-right groups. His resignation in early 1983 enabled Ronald Reagan to replace him with Paul Laxalt, a trusted friend, as overall party chairman.[11])

The strengthening of the Republican right also caused some problems for the administration elected in 1980, although

in many respects the right saw one of its own placed in the
White House. A parallel can perhaps be drawn between the
situation in the Republican Party in the aftermath of the
1980 elections and that of the immediate post-war period.
The moderates in the Republican Party in the 1950s may
have deplored much of what the right was then doing in
relation to the exploitation of such themes as communist
subversion and the China issue; but they saw the advantage
to be gained from hammering at them against a Democratic
administration. What did cause difficulty was the need to
suppress the promotion of certain right-wing ideas after
1952, once Republicans rather than Democrats formed
the administration.[12] Some examination of the ebb and flow
of policy arguments and of the influence of ideology upon
them will be given in the next chapter. Here discussion will
be directed towards the changes in the pattern of Republican
factionalism and the extent to which the 1970s and early
1980s saw the creation of a different balance within the
GOP.

The Nature of American Party Divisions

Party politics in the United States is, more than in most
political systems, a matter of building and maintaining
coalitions.[13] Although it is generally agreed that the Republican Party is now more ideologically cohesive than the
Democratic Party, it would be a mistake to see it as being
either a homogeneous or a united body, even prior to the
resurgence of conservative activity in the 1970s.[14] Its divisions are nevertheless qualitatively different from those of
the Democratic Party, which has increasingly seemed in
danger of becoming a coalition of interests so divergent
and contradictory that genuine party activity and leadership
have sometimes been rendered impossible.[15]

Writers on the Republican Party have commented on the
manner in which the GOP's factions are 'less visceral' and
more complex than those which exist in the Democratic
Party and have used a number of different categories to try
to explain the currents of opinion within GOP ranks.[16] Here
three simple categories will be used, although it must be

borne in mind that these are by no means precise or solid groupings. Indeed, the Republican Party, like the British Conservative Party, is difficult to analyze in terms of ideologically related measures, since most Republicans are pragmatic politicians oriented towards the practical side of politics. Rarely do Republicans produce coherent statements of political principles, although they may, of course, produce policy statements and personal apologias which allow the commentator to construct a description of the politician's ideological assumptions.[17]

Broadly speaking, the Republican Party can be divided into three tendencies. First, and most important, there is the Republican mainstream which occupies the center of the Republican Party's ideological spectrum and is characterized by a variety of compatible but not always explicit attitudes, orientations, and values. Secondly, there is the Republican right, which has a much more pronounced ideological character and a style which is distinctive if not downright aggressive. Thirdly, there is the liberal–progressive wing of the Republican Party, which has much in common with certain sections of the Democratic Party and is generally willing to contemplate and adjust to social change and to applaud governmental intervention on a case-by-case basis.

The Republican Mainstream

The mainstream of the Republican Party has changed as the burning issues of the day and the various personalities at the center of American politics have come and gone. While it may be true that a 'definitive history of the Republican Party' will never be written because of the need to assess the developments within the Party at so many different levels, there is none the less a distinctive Republican tradition which has generated loyalty both to the party as an institution and to a certain set of American political values.[18]

Historically, it was the Republican Party which represented the interests of business and capital and, although much of this was to be changed by the experience of the New Deal, it was the GOP also which was identified with the élites of the Yankee establishment. But there was a strand in the Republican tradition which reflected another aspect of American life. The small-town, middle-class, Protestant background that dominated much of the American scene in the nineteenth and early twentieth centuries produced Republican 'stalwarts' who reflected the ethos and prejudices of middle America.[19] Their background was most frequently in small business rather than in corporate finance, although the professional classes in the nineteenth and early twentieth centuries also tended to be solidly Republican. The interests of small and family-sized concerns in the Republican Party sometimes conflicted with those of the large corporations and trusts, so that appeals to Main Street did not always chime with appeals to Wall Street.

Although now committed to free trade, the GOP was generally in favor of protectionism; and at various times it was prepared to see other government intervention in the economy. Thus, although business in general naturally favored the Republican Party — and increasingly did so because of the growing role of organized labor — the party's mainstream was not necessarily wedded to uncritical *laissez-faire* free-market economics. After the Keynesian 'revolution' it accepted some forms of government intervention in the economy, and, although obviously more favorable to the Chicago school of economics than to Keynesianism, it did not become the prisoner of any economic doctrine. The debate about supply-side economics in the late 1970s, as one commentator noted, produced a good deal of nonsense about Republican attitudes to the economy in general and particularly about the views of President Reagan on the subject.[20] Republicans will tend to adapt whatever appropriate economic tools are to hand, but they have a general bias against government and government expenditure. In the context of the 1970s, with the much-publicized tax rebellions in states like California, the climate was ripe for a doctrine which stressed the importance of tax cuts in restoring economic prosperity. Indeed, even Republicans (such as New York's Barber Conable) who were deeply suspicious of deficits and had little enthusiasm for supply-side doctrines found it difficult in that climate to resist going on the record as favoring tax-cutting initiatives such as the Kemp–Roth bill.

Religion was an important factor in the mainstream Republican tradition. Most Republicans in the nineteenth century were of Anglo-Saxon, German, or Scandinavian backgrounds. The adherence to evangelical Protestantism led the Anglo-Saxon groups at least to be hostile to what they saw as the social evils of drinking, prostitution, and gambling. Until very recently one might have been accurate in describing this essentially mid-western constituency of the Republican Party — which was the driving force behind the bizarre attempt after the First World War to prohibit the sale and consumption of alcohol — as the base of the GOP and the source of its values.[21] The world of this section of society which formed the backbone of American Republicanism was beautifully captured by Sinclair Lewis in such novels as *Main Street*.[22]

Religion was also important as a method of establishing social status. Although the 1980 elections returned an unusually large number of Roman Catholic Republicans to Congress, for most of the twentieth century Protestantism was a feature which differentiated Republican Wasps from Democratic ethnics — be they Roman Catholic or Jewish.[23] Yet it is important not to be too cynical about the religious strand in the mainstream Republican tradition. The party had, after all, been founded on the issue of opposition to the extension of slavery, and the moralism inherent in that campaign reflected a genuine simple piety which informed later crusades. While the mainstream of the Republican Party was not enamoured of the civil rights revolution, it still looks towards the nineteenth- and early twentieth-century moral debates as a source of pride and inspiration. Despite the virtually monolithic support which blacks now give to the Democratic Party, there are still efforts by Republicans (albeit somewhat unsuccessful) through such groups as Blacks for Reagan and the Lincoln Institute to break the Democratic hold on that vote by reviving the memory of Lincoln and emancipation.

The ethnic composition of the mainstream of the Republican Party and its original geographical base in the mid-West affected the party's orientation in foreign policy. Thus, while significant sections of the Democratic Party, including the

South, were internationalist in outlook, the mainstream of the Republican Party has a tradition of suspicion about foreign-policy entanglements. In part this wariness stemmed from a general wish to maintain 'fortress America' free of overseas alliances; in part it reflected the natural unwillingness of many mid-western Republicans of German or Scandinavian extraction to support an alliance with the British Empire, because such an alliance would be directed against Germany.

The pragmatic nature of the mainstream of the party and the fact that it has been forced to take responsibility for the government of the country have inevitably meant that mainstream Republicans have tended to adapt their foreign-policy preferences in the light of changes in the international environment. Prior to the Second World War, the Republican Party's isolationist tendency was predominant, and this explained the rejection by the Senate of the United States' membership of the League of Nations. The rise of the communist threat, however, forced the vast majority of Republican leaders to accept the inevitability of a continuing American overseas involvement, although some did not accept that there was any greater reason to commit American troops to the defense of Europe than to the Pacific arena and there remained a lingering hostility towards the British in those parts of the GOP which were oriented towards the leading ethnic groups of the mid-West.

Thus, while the GOP came to accept the inevitability of international involvement, the underlying layers of contrary attitudes remained; when any crisis occurred which brought attitudes towards the international arena to the surface, what appeared among Republicans could still be isolationism, anti-Europeanism, and a certain degree of hostility towards the élites of the State Department and the Eastern Establishment, where it was thought that the true interests of America were sold short.[24]

The mainstream of the Republican Party generated in the post-war period a number of different kinds of politician, ranging from Robert Taft of Ohio — who so reflected the *mores* of the party that he was dubbed 'Mr Republican' — to the more internationalist Senator Vandenberg and the

procedurally skillful Everett Dirkson. (Taft's own hostility
to European entanglements appears to have come from his
experiences at the end of the First World War, when, although pro-British, he became disgusted with the squabbling
of the Allies during the peace conferences and doubted the
ability of the United States to settle the 'ancient animosities
of Europe'.[25]) Robert Taft, it is true, never won the Presidency, but he probably retained the affection of Republicans
to a much greater extent than did the man who narrowly
beat him for the nomination in 1952, General Eisenhower.

The Taft–Eisenhower battle for the nomination left a
lasting mark on the Republican Party. The GOP was split
into two almost equally powerful personal coalitions; but
although loyalty to a candidate was the motivating force
in each, the blocs which formed around the rivals represented many of the major cleavages in Republican ranks. Taft
tended to win the support of the more intransigent opponents of the New Deal and of the isolationists, and his
regional appeal was concentrated in the mid-West and South.
Eisenhower appealed to those who wanted a winning candidate rather than merely a true party man; and he tended
to win the support of the north-eastern internationalists.
Eisenhower's victory had the effect of installing the moderate
wing of the party in power, but at a price. For the men who
surrounded him tended to pay little attention to party
matters, and Eisenhower himself neglected the party organization at state and local level.[26] By 1960, therefore, not
only had the liberal and pragmatic wing of the Party not
developed leaders to succeed Eisenhower, but the liberals
could be charged with failure to nurture the GOP's grass
roots.

Loyalty to the Republican Party as an institution has been
a characteristic feature of its mainstream and it has created
both Republican dynasties and an emphasis on being a 'team
player'. The dynastic elements in the Republican Party are
well represented by Howard Baker, who married the late
Everett Dirksen's daughter, and by such families as the Tafts
and the Scrantons. The insistence on loyalty above factionalism is well represented in the attitudes of men such as Gerald
Ford, William Brock, and George Bush.

The Republican Right

In contrast to the mainstream faction of the Republican Party, which is itself by no means homogeneous, there has developed a faction or tendency which is much more clear-cut in character. This is the Republican right, which has gone through a number of incarnations over the course of the twentieth century. Thus, in the period prior to the Second World War it was determinedly hostile to the experiments of the New Deal. In part this hostility was a response to the ideas on which the New Deal was founded; in part it reflected Republican aggravation at being excluded from the power and patronage of government. In the years after 1945 the Republican right was fiercely anti-communist and dedicated to the rooting out of subversive elements within the United States. By the 1960s, with the rise of Barry Goldwater, it had extended its hostility to the federal government's general role as a social and economic regulator. The right had also become critical of the Supreme Court, both because of the substantive policies of the Warren Court after 1953 and because of the constitutional role which it was developing in relation to civil rights.[27] Care must be taken, however, in attributing to the right complete opposition to the federal courts. Orrin Hatch, for example, although deeply critical of the 1973 Supreme Court decision which held that there was a constitutional right to an abortion in the first three months of pregnancy, felt he could not join Senator Helms's attempt in 1981 to limit the jurisdiction of the courts in this matter.[28] He chose to promote legislation which would have allowed the states and Congress to prohibit abortion, whereas Helms continued to promote a much more sweeping constitutional amendment on the subject. Frequently the right finds itself divided over respect for the traditional institutions of the American polity and support for the actual policies handed down by them.

The development of the Republican right and the renewal of ideological conservatism went hand-in-hand in the 1960s, although the political strength of the right in that decade was much less than the renewed intellectual interest in conservative ideas.[29] Certainly it seemed novel in a political system which has eschewed ideologies and has not provided much opportunity for conservative parties to flourish. Although the Republican right took on a recognizably modern look in the period after 1964 (and also acquired by courtesy of Young Americans for Freedom some of its contemporary leaders), the defeat of Goldwater in 1964 was demoralizing; thus, while some would claim that the Republican Party has been controlled by the right since 1964, there has been more of an alternation between a Republican Party anxious to follow its ideological leanings and one anxious to regain power.[30] The choice of Richard Nixon as the presidential candidate in 1968 was the result of a desperate search for a winner rather than an indication that his policies were palatable to the right of the party.[31] And the success of the insurgent campaign of Ronald Reagan against an incumbent Republican President in 1976 — largely over *détente* with the Soviet Union and the Panama Canal Treaties — underlined just how torn the Republican right was between the urge for power and the urge for purity.[32]

Much of what has engaged the Republican right relates to style as much as to substance, for it has rejected the older notions in the legislature of 'going along to get along' and has sought to put forward very clearly defined Republican policies as an alternative to those offered by the Democrats. On some themes, such as the economy, the Republican right has for long had a difficult passage, given that there had developed a consensus behind the New Deal tradition of intervention in the economic life of the country. However, with what were perceived as the excesses of the Great Society programs and the intellectual debate about the efficacy of government intervention in the economy, a great change took place and the Republican right found itself able to adopt some positions which were no longer those of an embattled rearguard minority. The criticisms which the right had been making about the inadequacy of the defense budget and of the policy of *détente* became more widely accepted also. Nowhere was this more plainly seen than in the United States Senate, which over the decade between 1970 and 1980 was transformed from being one of the most liberal institutions in the federal system of government to one which was taking the initiative in hawkish policies.[33]

Much of the right's appeal originally was to the youth of the United States, who became organized through groups such as Young Americans for Freedom and the official Young Republicans.[34] The style of politics created on the right in the 1960s seemed at least as exciting as that on the left, although it should be noted that for both the Republicans and the Democrats the regular party machines paid a heavy price for the excitement. The fact that the right's agenda was not solely concerned with economic issues led some commentators to wonder whether the right might not be the cutting edge for a new alignment of political forces in America. Issues with a racial component seemed promising material for developing the strength of the Republican Party in the South, although it should not be forgotten that GOP politicians as far back as Taft had been concerned to protect the Republicanism of the South (they would not, however, have tolerated the exploitation of racial antagonism for political gain).[35]

The racial aspect of the right's creed and the heavy emphasis on limiting the jurisdiction of the federal courts and supporting states' rights have meant that many of the most obvious contemporary members of the Republican right hail from the South or the Southern Rim. Equally well represented, however, on the right of the Republican Party are the western and Rocky Mountain states, which seem to have produced a group of obviously conservative legislators, such as James McClure and Steve Symms of Idaho, Jake Garn and Orrin Hatch of Utah, Malcolm Wallop of Wyoming, and Paul Laxalt of Nevada. And while many of these politicians were initially seen as mavericks, Senator McClure and Senator Laxalt acquired general respect in the GOP during the 1970s, to the extent that the former was mentioned as a possible successor to Howard Baker and Laxalt was made Party Chairman on Richard Richards's retirement. These 'Rocky Mountain conservatives' were partly responsible for the incorporation of the range of themes discussed earlier as 'family issues' into the agenda of the Republican right generally.[36] Opposition to abortion, women's liberation, and homosexuality, and a desire to reintroduce prayer in schools, have all become themes which separate the right wing of the GOP from the mainstream, although it is perhaps now the case that it is the intensity with which such issues are pursued rather than the substantive opinions which often constitutes the dividing line in Republican ranks.

What is worth remembering, however, is that while there are visible proponents of the whole gamut of Republican right themes — and Senator Helms of North Carolina would be an obvious example — even within the ranks of the right there are divisions of opinion. Barry Goldwater, although instrumental in promoting members of the new right to leadership positions in the Senate, does not believe that moral issues should play the role they do in political debate within contemporary Republican politics, and there have been some marked differences of opinion on the authority of the government with respect to questions of personal morality and life-style. Indeed, *Congressional Quarterly* commented in 1982 that it was symbolic that the *coup de grâce* to the new right's social issues in that session of Congress should have been delivered not by liberals but by such figures as Senator Hayakawa of California and Senator Goldwater.[37]

The definition of the Republican right has primarily been undertaken on the basis of attitudes towards certain crucial issues of public policy, because until very recently — when the Republican Study Committee became a force in the House of Representatives and the Steering Committee became a major conservative force in the Senate — there was little organizational basis for the right wing of the GOP.[38] However, the use of transient issues makes it difficult to trace patterns over time, since, however similar a vote on, for example, taxation or a foreign-policy question may appear to be between one Congress and the next, there is always sufficient alteration in the parameters of debate to make precise comparisons misleading. Equally, what in one Congress may have been an indication of extreme conservatism may by the next Congress have been transformed into party orthodoxy. Thus, even Edwin Feulner, in his account of the development of the Republican Study Committee, is not entirely sure that the fact that 80 per cent of current GOP members of the House are affiliated to the Republican Study Committee is entirely a cause for congratulation. It may well be, as he acknowledges, that the Committee has lost its cutting edge and perhaps become an accepted part of Republican activity. This is possibly analogous to the transformation which came over the Bow Group in Britain: originally a pressure-group on the left of the British Conservative Party, it became an accepted organization within the Tory fold and lost much of its initial radicalism.[39]

During the 1970s several informal clubs sprang up in the House of Representatives to promote the discussion of conservative ideas and to facilitate cooperation on the floor of the House. This development presaged the major institutional change which occurred within the Republican Party, when it developed a formal organizational base for its right-of-center members in the form of the Republican Study Group. At the same time, Republicans became increasingly willing to challenge the established leadership both on substantive policy issues and on tactics.

The House, it must be remembered, is a much more anonymous body than the Senate, and even if the Senate ethos of a gentlemen's club has to some extent been eroded by the changes of the 1970s, the roles of party whipping, of caucus and conference, and of organization are much more important in the larger body than they are in the select institution of the Senate.[40]

The organization of the American legislature reached a watershed in 1970 because in that year the Legislative Reorganization Act greatly expanded the staff facilities available to members of Congress, and thus hastened a greater professionalization in the legislative process. Yet that professionalization increased the need for greater coordination, since it expanded the number of significant actors in the legislative process as senior legislative assistants and junior aides came to play an ever more important role in explaining, shaping, and advising the decisions open to Congressmen. The institutionalization of the right within the Republican Party in the House formerly occurred in 1973, when the Republican Study Committee was created. This organization was the result of discussions between Phillip Crane and two other Congressmen, the highly conservative Edward Derwinski (who in 1982 lost the seat he had held for twenty-four years) and Del Clawson. Like so many of the developments on the right in the 1970s, it owed much to the model provided on the liberal side of politics — in this case the Democratic Study Group, which had been the catalyst for many of the reforms within Congress which substantially modified the operation of seniority and the workings of the committee system.[41]

Much of the impetus to organize conservative Republicans in the House had come from the experience of Richard Nixon's second term in the Presidency, when two measures in particular — the Family Assistance Plan and the Child Development Act — had excited Republican rank-and-file anger on ideological grounds. The Republican Study Committee had to operate with a few individual members contributing the time of their personal staff, but it was able to appoint as full-time director Edwin Feulner, who subsequently became the director of the Heritage Foundation. After Feulner left the Republican Study Committee to head Heritage, Richard Dingman became its Executive Director. Dingman's position again underlines the preexisting links between the new right, the religious right, and the orthodox Republican Party. Dingman had worked for John Conlan, who had been involved in earlier efforts to forge an alliance between the Christian community and the right — most notably via the Christian Freedom Foundation. Dingman was invited to join the regular luncheons organized by Paul Weyrich and later became Chairman of the Kingston Group, which provided a forum for new-right strategy both inside and outside of Congress.

The development of an organizational base for conservative Republicans, who had increased in number as the 1970s wore on, the provision of an independent source of research and information that was separate from the party hierarchy, and the establishment of a network of contacts between House members, their staff, and the outside groups which were also developing at that time (such as the Heritage Foundation and the Committee for the Survival of a Free

Congress), represented a significant change in the Congressional milieu. The impact of the development of an organized right-wing Republican faction on the legislative output of the House is difficult to measure, but certainly it seems clear that the Republican Study Committee began to make itself felt during the years of the Carter Presidency.

In the Senate right-wing members conducted a successful filibuster against President Carter's Labor Law Reform Bill, while new-right forces in and out of Congress mobilized against the legalization of a form of picketing known as common situs picketing. The bill was designed to allow unions to picket an entire construction site regardless of whether the dispute was with a single contractor (in the United States such secondary picketing had been illegal since 1951). The campaign against this form of picketing was effected with the aid of the Chamber of Commerce and the Right to Work Committee.

The Senate Steering Committee was founded in 1974, and it has made a substantial contribution to the alteration of the attitude within the Senate to the question of defense expenditure, intelligence activities, and the general posture of the United States towards the Soviet Union. It may be that the personalities of certain new-right Senators, such as Orrin Hatch and Jesse Helms, make it easier for them to act as critics of legislative proposals or as 'gadflies' challenging existing assumptions and springing new legislative strategies on an unsuspecting body of Senators.[42] Certainly, once the Republicans had gained a Senate majority in 1981 the attempt by Helms and others to pass a substantive program of legislation on the basis of their family policies on abortion and school prayer ultimately came to nothing, although the abortion resolutions did reach the floor of the Senate. This failure suggested to many observers that their destructive capacity was greater than their constructive ability to build and maintain a legislative coalition. (In Helms's case there was much personal criticism of his handling in 1982 of the Agriculture Bill and speculation about whether, despite the enormous personal war-chest at his disposal, he would survive his next reelection race.[43]) Yet even if the successes of the Steering Committee and the new right have not been sustained, it would be a mistake to underestimate their joint role — together, it has to be admitted, with like-minded hawkish Democrats such as the late Senator Jackson — in reversing the mood of the Senate, particularly in relation to foreign policy, during the 1970s.[44]

The Republican right thus increased both its activity and its visibility in the 1970s, although the extent to which it remained a recognizable faction within the Congressional party was perhaps reduced by the manner in which the mainstream itself had shifted to the right.

Initially, the right's most controversial standard-bearers had seemed to be an irritant in GOP counsels; but slowly some of them gained intra-party respectability. In the 95th Congress, for example (1977–9), the Republican right gained access to a number of committees and leadership positions. According to a study of Orrin Hatch, this was partly because Carl Curtis of Nebraska (a conservative Republican who had once employed Paul Weyrich as his special assistant), the Chairman of the Republican Conference, selected Jake Garn, a conservative Senator who was also from Utah, as the Chairman of the Select Committee on Committees, which distributes committee assignments. Not only did this mean that a Senator sympathetic to the right was in a powerful position to promote freshmen; it also meant that Garn was able to substitute Hatch for himself on the Republican Policy Committee. As the same study has noted, some of the Republican professionals looked upon the new western conservatives — and especially Hatch — with misgivings because of their refusal to be apprentices. Certainly, such fights as that waged by the right of the Republican Party against the Panama Canal Treaties — in opposition to the then minority leader, Howard Baker, who supported Carter's treaties — revealed that the Republicans had acquired a more red-blooded political philosophy during the 1970s and that some at least were determined to press it even against their own leadership.[45]

The Liberal Republicans

The third strand of the Republican party which needs to be

mentioned is the liberal–progressive element. Just as the
GOP was divided in the early years of the twentieth century
between its progressive or reformist wing and the more
conservative mainstream, so there is a liberal tradition which
is today reflected in the politics of Senators Weicker, Mathias,
and Chafee. Sometimes this liberalism has been reflective of
a city constituency, and it is noticeable, for example, that
New York in the period after 1945 produced two controversial liberal Republicans, Nelson Rockefeller and Jacob
Javits. Both Rockefeller and Javits — like contemporary liberal
Republicans — were somewhat suspect within their own
party on domestic and foreign policy.[46]

A slightly different brand of liberal Republicanism would
be that represented by Bob Packwood of Oregon, who in
1982 criticized President Reagan's economic policies as
being too harsh on the underprivileged. Senator Packwood
(who was one of three Republicans targeted for defeat by
the new right) had condemned President Reagan for his
neglect of minority interests in America and for his insensi-
tivity to such issues as women's rights. Although Packwood
had been Chairman of the National Republican Senatorial
Committee (which distributes campaign funds to Senate
candidates), he was regarded as unusually moderate in his
views on the need for cuts in federal expenditure; and it is
noticeable that this element in the GOP — which has a
certain tradition of isolationism — wished to see the budget
deficit reduced not by cuts in domestic social programs but
by limiting the expansion of the military budget and raising
taxation. Indeed, Packwood's distance from his fellow
Republicans was underlined when he was ousted from the
Senatorial Committee position and replaced by Senator
Lugar, a figure whose right-of-center views made him much
closer to Reagan in outlook.[47]

Equally outside the mainstream of the GOP was Oregon's
senior Senator, Mark Hatfield, who cosponsored with Edward
Kennedy a resolution in favor of a nuclear freeze, thus
indicating his divergence from the Republican mainstream;
he had earlier cosponsored a resolution to withdraw American troops from Vietnam. In addition to this streak of
pacific isolationism, Hatfield had been active in the campaign

for tuition tax credits for parents who wished to send their children to private (mainly religious) schools.

Ideological differences are not the only points of distinction between the Republicans, especially since, as has been seen, these divergences are extremely fluid in the American system, and so cannot be delineated with very great precision. It is also important to note that a distinction must be made between the Republican Party at the Congressional level and the Republican Party in the states. Although it is within Congress that the tensions within the GOP ranks become most evident — and certainly provide the fare for its ratings by the various pressure-groups and lobbies — the party outside Congress is important, especially given the fact that in the post-war period Republicans have generally been a minority in Congress. The balance of power within the Congressional GOP may thus not be identical to that within other important political forums, and there are often slightly different nuances between the Republican Party in the House of Representatives and that in the Senate.

Thus, with respect to the liberal wing of the Republican Party, which has been on the defensive in both the House and the Senate, state-level contests have proved rather more encouraging than federal legislative contests. And during the 1960s and 1970s the Republican Governors almost became an identifiable liberal and progressive pressure-group within the GOP.[48] For example, in 1981 Reagan found opposition to his spending cuts in relation to Medicaid among a number of members of the National Governors' Conference who might in other respects have supported his brand of federalism.[49]

The Republican National Committee and the Electoral Dimension

The general weakening of political parties which had occurred over the period 1968–74 was to some extent reversed by the reforms undertaken by William Brock, who became Chairman of the Republican National Committee in 1976. It would be inappropriate here to detail all the changes which Brock introduced, but the most significant was the introduction of a major direct-mail fund-raising campaign, which placed Republican finances in a very healthy position by comparison with those of the Democratic Party. In addition, Brock sought to strengthen the Republican Party's chances of success by improving the caliber of the candidates running under the GOP banner. This was partly achieved by the establishment of a local elections division at the RNC, which could recruit and train candidates for state and local offices. Given the importance of legislative or administrative experience as a factor in determining whether a challenger can mount a good campaign, this development represented a good investment for the future of the Republican Party and its ability to have a pool of talented candidates available for federal races, even if it did not immediately pay obvious dividends. In addition to the establishment of this local elections division, the RNC established a Candidate Management College which could train Congressional candidates in the arts and wizardry of modern campaigning techniques.[50]

One major reason for strengthening Republican efforts at the state and local level in 1980 was the imminent electoral redistricting, which was largely over by 1982. Thereafter the local elections division changed its emphasis and devoted most of its resources to sending party advisers and operatives into the field to help the candidates and local party workers develop campaign skills.[51]

The strategy of the Republican National Committee in 1980 was thus to recruit able candidates and cater for the future recruitment of such politicians, and to provide the resources to support Republican standard-bearers directly. Although the strategy was modified to take account of the different environment of 1982, it still set a model which a chastened Democratic Party sought to emulate.

Even in 1980, however, not all candidates were equally supported. The party selected some seats in which they hoped to do well and concentrated their efforts there. (Similarly, in 1982 it was obvious that not every Republican candidate was favored with major Republican Party financial backing. For example, former Congresswoman Heckler was somewhat underfunded in her race against Barney Frank in Massachusetts even though the seat was an open one.)

In addition to the material aid provided by the Republican National Committee there was an obvious attempt over the period of Brock's chairmanship to develop a set of campaign themes and issue positions which would both be attractive to the American electorate as a whole and also enable the campaigns at the various levels to be integrated. Ironically, perhaps, the advantage felt by candidates who associated themselves with Reagan in 1980 was conspicuously lacking in 1982, as candidates sought to dissociate themselves from unpopular national economic trends and to localize their races.

The Republican National Committee devoted a good deal of attention during the period 1976–80 to improving its research and publicity. The provision of material for direct electoral use was one aspect of this, but so too was the enhanced role given to policy research and the establishment of a new Republican journal of opinion called *Common Sense*.[52]

By these initiatives the regular Republican Party was providing the kind of comprehensive and dedicated approach to elections offered by the pressure-groups of the new right, such as the Committee for the Survival of a Free Congress, NCPAC, and Senator Helms's Congressional Club; and it was also attempting to reassert the centrality of party in the funding of elections. The fact that the renewal of central-party activity by the Republicans occurred at the same time as the new right was seeking to maximize its electoral impact by targeting vulnerable members of Congress makes it difficult to disentangle the effects of the reforms in the Republican National Committee from the effects of intervention by the independent groups in the races, where in 1980 the Republicans had their major impact. However, as far as the balance between the parties was concerned, the GOP retained its advantage in fund-raising and services to candidates throughout 1982, so that not only were Republicans at a substantial advantage in the 1980 elections but arguably the party was able to moderate its mid-term political losses.[53]

Because both the GOP itself and many of the new-right groups which intervened to back selected candidates were working in 1980 in a common effort to reverse the liberal and Democratic tide, the contradictions and conflicts of priority in their approaches were muted in that year. Republicans could assail the Democratic record on the economy, on foreign policy, and on family or social issues. In 1982, however, the story was very different, and Republicans had to defend the record of the administration as well as broadening their appeals to keep their vote in a mid-term election year. Frequently, this meant a reduced emphasis on the family or social issues, even where a Republican candidate had received strong backing from new-right groups.

Not all of the Republicans who were elected or sought election in 1980 changed their style in response to the perception of a new mood in 1982. Some did tone down their social policy statements, with varying degrees of success. Thus, John Kasich of Ohio, who had a strong record of support for new-right hero Philip Crane and was a firm opponent of abortion and domestic spending, let his constituency set the agenda for discussion and succeeded in ousting a newly elected Democrat;[54] Mark Siljander in Michigan, although initially a fervent conservative, was forced by a strong primary challenge to broaden his party appeal;[55] and Christopher Smith managed to keep his New Jersey seat partly by reducing the emphasis on his own strong anti-abortion convictions.[56]

The general theme of the economy and employment would perhaps have dominated the campaigns of 1982 anyway; but there was a distinct shift of strategy in challengers' campaigns too. Thus, both Anne Bagnal in North Carolina and John Sonneland in Washington admitted a deliberate broadening of their campaigns away from such issues as abortion.[57] Both candidates had narrowly lost to Democrats in 1980, but their revised strategy did not help them in 1982 and neither was elected.

Some Republican candidates refused to water down their ideological message. Robin Beard in Tennessee, Vin Weber in Minnesota, John Paul Stark in California, and David Staton in West Virginia all kept a strong emphasis on social issues in their campaigns. Beard and Staton lost, although whether any conclusions about the significance of social issues can be drawn from their defeat is debatable.[58]

What may be concluded, then, about the extent to which
the Republican Party has been affected by the new issues
and themes raised over the period 1976–82? First, while
1978 and 1980 did bring into Congress a number of Republicans who had used social issues to secure election and who
were overtly conservative, the same was not so true of the
1982 intake. Some of the Republicans elected in the 1980
'Republican year' lost, and some changed their positions,
sometimes to the irritation of new-right groups which had
backed them. At the same time a second point has to be
recognized. Congress is now a career, and many of the
modifications which marked the positions taken by men
such as Senator Quayle, for example, represent the inevitable
transformation which occurs when a challenger becomes a
member of an institution geared to governing. Yet that does
not mean that the Congressman or Senator has fundamentally changed his position; the style is more accommodating
but the values have not changed. Thirdly, the use of social
issues to mobilize activists on behalf of candidates remains
important. As one Californian Republican commented on the
enthusiasm of anti-abortion activists, 'Right-to-life types will
quit their jobs and go to work for you 40 hours a week.
Their help is probably greatly disproportionate to their
numbers.'[59]

Congressional Management and Policy

The divisions within the Republican ranks which have been
mentioned were of potential electoral significance, but had
little direct impact on public policy prior to 1980 because of
the GOP's minority status. Matters inevitably changed when,
after the inauguration of President Reagan, a majority
had to be held in place to support the President's legislative
program, which, unlike many previous Republican agendas,
seemed based on an unusually explicit ideology and involved
a great deal of action to cut the budgets of various agencies,
departments, and bureaus.

The management of Congressional relations differs in the
House and the Senate. Fundamentally, however, it involves
two processes in both chambers. First, the troops of the

incumbent's own party have to be marshaled effectively; and secondly, appropriate coalitions have to be devised to make a majority for individual items of legislation.

As far as the cohesion of the Republican Party itself was concerned, the first two years of the Reagan administration registered a substantial degree of unity. In the Senate in particular Howard Baker developed a reputation as a highly efficient legislative leader, able both to deliver votes and to do so by a strategy which kept Republicans together and minimized the need for deals with the Democrats. However, with the recession and the onset of the 1982 mid-term elections, the inevitable tendency of both Senators and Congressmen to distance themselves from a potentially unpopular administration reasserted itself. And the liberal–progressive wing of the Republican Party was increasingly found after early 1982 adding its voice to the doubts which Democrats expressed about the President's economic strategy and objectives. Nevertheless, the degree of Republican cohesion in the Senate was still quite impressive, although it dropped from the unusual level of 81 per cent in 1981 to 76 per cent in 1982, and to 74 per cent in 1983.[60]

In the construction of a winning coalition to secure the passage of legislation Republican party managers obviously faced different situations in the Senate, where from 1981 they had a small majority, and the House, where they were still the minority party. In the House, Republican cohesion and support of the President were less marked than in the Senate, and after 1982 there was an unusual degree of democratic unity. Clearly, different situations faced party managers in the 96th and the 97th Congresses. In 1981 the Republicans were able to capitalize on the presidential victory, and the so-called 'boll-weevils' produced a margin of victory for a conservative coalition which was ideologically sympathetic to Reagan's policies. In the 1983 Congress, House Democrats reasserted their partisan identity by refusing to assign key committee appointments to southern Democrats unwilling to pay sufficient attention to the party line (for example, they removed Phil Gramm, the man associated with the first budget victories, from the Budget Committee; Gramm later became a Republican).

They also adopted procedural rules which limited the ability of Congressmen to attach non-germane riders to appropriations bills. The effect of these changes was to reduce dramatically the strength of the conservative coalition and to limit the opportunities for Congressmen such as Henry Hyde of Illinois to insert social policy riders into law, as he had done with the so-called 'Hyde amendment' limiting the availability of Medicaid for abortions.

Relationships between the Congressional Republican Party and the President, despite some disagreements over the budget and foreign-policy issues such as the sale of AWACS (which passed by the narrowest of margins), remained good since the President's congressional liaison staff, by comparison with President Carter's, were extremely professional and competent.

Both the image and the content of Republicanism were affected by the political developments of the period 1976–82, although, as has been seen in relation to the modifications which occurred in the 1982 elections, the course of the ideological movement was not by any means a straight or consistent one. Nevertheless, it seems fair to say that the Republican Party has eliminated much of its liberal and progressive wing and that it has moved to the right on the gamut of questions characterized as social or family issues. Clearly, this will bring it into conflict both with some specific sections of the population (e.g. women) and may push the party into an uncomfortable position with those groups known as 'Volvo Republicans', sophisticated GOP voters with a liberal approach to cultural issues and moral questions like abortion. The Republican Party has streamlined its organization and revived its finances in a way which the Democrats sought to emulate after 1980. And it has shaken off the albatross of Watergate. It may be, however, that the most enduring legacy to the character of modern Republicanism will be not the sum of attitudes and ideas espoused by its recent Congressional candidates but the set of policies adopted by the Reagan administration. It is to an examination of the ideological basis of those policies that we now turn.

CHAPTER V

Reagan, the Right, and Social Policy

When Ronald Reagan won the Presidency in 1980 it was clear that he intended to use his period of office to bring about a radical change in American public policy. Yet, as has already been seen, the victory had been the result of the coming together of a number of disparate forces in American society; and, while the Reagan coalition held together for the election campaign, it was by no means clear that it would do so once the President was installed in the White House. Moreover, although there might be differences as to how firm and ideologically rooted Reagan's own views actually were, there was no doubt that the attitudes adopted in the course of the election campaign would have to bend to some extent to the demands of the American political system.[1] The initial stages of the Reagan Presidency will probably long fascinate scholars and journalists alike, not least because it is unusual for a candidate to win election by offering Americans such a radical change of course. For the conventional wisdom has generally suggested that, while an administration may think it offers a fresh start, the transient nature of a Presidency inevitably reduces its impact.[2]

There could be little disguising the extent to which the brand of Republicanism which Ronald Reagan offered the American electorate in 1980 was a radical conservatism which involved an explicit rejection of many of the assumptions of the liberal Welfare State and the limited collectivism which had prevailed in America since the New Deal.[3] In the eyes of some commentators it was designed to be a counter-revolution.[4]

But promises to revive a different vision of America are one thing; implementing the concrete programs and policies which will dismantle a major bureaucratic structure quite another. In attempting to put into practice Reagan's brand

of radical conservatism, the American President faced difficulties which did not beset contemporary political leaders
with similar objectives, such as Margaret Thatcher. For
whereas the British system of government has a centralized
Cabinet structure and a unified Civil Service, and is as a
result usually an efficient agent of intervention in domestic
politics and a flexible instrument in foreign crises, the American polity is fragmented and decentralized, making it easier
to prevent action than to undertake it.[5] The British Parlia-
ment is normally an ally of the executive, not an independent
political force to be bargained with; but Congress, especially
since the reassertion of its powers in the 1970s and its internal changes, is not subservient to the executive in the same
way.[6] Not that relationships between President and Congress
are easily predictable or stable. Indeed, it is one of the ironies
of the American system that institutions and procedures
which in one period seem to work for one set of values can
be transformed into supports for an opposing set of preferences. Thus, the filibuster, long seen as the tool which
enabled conservatives to block change on the issue of civil
rights, was used in the early 1970s to prevent major damage
to the Great Society programs of Lyndon Johnson; and the
Supreme Court has swung from being a bastion of constitutional rigidity to being a major agent of social and political
change. The procedures introduced under the Congressional
Budget and Impoundment Control Act of 1974 were designed to strengthen the legislature's role in the budgetary
process; but, under Reagan, hitherto unimagined opportunities for executive domination of the process of budget
construction were revealed.[7] The extent to which a President
can exploit these opportunities clearly varies with political
circumstances; and neither 1982 nor 1983 followed the pattern
of 1981. Nevertheless, it became clear in 1981 that budgetary
bargaining would remain central to America's domestic
politics and that the outcome of each set of negotiations
would rarely be a foregone conclusion.

If structural and institutional factors in American policy-
making add their own constraints to the ability of a President
to push his policies through, so too does the political atomism
of American life. Congress itself, as was discovered by David

Stockman, the Director of Reagan's Office of Management and Budget and the man in charge of the cuts in expenditure, was still more likely to be moved by individual considerations of constituency interest than by free-market principles, even in the changed climate produced by the 1980 elections.[8] Indeed, no sooner had President Reagan won what seemed to be major victories in the fight to pass a program involving major cuts in public expenditure than some of his support seemed to fall away. New-right institutions such as the Heritage Foundation and Conservative Digest bewailed the fact that the Reagan cuts had not gone deep enough or been sufficiently extensive; but clearly for some Republicans, such as Robert Dole, the Chairman of the Finance Committee in the Senate, and the liberal Republicans in the House known as 'gypsy moths', the cuts were too harsh and too heavily concentrated on the poor and the needy.[9] In the first year the perception that Reagan had a mandate for drastic action created what was seen as a new political logic which took precedence over normal deals, demands, and accomodations.[10] As the second year of the Reagan administration arrived, however, with further demands for budget reductions, serious doubts were raised both about the ethics and efficacy of the Reagan administration's domestic policy in general and about its economic strategy in particular. Indeed, Congress reasserted its budgetary role and in many cases restored cuts it had imposed earlier, leaving observers at odds as to how radically the shape of the federal budget had been transformed. Thus, in September 1982, following another attempted round of cuts, Congressional Republicans and Democrats united to restore funding for a number of social programs and maintained that decision over the President's veto.[11] The decision to override the veto was intended to remind the President that any victories won on Capitol Hill had to be fought for; Silvio Conte, a liberal Republican with a reputation for tactical skill in relation to budget and appropriations issues, was quoted as hoping that Reagan had learned a lesson from the experience. The President, he suggested, had to appreciate that the House of Representatives was not composed of '435 robots' who were 'going to vote in lockstep'.[12]

The Style of the Reagan Presidency

Because so much of the success of any President depends upon the extent to which he can make an inherently inchoate system gel, it is worth isolating one or two of the character-istics of the new Reagan Presidency before any discussion of the policy themes which were taken up by the Reagan White House.

Perhaps the first feature of the Reagan Presidency was its emphasis on delegation. All Presidents when they first come to office have to decide what style of organization suits their particular personality, their staff, and, not least, their agenda. Eisenhower, who may have been unjustly criticized for political naïveté, was long thought to have imported into the White House the organizational habits of the army.[13] Kennedy, by contrast, was believed to have a more vigorous and personal organizational style which allowed him to intervene in decisions and problems at an early stage.[14] Carter was thought to be over-attentive to detail, a feature exhibited by the frequently quoted story that he took a personal interest in who was using the White House tennis courts.[15]

Reagan's administrative style had been influenced by his experience as Governor of California; but his own transition team — which was broadened to include other groups so as not to be dominated by Californian advisers — had given much thought to planning the organization of the Presidency. Reagan hoped thereby to avoid the personal and bureaucratic rivalries which had beset earlier administrations. His own preference for delegation as opposed to immersion in the detail of an issue or problem was seen by some commentators as a reflection of a certain degree of intellectual laziness.[16] And some saw it as an extension of his business-oriented approach, which entailed running the United States as a company managed by a board of very wealthy directors.[17] By others, however, it was seen as the result of a determi-nation to keep the Presidency free to mark out the general lines of political strategy and to retain an overall perspective on the multiple problems which crowd in on the chief executive.[18]

One of the perennial debates in relation to the organization of the executive has been the extent to which it is desirable or even possible to use the American Cabinet as a genuine forum of decision-making — a debate which became especially relevant as successive generations of the White House staff demonstrated the influence which personal advisers could exercise on policy.[19]

Initially Reagan attempted to use the Cabinet as a body for regular discussion, and apparently even encouraged Cabinet members to participate in debates on topics outside their immediate expertise.[20] He sought, as President Carter had done in the previous administration, a more explicit role for the Vice-President, making him responsible early in the administration for a Task Force of Regulatory Relief and placing him in charge of crisis management. And in the first year of the Reagan administration there was established a structure of five sub-Cabinet councils which were intended to ensure regular coordination between departments and agencies before the stage of Cabinet decision-making.[21]

Subsequently, however, the personal staff — and particularly the key aides, James Baker, Michael Deaver, and Ed Meese (before being nominated as Attorney-General in 1984) — came to exercise greater influence. And in the first year at least the key position of Director of the Office of Management and Budget was perhaps the most influential of all, though its incumbent, David Stockman, lost political influence after he was revealed to have leaked doubts about Reagan's economic policies to a magazine.[22]

Some of these aides were looked on with suspicion by elements of the right, so that, although Ed Meese was viewed as a conservative loyalist, the role of James Baker (who had the task of controlling personnel) was often under fire because he had been a partisan of George Bush. Altogether, however (with the exception of Stockman, whose post is in any event subject to Congressional confirmation), Reagan's personal appointees were much more conscious than those of either Nixon or Carter of the need to subordinate their own roles to that of the President.[23] Thus, although there was a swing back towards a greater dependence on the personal staff than early discussion of the Reagan White

House suggested, the administration of Reagan was one where there was far more collective decision-making and discussion than under his immediate predecessor.

A second aspect of the Reagan presidential style was exhibited by the fact that he acted quickly in the first year of his administration to set in motion the policies for which he believed he had a mandate. One scholar has emphasized the extent to which Reagan coordinated legislative and administrative methods for obtaining his domestic objectives, and has labeled this a 'dual approach' to policy-making.[24] What this meant was that the President realized that legislative methods would not be sufficent to bring about the political changes required, and that in so far as Congressional action could be taken it would have to be done early in the term while the presidential mandate still appeared fresh. Certainly, David Stockman acted on the assumption that cuts of the scale required to change the political climate had to be imposed before members of the Cabinet were captured by their departmental bureaucracies.[25]

The speed with which the administration acted to reorder federal priorities did indeed have the advantage of catching the special interests off guard. Special-interest groups which might have been especially active in the defense of programs designated for the axe — the welfare lobbies and the cities whose urban renewal programs were under threat — had no real opportunity to organize.[26]

To supplement the legislative means at Reagan's disposal, full weight had to be given to the administrative powers available to the executive, both to bring about substantive policy changes and to imprint the President's personal style on the whole administration. Indeed, the same analysis brings out the paradox that, while new-right critics of the administration were castigating the Reagan team for not paying enough attention to personnel, the Reagan White House was slowly infiltrating the bureaucracy with loyal adherents to an extent which was highly unusual in American government.[27]

A third aspect of Reagan's approach to his office was the emphasis on communication and efficient liaison with Congress. As a result, the President, despite having no majority in the House of Representatives, was able in the first year of his administration to inflict some potentially unpopular cuts on a range of domestic programs as well as to survive the exposure of a number of glaring contradictions in his economic policies. Initially, this was made easier by the existence of the House Conservative Forum — an organized group of Democrats in ideological sympathy with the Reagan program; but it still required a good deal of skill to keep the lines of communication to these mavericks open at the same time as the President's own troops were being kept in line on partisan grounds. Whatever view is taken of the merits of his policies, one of Reagan's achievements was his success in retaining so much of his personal popularity while coping with a recession which produced the highest rate of unemployment since the Great Depression.[28]

The Front Burner

One of the unusual features of the early part of Reagan's Presidency was that it was more clearly concerned with domestic issues than foreign-policy ones. Certainly, America's role in the world had been an issue during the campaign and Reagan was committed to a major expansion of the military. But the primary domestic problem, in his view, was the restoration of American economic prosperity and the elimination of inflation. This aim was to be achieved by an economic program which combined some extremely risky experiments based on supply-side arguments with more familiar economic themes. The glue which held them together, however, was the strong belief that government was itself a major cause of the United States' economic decline and that there was little that government could do which would not be better done by private enterprise and the free market. Bolstering this assumption was a rejection of the idea of using the federal government to promote the goal of substantive equality and an explicit dislike of redistributive mechanisms such as the progressive income tax and welfare expenditure.

The Reagan economic package had three facets: it reduced

direct taxation; it sought to cut federal government expenditure; and — although the President's influence is limited in a system where the monetary policy is the preserve of the highly independent Federal Reserve Board — it encouraged the placing of a brake on the growth of the money supply.[29]

The most unusual aspect of the strategy was the commitment to the major tax cuts which the supply-siders had recommended and which were contained in the 1981 Economic Recovery Tax Act. Reagan and supply-side advocates had wanted a 30 per cent reduction over three years; after compromises necessitated by Congressional politics and the realization by some of the size of the impending budget deficits, the reduction was agreed at 25 per cent over three years. Across the Atlantic Mrs Thatcher, despite her pronounced belief in reducing the levels of personal taxation, managed to achieve a major tax cut only once, when at the beginning of her 1979 administration the base rate was reduced from 33 per cent to 30 per cent. And even then income bands were not amended to take account of inflation, so that, as many commentators were swift to point out, the Thatcher brand of conservatism had seen taxes rise over the period since 1979.[30]

The structure of a country's system of taxation reveals much about its underlying values and priorities. With the 1981 Act a measure was passed which earned the epithet of the 'biggest tax cut in history' and which was clearly designed to have a major impact on the nature of American government. But such cuts were not directed towards reducing the inequalities in American society.

On one level there was the appeal of tax cuts which could be seen to benefit everyone even if — as they manifestly did — the very wealthy individuals and corporations benefited to a much greater extent than lower- or middle-income groups. And on another level they might be defended as offering inducements both to those sections of society likely to consume their additional disposable income and to the section most likely to invest it. David Stockman cynically admitted that this was a motive when he suggested that across-the-board tax cuts were simply a Trojan Horse for reducing the top rate of taxation.[31] Yet he was perhaps saying more about American political culture generally than about the clandestine purposes of the Reagan administration. Direct personal taxation came late to the United States; the country has only a weak tradition of social welfare; and arguments about fairness and equality seem abstract and alien to a large part of the population. Thus, while it is possible to argue that the cuts were geared to the Republicans' own constituency — the wealthy — it should not be forgotten that there is a much broader section of American opinion which would applaud the idea that differentials in income are not merely to be tolerated but even encouraged.

The debate about tax cuts in Congress also underlined the extent to which the Reagan administration's initial ideological clarity had enabled it to take the initiative, and showed how the lack of a focused and coherent opposition party can work to the advantage of a determined President. In marshaling a majority, few wanted to be seen to be against tax reductions which benefited everyone, although it is clear that many legislators realized that they were acting irresponsibly in voting them through with some additional concessions to special interests. Altogether the passage of the cuts was reckoned to be the functional equivalent of a loss of $750 billion to the Treasury over five years.[32] The size of these tax cuts necessitated major cuts in domestic public expenditure and a retreat from the paternalist role which, in the view of many Americans, was illegitimate.[33]

The initial strategy for reducing the growth of federal expenditure involved a package of cuts designed to control the amount which they claimed from the federal budget, and in some cases to eliminate them from federal government responsibilities. Two problems beset the process, however. First, Reagan was committed to increasing the defense budget, so that not only was one of the largest items of expenditure deemed sacrosanct but the scale of domestic cuts had to take account of plans to increase one area of spending very heavily.[34] Secondly, whatever Reagan's own view of the system of retirement benefits known in America as social security, he realized that direct attempts to alter the basis of the scheme would be politically disastrous. (The scheme had run into funding difficulties for demographic and other reasons, and after two futile efforts to introduce reforms a bipartisan commission was appointed to effect change.[35])

Initially the administration declared that it would not touch the range of social safety-net programs and would concentrate on cutting the frills of domestic expenditure. What precisely was to count as a safety-net program was inevitably rather arbitrary and, although the basic support systems — such as Social Security itself, Medicare, and unemployment benefits — remained relatively untouched in the first round of cuts, they were not deemed sacrosanct thereafter. Not only did the range of programs included in this category get smaller, but with some benefits (such as unemployment pay) the amount available was actually reduced.[36]

The programs that were the obvious first target for the administration were those which had come into being as a result of the Great Society's efforts to reduce poverty under President Johnson's Great Society program. Some, such as the various nutrition programs for mothers and children, food stamps, Medicaid, and Aid to Families with Dependent Children, were cut by the strategy of altering the eligibility requirements. Others, such as job training schemes, were simply cut. These programs had only recently been adopted by the federal government and it was against them that the most frequent accusations of fraud and waste were leveled.

It may be that the public had never accepted a general commitment to these programs, and even under President Carter the federal government had been reducing its financial obligations in the field of social welfare generally and attempting to shift more responsibility on to the states. However, the Reagan administration not only accelerated the pace of federal withdrawal from the general field of social provision but combined it with an explicit rejection of the notion that there was a federal obligation to reduce American poverty.[37]

The policy of reducing the growth of federal expenditure by transferring responsibility for many programs to the states was a key element in Reagan's domestic strategy. In addition to its financial advantages, Reagan had always wanted to allow the states more autonomy and to eliminate what was seen as unnecessary bureaucracy in the joint administration of programs. An important part of the first Reagan budget, therefore, was the consolidation of a number of categorical — i.e. specific — grants in the areas of health, education, and the social services into nine block — i.e. general — grants which would enable the states themselves to allocate priorities.[38]

A principal problem with such a revival of state autonomy, even in the changed circumstances of the 1980s, was that within any individual state it was difficult to secure support for minority programs. Many of the innovations in the field of social provision subsequent to the New Deal had occurred because of federal government pressure to provide hitherto neglected services and to raise the overall standard of health and wellbeing of the American people. In education, for example, it was the federal government which had put pressure on states to make provision for the handicapped and the disadvantaged. Only a few states, such as California, had exhibited much initiative of their own, and many persistently struggled to avoid federal government guidelines with respect to welfare payments and services.

Naturally, with federal financial payments went federal control, but until the Reagan administration a general concern with the quality of social provision outweighed dislike of the enhanced power of federal government, even among many conservatives. Thus, Richard Nixon's 1972 General Revenue Sharing scheme — which was a method of handing federal money to the state and local governments in order to allow them a greater power to determine their own political priorities — did not really remove federal oversight powers. (Many states used their additional revenues to hold taxes down rather than develop new programs.) The Nixonian new federalism was very obviously conservative in design, since it was assumed that by reducing the power of the federal government to control individual programs and by enhancing the powers of the states, the subunits of the American system would be made even more cost-conscious than they had hitherto been and certainly less prone to extravagance than the federal government. (American state government is of course restricted in its ability to run deficits both by the political climate of most state capitals and by the fact that deficits are explicitly prohibited by many state constitutions. In addition, there is in many constitutions a provision for an item veto, which allows a Governor to veto some parts of a budget without creating chaos by vetoing the whole package.)

The budgetary policies of the Reagan administration would by themselves have shifted power of a sort to the states since they unilaterally forced states to adjust to the new economic environment and signaled an intention to withdraw federal aid from a number of areas. However, in his 1982 State of the Union message Reagan indicated his intention to take the concept of a new federal relationship even further than Nixon and, although the proposals were not developed into concrete policies, they indicate the administration's still evolving assumptions about the future direction of the federal system in America.[39]

The major premise of Reagan's 1982 address was that the growth of federal grants-in-aid had become uncontrolled and that this was especially true of the most monitored form of federal assistance, the categorical (or specific) grant. Congress, according to the President, could neither exercise oversight of the programs themselves nor of the money spent on them:

In 1960, the federal government had 132 categorical grant programs costing seven billion dollars. When I took office, there were approximately 500 costing nearly 100 billion dollars — 13 programs for energy conservation, 36 for pollution control, 66 for social services and 90 for education . . . Here in Congress it takes at least 166 committees just to try to keep track of them. You know and I know that neither the President nor the Congress can properly oversee this jungle of grants-in-aid; indeed the growth of these grants has led to a distortion in the vital functions of government . . . The growth in these federal programs has . . . in the words of one intergovernmental commission . . . made the federal government 'more pervasive, more intrusive, more unmanageable, more ineffective, more costly and above all more unaccountable.[40]

The solution, according to Reagan, could be achieved with a 'single bold stroke'. What it was necessary to do was to transfer approximately $47 billion of federal programs back to the states and local government and take federal government out of a number of areas altogether — especially some in which it had only recently begun to intervene at all.

The initial suggestions for a transfer of responsibilities clearly reflected the administration's distaste for federal expenditure on the more recently accepted forms of welfare provision. The responsibility for relief programs in cash or kind, such as food stamps and Aid to Families with Dependent Children, would be given to the states. In return, the federal government might assume the full responsibility for Medicaid, which, unlike Medicare, was not fully funded by the federal government. In the President's view the proposed transfer would make welfare less costly and 'more responsive to genuine need because it will be designed and administered closer to the grass roots and the people it serves'.[41]

The finances of the proposal were hazy and complex. Initially, it seemed that for the fiscal year 1984 a trust fund would be established for the non-federal levels of government and that certain tax revenues would be assigned to it. The states could then decide whether to use the trust-fund money allocated to them to continue a federal grant program or abandon it and substitute some different combination of programs of their own choosing. After a transition period (which was to last for four years) the states were to have total control over some forty programs and the trust fund would be phased out. At that point it was suggested — but the financial implications were never entirely clear — that the states would be given excise tax revenues and a tax on oil company profits, and that all responsibility for funding the programs would henceforward devolve upon the states and local units of government.

Not unnaturally, these proposals received a good deal of criticism, some of it inspired by the fact that the plans for transfers of functions appeared to have been developed without detailed consultations. Three particular sources of disapproval quickly emerged.

First, the states were not at all convinced that the exchanges proposed were to their advantage. The National Governors' Association seemed to think that if any transfers were going to occur then the states should be given services relating to education and transport, and not the generally unpopular programs for the poor. Equally, it was difficult for the states to estimate the full financial implications of the maneuver. And because the new federalism outlined by Reagan in 1982 followed hard on the heels of a round of spending cuts which forced the states to decide whether to step into areas where federal presence was reduced, it was difficult for the National Governors' Association to view the exercise as anything but another way of reducing the federal budget.

A second set of objections came from policy experts and from those welfare rights groups which had become increasingly active since the mid-1960s. The assumption of welfare responsibilities by the federal government had occurred initially as a response to the Great Depression, when the states and the localities were unable to meet the demand for relief. But, as one authority has observed, the continued participation by the states in the administration of welfare meant the loss of benefits to the indigent who happened to live in poor states or in those which were indifferent to welfare.[42] And another scholar in the field has noted that in the 1960s all but six states set their standards for Aid to Families with Dependent Children at below the federal definitions of poverty, while all but sixteen failed to appropriate the money necessary to 'meet their own low standards'.[43]

In the early 1970s, some observers detected a trend towards greater equality of provision regardless of residence, but that has not continued. It seemed inevitable, therefore, that any extensive implementation of greater devolution to the states along the lines outlined in Reagan's speech of January 1982 would produce further variations in welfare provision across the United States. As the *Washington Post* commented, the case for national standards was both 'practical and moral'. It would be 'grotesque', the paper suggested, to invite those states with a tradition of social conscience to 'take disproportionate burdens of the nation's poverty as helpless people fled to them from the penury of the less generous'. In order to remind readers that some wealthy states were indifferent to welfare, the *Washington Post* pointed to Texas as an example of a state which remained remarkably mean in its treatment of the poor and allocated a family of four $140 per month on which to live.[44]

A final objection to any further devolution of domestic responsibilities came from the groups which had been particularly hard hit by the spending cuts and by changes in the administration of benefits. Blacks in particular had good reason to believe that changes along the lines suggested by Reagan in 1982 would be more than institutional tinkering and would hit them especially. The whole history of blacks in America has been one of federal government redressing the wrongs done by state and local government, so that it is hardly surprising if even three decades after the leading case of *Brown* v. *Board of Education of Topeka* had inaugurated desegregation in the South blacks feel less trusting towards state and local government than towards the federal authorities.[45]

The role of minorities in a federal system is, of course, a peculiarly sensitive one. Minorities whose causes are unpopular — and both blacks and the poor fall into this category in the climate of the 1980s — can generally only make their voices heard by combining at the federal level or by bypassing the more political branches of government and appealing to the courts. At the state level such groups are generally too fragmented and weak to make much of an impact. Inevitably, black spokesmen assumed that the effect of major transfers of powers would be policies which, while more responsive to majorities, would be less responsive to the very minorities which those policies were designed to help.

Thus, whatever the intentions of the Reagan administration and the motives for its policies, the impression which it had come to give after a couple of years in office was that its priorities on the domestic front would be pursued ruthlessly even at the expense of the young, the elderly, and the sick, and that, so far from regretting the inability of the State to provide protection in the event of misfortunes such as unemployment, it was the intention of the administration to discourage citizens from thinking of the federal government as having that protective role.

For some neo-conservatives, such as Senator Moynihan,

who had encouraged greater realism about the need for efficiency in social policy, this was too extreme an approach, although others, such as Michael Novak, continued to argue against the assumption that government had an obligation to protect individuals against all forms of personal misfortune. (Novak wanted the community rather than government strengthened, through greater reliance on such institutions as Church and family.) Equally important, some Republicans faced with reelection battles in the midst of a recession found the administration's policies unpopular, even though many were prepared to defend the Reagan approach as a necessary step to recovery. Thus, a Republican like E. Clay Shaw found himself forced as a Representative from Florida to vote against Reagan in 1982 because of the threat to the elderly that was implicit in Reagan's policies, although previously Shaw had been an advocate of Reagan's economic package. And mainstream Republicans such as Gary Lee of New York explained their defections in mid-1982 by reference to the damage which cuts threatened to inflict both on the elderly and on education.[46]

As a result, although Reagan achieved his first round of cuts he had to fight extremely hard for the rest; Congress became increasingly unwilling to grant further cuts and indeed reversed some of those made in 1981. Yet even if the logic of the administration's economic policy was no longer compelling after 1982, the implementation of the ideas behind it changed the American environment — quite apart from the substantive effects of the cuts which did occur. Democratic critics might charge the administration with unfairness and a lack of social concern, but it was noticeable that few politicians wished themselves to be labeled as advocates either of high spending programs in the field of social welfare or of an enhanced role for the federal government. To that extent the highly unusual budget of 1981 and the general attitudes which it inspired may have made a permanent mark on the American political scene.

Deregulation

Throughout the 1970s it had become a matter of common

belief that the efficiency of a wide range of industries was being impaired by the extensive network of government regulations that affected their functioning. Indeed, President Nixon, President Ford, and President Carter all placed a great deal of emphasis on the need to avoid unnecessary regulatory activity which might engender inefficiency.

In this sense, therefore, the Reagan administration came at the end rather than the beginning of an intellectual movement. Yet in practice it saw further deregulation as central to its philosophy and identified it as a pivotal part of its economic strategy and its policy of reducing the role of government.[47]

The establishment of a special Task Force on Regulatory Relief under George Bush was effected by Executive Order in the first month of the administration. The Office of Management and Budget was then given the power to review all regulations, so that no new regulation could be published in the Federal Register until this had been done. Major rules had to be accompanied by a statement describing the reasons for the promulgation of the rule and giving a cost-benefit analysis of its impact. This procedure, together with the fact that the administration imposed a freeze on the promulgation of rules that were in the pipeline when it took office, clearly signaled an intention to place the burden of proof on a regulatory agency or department to show why a particular rule was necessary.

In addition to these institutional developments, the Reagan administration appointed to the regulatory agencies men and women who were not merely hostile to excessive bureaucracy and regulatory control but who were often sympathetic to the sector that was to be regulated. The philosophy of the administration was thus that industry should be allowed to monitor itself as far as possible and that only where extreme public damage could be caused was there a case for government intervention. Such a withdrawal meant a relaxation of anti-trust prosecutions and federal government intervention in the economy, and also a public display of lack of interest in consumer protection and environmentalism.

The origins of this philosophy are complex. Clearly it is

not entirely based on free-market principles, since the existence of trusts and the absence of competition in an industrial
sector are anathema to free-market economists. It is rather
that the debate in the minds of the administration, although
not in the writings of such groups as AEI, has been cast into
a simple mold of federal government versus industry, and in
that debate the Reagan administration favors industry.

Much of the impetus for deregulation came from free-
market economists and think-tanks such as AEI, but much
of the virulence with which the new right has pursued the
topic has also come from the dislike of the public-interest
and consumer movements of the 1960s and 1970s. The
appointment of James Watt at the Department of the Interior
was more than simply the appointment of a controversial
politician to reverse existing policy. It was also the symbolic
rejection of a range of values seen as alien to the new right
in particular: conservation, environmentalism, and federal
regulation of private interests.[48]

Civil Liberties

The treatment of civil liberties under the Reagan administration was influenced by a number of factors. On one level,
although this was probably the least important, the arguments about the effectiveness of such policies as affirmative
action had made an impact on those who would anyway
have been suspicious about additional federal intervention
in the social arena. On another level, there was a belief that
the civil liberties groups had succeeded in pushing the balance
too far in their direction and that on issues such as criminal
procedure groups like ACLU were out of touch with public
opinion. Finally, there was an element of populism which
made Reagan's Republican Party hostile to such causes as
women's liberation, gay rights, legal services for the poor, and
any attempt to elevate minority racial groups to a protected
position.

The 1980 Republican platform took a very strong stand
on affirmative action, a policy which neo-conservatives and
Republicans alike believed ran counter to most Americans'
sense of natural justice. Attorney-General William French

Smith announced that the Justice Department would no longer pursue policies which sought to advance one group over another by such strategies as quotas, and on 25 August 1981 Reagan's then Secretary of Labor, Raymond Donovan, announced new regulations which would weaken the affirmative action steps required of those seeking government contracts.[49] But the administration did not actually reinstate the Civil Service admissions tests which the Carter administration had abolished, and did not remove the requirement that the federal Civil Service be representative of the population at every level of employment. In fact, some critics suggested that the Reagan approach in this sphere had been subtly transformed from opposition to affirmative action on grounds of principle to a more pragmatic opposition based on the additional administrative burden which affirmative action programs involve.[50] Overall, however, there was little doubt — whatever confusions occurred about administrative policy on this issue — that the levers available to an administration to help minorities were not actually being pulled.

Although the administration did ultimately renew the Voting Rights Act of 1965, it did so after such delay that the impression given was that it cared little for the measure, although it had been described as one of the most important steps towards black equality ever taken.[51] And on issues such as criminal protection, the role of the CIA, and freedom of speech it has moved to strengthen the hand of governmental authority rather than the rights of the individual.[52]

The image of an administration which was torn between its own ideological sympathies and the constraints of the law and existing governmental practice was reinforced by the controversy surrounding the tax-exempt status of private schools. The protection of these schools had been the cause which mobilized a number of Christian Protestants in the 1970s as a result of the IRS's decision in 1970 that it would no longer grant tax-exempt status to private schools which discriminated. Initially, the Reagan administration had the confidence to announce that it was simply going to reverse the ruling; but when civil liberties groups reacted unfavorably to that announcement of January 1982, the administration attempted to transfer the responsibility to Congress by asking the legislature to authorize the IRS policy. Congress refused to do this on the grounds that the IRS already had legal authority for its policy. The position was further complicated by the fact that at the time of the Reagan administration's announcement of a shift of policy in January 1982 it was already known that there were challengers to the legality of the denial of tax-exempt status before the courts. In the end the administration was left in the unhappy situation of having to abandon its own agency (it had to ask the Supreme Court to appoint someone to argue the IRS case) and ultimately of having lost the case by an 8 : 1 decision.[53]

Social Issues

The new right and the religious right had, as has been seen, their own particular agenda for legislative action, and one of the initial fears of the Reagan legislative and political strategists was that this agenda might impede the conduct of the administration's economic program. The attention paid by the Republican leadership to Congress and the fact that the new right in the Senate could not itself agree upon a strategy meant that the social issues — abortion, school prayer, and busing — were subordinated to the questions of economic policy and foreign policy. In addition, the fact that the administration would have had to back constitutional amendments limiting the jurisdiction of the courts in these areas in a sense made its life easy, since the passage of a constitutional amendment is difficult even where, as seemed at first to be the case with the Equal Rights Amendment, there is a substantial degree of consensus on the need for the change. Reagan was willing to make a move towards the introduction of an amendment to permit voluntary school prayer, but on the social issues he has generally relied not on legislative methods but on the other remedies available.

Obviously, the appointment of federal judges is significant and over time the administration may expect that it will indirectly be able to influence the courts in a conservative direction. But more significantly, perhaps, the administration may use its discretion as to whether to pursue integration cases and enforce the existing law.

Conclusions

The domestic policy of the Reagan administration was a mixture of free-market economic theories, hostility to government, and populism. As the theoretical rationale for much of its overall economic strategy disappeared, what was left was an attitude that combined antipathy to government with support for industry and existing economic interests. The populist appeal was reflected in a call for stronger action against crime, stronger efforts to remove fraud and waste from the welfare system (even though, as with the imposition of tightened AFDC regulations, this meant additional regulations), attempts to disband the Legal Services Corporation, and a general rejection of minority concerns in the field of civil liberties.[54]

Many of the individual policies could be justified on their merits rather than as prescriptions derived from a highly conservative set of values. Many Republicans, indeed, sought to defend the administration's record in that way and to play down the extent to which its policies were inspired by ideology. Yet it will be difficult for Republicans in the future to convince those who felt most aggrieved by the administration's policies — minorities, the poor, and supporters of civil liberties — that the GOP really can be even-handed in defense of their interests. To that extent the legacy of the Reagan administration and Reaganism may be a difficult one for the Republican Party to disown.

CHAPTER VI

Reagan, the Right, and Foreign Policy

Just as the 1980 presidential elections seemed to presage a radical change of course in American domestic politics, so they appeared to be the prelude to a major reorientation of foreign and defense policy. The rhetoric of the Reagan candidacy, the appointment of prominent neo-conservatives such as Jeane Kirkpatrick to sensitive positions in the administration, and the flavor of a range of policies enunciated early in the administration's life all suggested that there would be a sharp break not only with the policies of the Carter administration but also with those of the Nixon and Ford Presidencies before 1976. Clearly there was heightened awareness of a global ideological confrontation within the Reagan administration and a determination to change the direction of foreign policy. The redefinition of priorities signaled by the first Reagan budget underlined the perceived need to strengthen defense, and some commentators made explicit the links between the philosophy of the Reagan administration on international issues and its approach to economic policy.[1]

Not long after the Reagan administration took office, however, much of the sense of coherence had been lost from its foreign policy and contradictions in the approach to a range of topics — as well as personality clashes — soon became evident. By the time President Reagan had passed the mid-term elections of 1982, it had become clear that there were limits to the ability of a revived conservatism to provide the basis for a comprehensive American foreign policy. Formerly enthusiastic supporters of the assumed change of direction publicly expressed anger as well as disappointment. Thus, Norman Podhoretz, in an article originally written for the *New York Times* but widely circulated by the Committee for a Free World, suggested that many of the people who had initially been hopeful of Reagan's ability to reassert American power had sunk into a state of near total despair.[2] Podhoretz's criticisms ranged widely over the gamut of international issues, but he was especially scathing about the Reagan administration's lack of an overall strategy and of its refusal to 'move quickly and decisively in shoring up the American position in the Caribbean and in the Persian Gulf'. Podhoretz was also critical of the failure to support Israel and of Reagan's attempted use of the Saudis as surrogates in the Gulf, as well as of the administration's general failure to respond forcefully to events in Poland and Latin America.

The structure of the American foreign-policy process had added its own uncertainties to the implementation of the administration's choices; and the character of the mandate for what Podhoretz had called in 1980 'the new nationalism' was rendered even more ambiguous by the actual results of the 1982 elections and by the passage across the United States of a series of initiatives and referendums calling for a nuclear freeze, although Reagan himself tried to diminish the significance of the freeze movement by suggesting that it had been orchestrated by communists.[3] By 1983 some commentators had come to emphasize not so much the distinctive characteristics of the Reagan foreign policy and its roots in a revived conservatism but the elements of continuity of policy between the Reagan administration and its predecessors.[4] Other writers, however, stressed the extent to which under Reagan the United States had consciously reassumed the role of world policeman and had attempted to mold international affairs to suit its preferences.[5]

Domestic politics and international events inevitably constrained any capacity on the part of the President or his most ideological supporters to pursue a counter-revolution in foreign policy. Within the administration, too, there were pragmatic politicians who, while sharing some of the President's beliefs, were unlikely to act incautiously in advancing them. Yet for outside observers the administration's reactions to events seemed oddly schizophrenic. Some of the campaign rhetoric of 1980 lingered on, and while references to 'evil empires' could be dismissed as tailored for domestic consumption, there was no indication of any extensive alternative strategy behind the administration's thinking on foreign policy.[6] President Reagan's attitudes explicitly represented to many scholars an attempt to regain American dominance in the international system and as such were bound to fail.[7] What was less clear was what the cost of that effort would be — or its consequences.

Although it is necessary to recognize that some modification of the Reagan administration's hopes was produced by the realities of the international order, and even that there had been a substantial amount of continuity in American foreign policy between administrations, it is important not to underestimate the changes brought about by the advent of the Reagan administration. The impulses of neoconservatism as well as of movements within the Republican Party were reflected in the style of Reagan's foreign policy and his expanded defense commitments. Whatever else it did, the Reagan administration soon ensured that the mood of the United States on international issues was very different in the early 1980s from what it had been in the 1970s, and it reasserted the legitimacy of a foreign policy based on national self-interest.

The Carter Legacy

During the Carter administration foreign-policy and security issues had generated substantial controversy and stimulated critics to organize themselves on a range of issues.[8] The criticisms, however, came from a variety of perspectives even on the right, so that, as with economic policy, they could not automatically be incorporated into a positive policy once the new administration came to power. The reasons for the opposition to the foreign policy of President Carter varied, but, as Zbigniew Brzezinski, his National Security Adviser, admitted, much of the coherence and momentum which President Carter's policy had contained in 1976 was lost by the end of his period of office.[9] Opposition to Carter's foreign policy had emerged over the relationship between the United States and the Soviet Union and the role which arms limitation could play in that relationship. It had also emerged on a number of other issues, such as human rights policy, the status of the Panama Canal, policy towards Latin America, and the question of Rhodesia/Zimbabwe. The situation in Iran proved highly embarrassing for the United States and generated a major political problem when the United States Embassy was seized and its residents taken hostage. And the Middle East remained sensitive because of the inherent intractability of the situation and because of the domestic repercussions of American policy there.

More damaging even than the host of specific problems which plagued Carter was the general perception that America's position in the world had declined and that she had militarily become only number two in the world.

President Carter had sought to reduce the emphasis on the cold-war conflict with the Soviet Union and to give more priority than in the past to North–South, as opposed to East–West, issues. But the actions of the USSR and the attempt to negotiate arms control agreements in the wake of mounting evidence of Russian adventurism made such a shift of emphasis seem foolhardy. In response Republicans, neo-conservatives, and the new right mobilized their forces both inside and outside of Congress. Indeed, so extensive was the lobbying and campaigning while the administration was fighting to get SALT II ratified by the Senate that the battle was not merely described as the 'debate of the decade' but was judged by *Congressional Quarterly* to have generated one of the 'largest and most sophisticated campaigns in recent times'.[10]

In the elections of 1980, the American public exhibited a strange ambivalence towards the candidates by recognizing the appeal of Carter as the man most likely to keep America out of war while at the same time identifying Ronald Reagan as the man most likely to restore America's military position.[11] Although Carter had himself set in motion a drive for rearmament, the climate of foreign and national security policy had changed and Reagan articulated that movement. The Soviet invasion of Afghanistan legitimized the expression of a militant anti-Russian ideology and it destroyed much of the credibility of Carter's approach even in Democratic circles; among the general public it made

Reagan's well-established hostility to communism seem more justifiable than the *détente*-oriented policies of previous administrations.[12]

Foreign-policy issues therefore generated a good deal of activity on the right in the late 1970s, both as a result of these developments and as a part of the general mobilization of conservative opinion. The attempt to normalize relationships with Panama and to pass the SALT II Treaty provided opportunities to put together coalitions with sections of the Democratic Party which often found themselves more hawkish than the Carter administration. The late Senator Jackson was able to mobilize a formidable group of opponents to arms control agreements, and his principal aide, Richard Perle, continued within the Reagan administration to display attitudes on the subject which were more hardline than those of many Republicans.

Organizations formed to lobby on foreign policy included the Madison Group, which consisted of Congressmen and their aides; its weekly meetings at Washington's Madison Hotel underlined the growing concern within the legislature during the 1970s on foreign-policy and security issues. New-right groups, such as Paul Weyrich's Committee for the Survival of a Free Congress, also organized regular luncheon meetings on foreign-policy issues and briefed aides and Congressmen on defense and foreign-policy topics. And the Committee on the Present Danger, which was formed in 1970, mobilized formidable financial and intellectual opposition to the SALT II Treaty, while the American Security Council conducted a more general campaign to mold public opinion. Other groups which formed over the period or quickened their activities included the Advanced International Studies Institute at Bethesda, the Ethics and Public Policy Center in Washington, the Institute for Foreign Policy in Philadelphia, the Institute for Foreign Policy Analysis in Cambridge, Massachusetts, and the New York-based National Strategy Information Center. Although many of these institutes and organizations were very small, they had a cumulative impact and developed during the Carter Presidency a network of ties which gave them access to the Reagan transition team and later to the administration.[13]

The Committee on the Present Danger (in many ways a recreation of a committee of the same name formed in the early 1950s for many of the same purposes) alerted the American public to the deficiencies of the Carter approach to the defense budget and to the dangers of arms negotiations from a state of weakness. It gained the support of a wide range of influential academics and politicians, and it has been estimated that when President Reagan first took office there were thirty-two members of the Committee on the Present Danger who were given significant appointments in the foreign-policy and defense sphere. Thus, Paul Nitze, the Director of Studies for the Committee, was appointed Chief Negotiator for Theater Nuclear Forces, Fred Iklé was appointed Under-Secretary of Defense for Policy, Richard Perle was appointed Assistant Secretary of Defense for International Security Policy, and W. Glenn Campbell was appointed Chairman of the Intelligence Oversight Board. At the Cabinet level Reagan himself, Richard Allen (his first National Security Adviser), John Lehmann, and Jeane Kirkpatrick had all been members of the Committee.[14]

Criticisms of the strategic balance between Russia and America were offered by the other think-tanks, committees, and pressure-groups, and gradually their arguments changed the climate of élite opinion in a way which was difficult for the Carter administration to counter. For example, the Institute for Contemporary Studies, a San Francisco-based think-tank, in its first venture into foreign and military policy published *Defending America*, which (together with a later collection, *From Weakness to Strength*) set the intellectual right's agenda on international and defense issues.[15]

It was not merely the intellectual right, however, that developed the attack on Carter's foreign-policy record. The religious right also took issue with a number of his policies and Christian Voice made support of the Taiwan Treaty one of the key issues on its score-card for determining whether or not a Congressman or Senator was worthy of Christian support.[16] (President Carter, following the Nixon opening to China, had broken off full diplomatic relations with Taiwan and abrogated a treaty which committed the United States to its defense.) Indeed, the attempts by the

Reagan administration to reconcile support for Taiwan —
including arms sales — with the need to prevent a *rapproche-
ment* between the Soviet Union and China caused a good
deal of anger on the right as initial promises to upgrade the
American liaison office at Taipei to formal representation
were abandoned, and sales of arms to Taiwan subordinated
to wider diplomatic concerns.[17]

The Character of Reagan's Foreign Policy

Although the plethora of pressure-groups campaigning on the
right on foreign-policy issues during the Carter administration
and the broad trend of Republican thinking were in harmony,
there was no unanimity on the details of foreign policy in the
Republican Party during the 1970s. The issue of competence
in their handling enabled Reagan as presidential candidate —
and Republicans generally — to have a fine time attacking
Carter and the Democrats.[18] Nevertheless, simple opposition
to communism and Soviet expansionism was clearly not in
itself enough to generate an understanding of international
complexities. Reagan's own interest in foreign policy and
national security was limited; and his initial team of experts
— Alexander Haig, Caspar Weinberger at Defense, and Richard
Allen as National Security Adviser — were deeply divided on
a number of issues. Moreover, the election results, while they
could be interpreted as a mandate for a military build-up,
gave no indication that there was any direct support for
military intervention by the United States in any of the
trouble-spots of the world.

William Schneider has drawn the important distinction
between isolationists in America — whom he sees as having a
principled opposition to international involvement — and non-
internationalists.[19] The latter group, he argues, has a much less
active and informed approach to foreign-policy issues and
could be mobilized for additional military expenditure or for
a reduction in it. In 1980 he suggested that Reagan won the
support of this group but for reasons which did not necessarily entail a comparable willingness to incur additional
obligations:

Non-internationalists voted heavily for Reagan in part because of his promises of a defense build-up and a tougher line with the Soviet Union. This constituency likes strength and toughness in foreign affairs because that increases our independence . . .[20]

The contradiction between what many on the right think could be done by stepping up the fight against communism and what public opinion will allow is a substantial limitation on the methods available to an American administration. Covert aid and assistance may perhaps be given; direct intervention is always a political gamble of the highest order.

Moreover, in 1980 the Republican Party divisions on foreign policy brought their own difficulties for an administration with only a slender majority in the Senate and no majority at all in the House. Some parts of the GOP — and this was especially true of the Republican right — were less concerned with Europe and NATO than they were with policy towards China, Japan, and Central America.

To some extent this reflected a regional division between east-coast and west-coast representatives, but it meant that there could be no easy assumption of support for the Atlantic Alliance.[21] Other regional divisions also had foreign-policy and national-security implications. The question of whether to have (and, if so, where to site) the MX missile arose under President Carter. Carter's original decision involved the siting of the missile in the public lands (i.e. federally owned areas), of the West, especially Utah and Nevada. This possibility further fueled the already burgeoning sage-brush rebellion, and even after Reagan had taken office his close allies from the western states, Jake Garn and Paul Laxalt, had to be cautious on this issue for fear of home-state repercussions.

Other divisions in Republican ranks arose because some Republicans did not actually share the Reagan outlook on the world. Senator Hatfield, for example, was the joint sponsor with Edward Kennedy of a nuclear freeze resolution, and among the Senate's leading Republican foreign-policy figures there was less than total support for right-wing Republicanism. Thus, Senator Percy, who chaired the Foreign Relations Committee, was seen as being a liberal on many issues and Howard Baker, although he became a loyal leader of the Senate for Reagan, had afforded President Carter a crucial degree of support as minority leader. Indeed, Baker incurred a good deal of venom from the Republican right for the major role which he played in getting the Panama Canal Treaties through the Senate, as did the then Chairman of the Republican Party, William Brock, who found his advocacy of ratification of those Treaties countered by Reagan 'truth squads' during the debate in the country. According to Zbigniew Brzezinski, it was primarily the President's personal hostility to Baker which prevented further cooperation between 1976 and 1980, when Brzezinski would have liked to establish a bipartisan foreign policy.[22]

Even before the Reagan administration was installed, disagreements over the substance of policy and personnel appeared. There were bitter divisions of opinion within the transition team as Caspar Weinberger, Reagan's choice as Secretary of Defense, and William Van Cleave, Professor of Political Science and Director of International Relations at the University of Southern California and a long-time right-of-center intellectual with interest in defense policy, quarreled over the percentage of GNP which should be allocated to defense. (Weinberger, although a hard-liner in some respects, preferred to have Frank Carlucci, a professional foreign-policy manager, as his deputy, and thus apparently rebuffed Van Cleave.[23]) There was also a series of delays over appointments as Senator Jesse Helms, a highly conservative Senator from North Carolina, tried to delay the confirmation of a number of State Department nominees on ideological grounds. Thus, in September 1982, in moves applauded by the Heritage Foundation, among others, the nominations of Robert Grey as Deputy Director and Norman Terrell as Assistant Director in charge of Nuclear Weapons appeared permanently locked up in the Senate because both men had been close to Democratic Presidents. (Helms, who became the Chairman of the Sub-Committee on European Affairs, had been the only member of the Foreign Relations Committee to vote against the Panama Treaties.)

The tactic of opposing appointments was not, of course,

something which was open only to conservative critics of
the administration, and the Democrats were able to block
or delay nominations. Thus, Ernest Lefever was prevented
from becoming head of the Human Rights division of the
State Department and Kenneth Adelman experienced a
very protracted struggle to secure confirmation as Director
of Arms Control following the 'resignation' of Eugene
Rostow. Dissatisfaction with the pace of arms control negotiations and concern about the level of Adelman's expertise
were the cause of delay in his case, and in fact the appointment was confirmed only after the issue had been removed
from the Foreign Relations Committee and taken to the
full Senate in April 1983.[24]

One continuing problem within the range of debates about
the specifics of foreign policy — be they the nature of containment, the size of the defense budget, or the posture to
be adopted towards the Soviet Union — has been the recurrent American attempt to frame its policies on idealistic
grounds rather than simply pragmatic or *realpolitik* ones.
The Carter human rights strategy, though in many ways a
response to initiatives already taken by Congress, was a
reflection of the perceived need to inject a visible moral dimension into American foreign policy. The neo-conservative
critique rejected much of that strategy as damaging to the
interests of the United States and the long-term chances of
securing democratic development in the Third World. But
however much the Reagan administration would have liked
to adopt such a hard-headed approach to foreign policy, it
had to live in a system where idealism was not merely ever-
present but could also be backed by institutional power.
The administration could and did issue certificates that a
regime such as El Salvador's had made progress in human
rights and therefore qualified for American aid; it remained
at the mercy of Congress as to whether or not that aid
should be supplied and in what amounts. Indeed, it was
noticeable that when the Kissinger Commission attempted
to mobilize support for a massive extension of aid to Central
America, it felt it necessary to insert the caveat that such
additional aid should be made dependent on the human
rights record of recipient countries.

The tension between moralism and pragmatism in foreign policy is not simply a problem for the American left. The right also likes to feel that its policies are grounded in idealism and high moral principle. The challenge to President Ford from Ronald Reagan for the Republican nomination in 1976 was based on the belief that the Republican record in foreign policy had not been sufficiently based on principles. Although Ford eventually won the nomination, his platform was changed to include what has been called a 'moral amendment' on foreign policy, and with the defeat of Ford in 1976 the foreign-policy rhetoric of the Republican Party became more ideological. What made the Kissinger-style *détente* policy so unpalatable to many Republicans was its very failure to address the moral aspects of international politics and its completely pragmatic approach to the Soviet Union. In fact the Reagan administration proved to be extremely hard-headed — some would say amoral — in its foreign policy, permitting, for example, an expanded range of arms sales, an extended use of subversive activity to destabilize regimes of which it disapproved, and, subject to Congressional acquiescence, a restoration of aid to countries with poor human rights records.[25] One of the key questions asked about the incoming Reagan administration was whether it would be able to convince its allies and enemies alike that it would be prepared to use military force to defend either its own or an ally's interest. The experience of defeat in South-East Asia was thought to have paralyzed the United States, so that even where the administration wanted to give military support, as in El Salvador, it has had to proceed very cautiously indeed.[26] The decision in July 1983 to appoint a commission headed by Henry Kissinger to examine the policy options for the USA in Central America represented both the administration's perception of how difficult intervention in that area would be and perhaps also a belated recognition of the limits of its own tough, ideological approach to the area. Ironically, the appointment itself, so far from signaling the need for consensus in the area, immediately seemed to create a consensus only with respect to the dislike which all parties had for Kissinger himself, who had at the time just been the subject of a savage study.[27] The

Commission's conclusions, when they did appear in 1984, did not dispel the widespread doubts about the wisdom of extending the United States' commitments to Latin America.

The difficulty of selling any policy which involved the use of American troops initially seemed to have been overcome to some extent with the acceptance of the commitment to provide part of the Lebanese peace-keeping unit in September 1982. And when Grenada was successfully invaded and a left-of-center government ousted in 1983, it seemed that public opinion might be moving away from the implacable opposition it had displayed after Vietnam to any long-term overseas intervention. The early doubts about the wisdom of the Lebanese commitment — exacerbated by the Beirut massacre — spread throughout the House of Representatives and the Senate; eventually the situation became untenable and the marines were withdrawn in February 1984, thereby removing one foreign-policy embarrassment in an election year.

The reassertion of Congressional power in the foreign-policy process during the 1970s had been at the expense of executive leadership. The climate of the late 1970s and early 1980s was admittedly very different, and the legislative veto, one of the principal mechanisms of Congressional participation in establishing foreign policy, was struck down in 1983 as unconstitutional.[28] Reagan's attitude to Congress proved to be mixed: he had been prepared to cultivate good relations on the Hill in foreign policy, but it was noted that he had avoided using the provision of the 1973 War Powers Act when he sent the marines into Lebanon,[29] despite strong demands from within his own party that the move be made with Congressional support.

The Reagan administration has moved away from one of the other taboos created by the Vietnam era, namely the dislike of subversive activities and a strong role for the intelligence services. The perception that American entanglement in Vietnam could have been prevented if the 'system' had displayed greater openness (which was compounded by the Nixon administration's conspiratorial style) produced greater accountability and control of the intelligence services and diplomatic negotiations. It is, however, arguable that in the American polity these areas are already unusually democratic by comparison with other Western countries and that to introduce further openness would make American handling of them even more unwieldy.[30] It is also somewhat ironic that former Senator Frank Church, a long-time opponent of the Vietnam War and from 1978 to 1980 the Chairman of the Senate Foreign Relations Committee, should have lost his seat in 1980 as a result of a campaign in which his liberal foreign policy and his attitude towards the Central Intelligence Agency were made major objects of attack by the National Conservative Political Action Committee.[31] Regardless of whether Church was always an unusual Senator for a state as conservative as Idaho, the fact is that the contest was one of the most acrimonious Senate races in 1980 and revealed the extent to which attitudes on foreign and defense policy had changed, leaving Church with a record which proved to be an electoral liability which the new-right organizations such as NCPAC and the Republican Party could exploit.[32]

Soviet–American Rivalry

It has already been seen that much of the right-wing criticism of President Carter's foreign policy was occasioned by his alleged underestimation of the ambitions of the Soviet Union. *Détente* — the policy first associated with Henry Kissinger but then accepted tacitly by President Carter — had become a taboo word in most conservative circles by the time of the 1976 election campaign. Indeed, so aware had President Ford become of the opposition to *détente* within his own party that he had apparently banned the very use of the word in 1975–6.[33]

The rejection of *détente* by American policy-makers themselves was a long time in the making. Zbigniew Brzezinski has suggested that in retrospect the idea may have been 'oversold' to the American people and he makes the point, somewhat self-servingly perhaps, that during the Carter years he was anxious that *détente* should be comprehensive and reciprocal, whereas Cyrus Vance and the State Department were much more influenced by pro-*détente* thinking and less critical of the way the Soviet Union was interpreting *détente*.[34] According to Brzezinski, it seems that some advisers within the Carter administration were anxious to redefine *détente* as a process which involved the Soviet Union to a much greater extent in obligations and responsibilities, rather than simply being open to exploitation by the Soviets. But even if there was a movement towards taking a tougher line with the Soviet Union, the overall impression given by the Carter administration was that it was internally divided on one of the most crucial aspects of American foreign policy. Given the clear signals about disengagement from local military struggles after Vietnam and the reaction to Watergate, as well as these divisions, it is hardly surprising that the Soviet leadership should have taken advantage of American debility and probed the possibilities for extending its power in a number of areas of the world, whether directly, as in Afghanistan, or indirectly through the use of surrogate forces, as in Angola and the Horn of Africa. At the same time the Soviet Union continued to increase its expenditure on its armed forces, building up its nuclear and conventional forces and developing a major navy.

While the Carter administration had towards the end of its period of office acknowledged the need for an extensive modernization of America's fighting forces and those of NATO and recommended an increase in the defense budget, the many critics of the Democratic administration doubted whether this late conversion was genuine and whether it could in fact fulfill the promises of its more hawkish proposals.

And others doubted whether even the amount of money envisaged by Carter at that point was sufficient for the task or would do more than keep up with inflation. There were major hawks within Carter's own party, such as Senator Jackson and Senator Nunn of Georgia, whose values presaged some of those of the Reagan administration. Overall, in Senator Nunn's view, the United States had been guilty of 'misplaced priorities' because the federal government had usurped areas of responsibility that were 'best left to local and state governments' and had neglected responsibilities in areas which were 'uniquely the constitutional responsibility of the central government — specifically, national defense'.[35]

(Nunn did, however, become somewhat dissatisfied with the Reagan approach to defense expenditure and suggested that the increases in defense spending were ineffectively deployed.)

The determination to reorder defense priorities was inherent in the philosophy of the Reagan administration. In 1980 the President felt he had a mandate to spend more on defense and maintained that view even against his own Director of the OMB, David Stockman — who was suspicious of the Pentagon's claim to be able to escape the cuts that were being imposed immediately elsewhere.

The trend of defense expenditure under successive administrations since the Second World War has been extremely uneven. During the Vietnam War the competing claims of military expenditure and the Great Society programs were most apparent, and in 1968 the federal budget outlays on defense constituted 43.3 per cent of all federal outlays and 9.3 per cent of GNP.[36] Thereafter guns claimed a decreasing share of both federal outlays and GNP, so that in 1978, half-way through the Carter Presidency, only 22.8 per cent of all federal outlays was absorbed by defense, a figure which represented 5 per cent of GNP. At the end of the Carter Presidency there was an attempt to compensate swiftly for the decline of American military strength. But President Reagan moved even more quickly to increase the defense budget, revising Carter's budgets for fiscal years 1981 and 1982 as well as raising the total obligational authority over the five years 1981–6 by some $195 billion.[37] The amendments to Carter's last budget which President Reagan introduced thus envisaged an overall increase in defense spending from 5.6 per cent of GNP in 1981 to 7 per cent in 1986 — by comparison with Carter's efforts to take defense outlays to 5.9 per cent of GNP.

The Reagan administration moved quickly to modernize its strategic forces and to develop new systems. On 2 October 1981 the President presented a plan which included the development of the B-1 bomber, further research on 'stealth' aircraft, the development of the MX missile, the construction of Trident II as an improved sea-launched ballistic missile system, improved radar and satellite systems, and an enhanced strategic defense system. Congress approved the President's program and voted the administration for the fiscal year 1982 a budget of $199 billion. However, in the next year he wanted a further increase of 18 per cent, with still more for 1984. Overall it has been calculated that Reagan's plans involved the increase of the military budget from 24 per cent of the total federal budget (as it stood under Carter) to 32 per cent.[38]

As the euphoria of the first year wore off, it proved increasingly difficult to persuade Congress that such a massive military build-up was really necessary. Even those who wanted more guns began to ask whether the money was being spent effectively (indeed, some doubted whether much of the money voted could be spent at all); and some sceptics queried whether there was any strategic logic behind the requests for additional money[39] — doubts about the balance between military and domestic spending in the President's budgets came from the Democrats and from liberal Republicans.[40] There were, however, still those on the right who wanted to speed up the process of modernization and rearmament, so that in 1982 the still active Committee on the Present Danger called for more effort on the administration's part to raise defense spending quickly to 7 per cent of America's GNP.[41] However, if enthusiasm for an increasing expansion of the defense budget had begun to diminish by the middle of the Reagan administration, it was too late at that point to effect a change of policy. New systems had been approved and the commitment to a vastly enhanced armaments bill had already been made.

The Carter administration's recognition that it was necessary to increase military expenditure had been coupled with a commitment to arms negotiations. For the Reagan administration, however, arms control was not a process that was taken seriously. Perhaps this was because so much of the administration's thinking had been shaped by the debate about SALT II; perhaps it was because of the genuine belief that no treaties should be negotiated with the Soviet Union until the United States was in a manifest position of military parity, if not superiority.

Reagan himself exhibited a dismissive attitude towards

arms control — an attitude which was complemented by the traditional scepticism of the Republican right towards international agreements and international institutions such as the United Nations and agencies like UNESCO.[42] Within the administration arms control policy was caught between those who thought some limited progress could be made and those who believed that any agreement would be worthless in the existing climate. The policy may have been determined by a realistic appreciation of the chances for a comprehensive agreement, but it undoubtedly fueled anti-nuclear sentiment within the United States and Europe.

Human Rights

The Reagan administration viewed the Carter administration's approach to human rights as completely erroneous because of its tendency to destabilize large parts of the world and to undermine regimes friendly to the United States.

Mrs Kirkpatrick brought to the Reagan Cabinet very clear views about the need to avoid further mistakes of the kind that occurred when the United States put pressure on the Shah of Iran to reform his government. Her analysis of the 'destabilization syndrome' was important not merely as an indication of the tougher attitude to be taken towards dictatorships and reform movements but because it brought to the surface doubts about the role of the State Department. Suspicion of State Department personnel has long been a feature of right-wing American administrations, and there opened up within the Reagan administration a division between the Department and the rest of the government. Area and functional specialists were viewed with suspicion as being more committed to the fields they were assigned to than to the immediate interest of the United States.

The arguments advanced by Ambassador Kirkpatrick had two important aspects. She believed that American national interests should not be undermined by support for movements in other countries likely to produce regimes hostile to the United States. But she also believed that it was in the best interests of freedom and democracy in the countries themselves that left-wing communist forces should not be encouraged even against dictatorships and regimes of a dictatorial nature. This argument was rather more sophisticated than the reaction of Reagan himself to the Third World's revolutionary developments. For the President was overwhelmingly influenced by hostility to communism and to what he regarded as leftist movements generally. Inevitably, he would not draw distinctions between types of reform movement and he was especially unwilling to do so in Latin and Central America, the area where American policy was most controversial.

Central America came to be recognized as the region where many of the basic tenets of President Reagan's foreign policy, as well as Ambassador Kirkpatrick's arguments, would be most sorely tested.[43] Here is a region of obvious strategic interest to the United States: administrations since Monroe's have declared the whole continent to be within the American sphere of influence. The policies of the Carter administration, by focusing on the local and regional characteristics of Central and Southern America, neglected both the global significance of the conflicts that erupted particularly in Central America and the vital interest of the United States in having no hostile leftist forces on its doorstep. Human rights, however worthy a cause, had to take second place in the construction of policy for the region — whatever the Democrats or Congress might say. The rhetoric of the Reagan campaign of 1980 and the writings of most of the prominent figures within the Reagan coalition made it perfectly clear that if backsliding was to occur anywhere it could not be in Latin America. Yet even in Latin America the clear lines of the Reagan approach to foreign policy became blurred with time, and divisions opened up on the conduct of Latin American affairs precisely because it was seen as the touchstone of Reagan's fidelity to Reaganism. The initial approach of Reagan's first Secretary of State, the pro-NATO Haig, was to see the problem primarily in military terms, but Shultz modified this perspective and adopted a more political stance. Even in 1983, when there appeared to be a wholesale rearrangement of the United States' diplomatic representation in El Salvador, some interpreted this not as a hardening of policy but rather as a reflection of the White House and the State Department's anxiety to maintain closer control over the course of policy in the country than Thomas Enders's presence perhaps allowed. The use of military aid ran into problems with Congress, although it should be noted that it was not until December 1982 that Congress finally voted to cut off all aid designed to facilitate the overthrow of the Sandinista regime in Nicaragua. Military aid to Honduras from Washington had in fact been tripled in 1982 — an investment which could be attributed both to Honduras's position as a base for the training of anti-Sandinista forces and to its very vulnerable border with El Salvador.[44]

El Salvador presented a situation which underlined the limitations of Reagan's foreign policy. This was founded on the premise that American military power should be used in appropriate circumstances, and yet the administration was reluctant to become involved militarily in a war where the objectives would be unclear and the possibility of a meaningful victory uncertain. The local situations in Central America may thus be part of a wider global pattern, but pursuing global policy in the jungles of Central America is difficult. The impossibility of a quick or final solution made it all the harder to keep public opinion behind an assertive policy, so that support for prolonged involvement appeared to be a political cost that the administration would probably be unable to pay. Unfortunately, the political costs of defeat in this situation were also high, in terms both of morale and of real strategic interests. It was an indication of Reagan's belief that American opinion on Central American issues needed to be molded that he made a special address to Congress on the subject, although whether such efforts to win converts for a more active policy had any success may be doubted.

However, if the attempt to reassert American power within the Americas runs into the impediments of complex local situations, national hostility, and uncertain domestic opinion, so too does American policy towards the Atlantic Alliance. The reaffirmation of the centrality of the brute facts of Soviet power in all international relations might have been expected to revive the alliance, just as President

Reagan's determination to provide the West with firm leadership might have been expected to reinvigorate a NATO
demoralized by a series of crises, disasters, and misunder-
standings. In fact, however, the tensions within the alliance
appeared to be greater in the early 1980s than at any time
since the foundation of NATO, and there is on the American
right a demand for policies which would disengage the
United States from the nuclear and conventional defense of
Western Europe — not so much because of hostility to
Europe, but rather in recognition of changes which have
occurred in the needs, values, and priorities of both the
United States and Europe. The disharmony within the
alliance occurred because of the way a number of themes
of international politics have interacted during the past
decade.

With regard to the American right's contribution to that
disharmony, three themes deserve especial attention. First,
the concentration on the aggressive nature of the Soviet
Union became the starting-point of American foreign policy
under President Reagan. Economic policy became a weapon
to be wielded against the Soviet Union as 'economic *détente*'
was transformed into 'economic warfare'. Moreover, many
of the decisions to explore new weapons systems seemed
designed as much to put pressure on the USSR as to serve
some intrinsic goal of American defense policy.[45] Although
many Europeans do indeed share that outlook on Russia,
the more extensive contacts of all Western European nations
with the Soviet bloc are bound to give them a different
perspective on the USSR. The Europeans have long appreci-
ated the need to reach an accommodation with the Soviet
Union and can see little use in emphasizing ideological
divisions. Frequently, therefore, the rhetoric of the American
right strikes European politicians as unhelpful even when,
as is undoubtedly true of Mrs Thatcher, they sympathize
with its spirit. By the same token, some members of the
American right suspect that Europeans are soft on communism, a suspicion which is fueled both by the development
of peace movements and by the perceived refusal to sacrifice
welfare expenditure for military spending.

Secondly, differences of an acute kind have arisen between

Europe and the United States in relation to the Middle East, and those differences have affected the attitudes of the right to other international issues — notably NATO. The oil crisis of 1973 and the increasing awareness of Europe's dependence on the region for energy produced a trend towards a pro-Arab stance in foreign policy in that area. The United States has a special relationship with Israel, which became stronger after the deterioration of the situation in Lebanon. Initially, the Reagan administration looked as though it might be less committed to Israel than is usual for American governments, especially after Haig's pro-Israel influence was no longer there to balance the pro-Arab impulses of Weinberger. But in fact the military links were upgraded, and although it is also American policy to improve relations with conservative Arab States, such as Saudi Arabia, in the case of a conflict there is no doubt where political pressure would be felt.[46] European sympathy for the Arab cause and the independent stance taken by the Common Market over the peace negotiations in the Venice Declaration have angered many Americans on the right. The neo-conservatives are strongly pro-Israel and, while they might argue (as Podhoretz does) that the American commitment to the Israeli State results from its democratic rather than its Jewish nature, there is no doubt that the issue is a very sensitive one for them. The perception of Europe reassessing its own commitment to Israeli security may have reinforced a developing anti-Europeanism in the minds of many Americans. The question 'Why should we support Europe militarily if Europe will not support Israel?' is not one that is generally asked in those terms, but it is a factor in the attitudes of some neo-conservative critics of the existing shape of the alliance.

One final theme which has led to discord has been the attempt to use economic transactions as a political weapon. Trade between European countries and the Eastern bloc caused friction as the Reagan administration attempted to regulate the exchange of dual-use technology and to prevent the West supplying the Soviet Union with commodities which its own economy was unable to produce. What especially made this policy divisive was the fact that domestic

pressures ultimately limited the application of a grain em-
bargo *vis-à-vis* the Soviet Union, while the United States
nevertheless still felt able to try to make Western European
governments revoke contracts to supply technology for a
pipeline across Siberia to supply gas for their own economies.
Indeed, it could be argued that the issue of the Trans-Siberian
pipeline both epitomizes the different orientations of the
United States and Europe towards trading relations with the
USSR and exhibits the extent to which the foreign policy
of the United States appears to many outsiders to be un-
predictable and illogical.[47]

Behind the specific irritations of American–European
relations there lies the broader issue of nuclear strategy.
The open debate over the viability of MAD (Mutual Assured
Destruction) as a doctrine, the increased discussion of the
feasibility of fighting a limited nuclear war in a European
theater, the peace movements which have erupted in Europe in
response to the NATO decision to station Cruise and Pershing
missiles on European territory — all these have removed
some of the comfortable certainties of an alliance where it
was assumed that an attack on any member of NATO would
be regarded as an attack on the whole alliance, including
the United States. In such circumstances it is hardly surprising if on the right there are those who wish to push
the logic of unilateralism to its conclusion and who urge
each member State of Nato to promote a European deterrent
rather than rely on the American umbrella.

The Reagan administration did not itself express any
support for those on the right who agreed with many on the
left of the American political spectrum that the alliance
has to be reframed and that the United States should consider playing a greatly reduced role. However, it would be a
mistake to neglect the strength of the forces within the world
of American foreign policy who wish to see such an outcome
and who will maintain a dialogue with any administration
on this issue.

Ultimately, foreign policy, as the Reagan administration
discovered, cannot easily be fitted into an ideological framework or a preconceived set of priorities. The innumerable uncertainties of local conditions in the real world inevitably

constrain the translation of deeply held values and intuitive reactions into specific and detailed policies; and they upset even the best of international strategies, just as on occasion they may cause even the most committed of partisans to question his ideas. In the United States these generalizations about the difficulties of making foreign policy are compounded by the country's fragmented decision-making structure. Internal divisions over policy and Congressional resistance to executive dominance plague Republican and Democratic Presidents alike — to the frustration of the incumbent of the White House and the puzzlement of America's allies. Behind both President and Congress there is the major force of public opinion, which, equally irritatingly, needs neither to act itself nor to obey the canons of logic. In these circumstances it is somewhat Utopian to demand coherence and continuity from American foreign policy. Yet, when that is said, the experience of the years 1981–4 does seem to suggest that the Reagan Presidency has been a watershed in American foreign policy. The United States did commit forces to two trouble-spots — Lebanon and Grenada; and the administration's approach to Latin America generally indicates that it might be ready again to contemplate the kind of involvement which Vietnam had made so unpalatable. It did accelerate defense spending — though whether Congressional support for it can be maintained is open to question. And it did articulate once again in ringing, if not strident, tones the need to resist communism and to discharge America's responsibility as the leader of the Western world.

If this was still less than many conservatives wanted, it did create at least the impression that the President had determined to reverse the policies of his immediate predecessor. Reagan, it has been noticed, came to office more interested in domestic than in foreign policy, unlike President Carter, whose interests and energies were increasingly consumed by events in the international arena. While it is unlikely that Ronald Reagan will ever himself take major initiatives in foreign policy or display the detailed interest in international affairs which Carter did, this aspect of the Presidency seems to have acquired greater salience for him. A second term might see even greater personal attention to international issues. Whatever the outcome of the 1984 election, however, it will for some time be difficult in foreign policy, as in social policy, for the GOP to dissociate itself from a set of policies and assumptions which, even if more distinctive in style than substance, nevertheless represent an attempt to set American foreign policy on a new and more conservative path.

CONCLUSION

The resurgence of the American right has raised a number of questions about American values, about the style of American politics, about the role of religion in American life, and above all about the structure of American party competition. There may be those who hope that it is possible to provide the scholarly equivalent of the bottom line in relation to at least some of these issues. Unfortunately, as I hope the discussion has already demonstrated, the conservative revival is a multi-faceted phenomenon and simple answers to straightforward questions such as whether it will last are inappropriate. Nevertheless, although it is not the task of the political scientist to make predictions about the future of American politics (especially in the midst of a primary season which, with the emergence of Gary Hart, has already underlined the element of surprise inherent in the subject-matter of the discipline), some general conclusions may be in order at this point. If they are posed in what may seem to the general reader to be rather negative and tentative terms, that is sadly a reflection of the fact that this book has been written by a sceptical academic rather than a committed politician or journalist.

For most people concerned with developments on the American right the central question is presumably its electoral impact. Are we in the course of a realignment analogous to that of the New Deal period and is a new coalition being built which could produce a natural Republican majority for at least a generation? Such questions are in my view misguided because they assume that the political loyalties and allegiances of an earlier period can be reproduced in today's altogether more fluid and fast-moving environment. Dealignment of the electorate in the United States, as elsewhere, is a product of greater education and of the failure of the regular parties to maintain their hold over successive generations of voters. To say, however, that the prospect of a durable switch in partisan loyalty is remote is not to deny that the political environment has become much more accommodating and encouraging for Republicans. And it has arguably become especially encouraging for a party which can live with, if not exploit, the breakdown of traditional alignments and the increased importance of pressure-groups, Political Action Committees, and the media in political life. It may be that the Democratic Party will prove as adept at doing this as the GOP has recently seemed to be; but on every level the Democrats, while in theory commanding the electoral numbers, have apparently not been able to mobilize their natural strength. Thus, within the framework of a more volatile politics in which votes are there to be fought for and the existence of latent electoral support is not itself a guarantee of success, the GOP seems likely to have a rosier future than would have been predicted in the early 1970s.

A second concern which has arisen in relation to recent developments on the right of American politics has been the extent to which the character of Republicanism — and indeed of American political life — has been changed by the tactics employed by the new right in its campaigns and by the kinds of issues which both the new right and the religious right have emphasized. It is my belief that the Republican Party has indeed been changed by the events of the 1970s and by the experience of the Reagan Presidency. At the level of ideology and image the GOP has been tilted towards a radical populism which, while still liable to be held in check by other elements in the party, is nevertheless going to be a dominant feature of the GOP for some years to come. Certainly the contribution of the neo-conservatives to the character of Republicanism was to change the intellectual climate and to legitimize the broader coalition of the right. And it was also to make plausible the claim that the GOP was a reasonable option for moderates who might otherwise have stayed with the Democratic Party, despite increasing doubts about the direction of that party's policies. But one now has the feeling — to borrow one of Oliver Wendell Holmes's analogies — that the acceptance of so many of the neo-conservatives' ideas, however good, has made them appear somewhat flat, just as even the most effervescent champagne can lose its sparkle after a period of exposure to the air.[1] The new right and the religious right, by contrast, represent a cruder and older vintage, and their contribution — which has been to strengthen the populist appeal of the GOP — will consequently last longer.[2]

In identifying the new right and the religious right with populism I am, of course, aware of the fact that populism is a difficult term to define. However, there is little doubt that the appeal of the new right on social issues such as busing, taxation, and law and order — as well as on the whole gamut of moral themes from homosexuality to abortion— reflects a peculiarly American tradition of anti-intellectualism and hostility to government which, like isolationism, could be given a bias to either the right or the left of the party system, but which has essentially transcended it. Whether this strand of thought will remain dominant in the Republican Party remains to be seen; certainly the geographic movement of GOP support — towards the southern and western areas of the United States — suggests that it will. But what the period under discussion has revealed is that the populist constituency can be married with more traditional conservatism and Republicanism to form a coalition which it may require effort to keep together but which can survive. And it has demonstrated the difficulty of translating American ideologies into European understandings of right and left.

One aspect of the new right's strategies which caused particular controversy was its hard-hitting negative campaign tactics, which were first felt in the 1980 election and especially in those Senate races where well-known liberals such as Frank Church and George McGovern were targeted for defeat. The fact that such extreme tactics proved counter-productive in 1982 will almost certainly mean that the new right's tactics will be refined in future; it does not necessarily mean that the new right's emphasis on organizational skill, or its determination, will cease to be a factor in campaigns.

The religious aspect of the right-wing revival remains problematic. The major significance of the attempt to mobilize religious groups into the politics of the right was not perhaps the greatly exaggerated claims about registration and voting effects, but rather the *indirect* impact on a morally conservative culture such as that of the United States of bringing the conservative evangelicals and fundamentalists back into politics. Fear of what an aroused conservative religious community might do is perhaps sufficient to prevent politicians raising issues of a controversial nature, and hence questions — often of major importance — will be ducked. The present situation in relation to abortion, for example, where it is available to all who can pay, seems anomalous — but it is an anomaly unlikely to be corrected by politicians fearful of pro-life sentiment in their constituencies.

Finally, there is the question of whether the effect of a Reagan administration dedicated to avowedly conservative goals has really been all that great. Has the ideological color faded, leaving a Republican President not so very different from Eisenhower, Nixon, or Ford? The answer is perhaps that the legacy of the Reagan administration which took office in 1981 must be assessed in broader terms than the simple numbers of programs that were passed or even the number of programs and budgets which were *not* passed.

The Reagan administration has wanted to bring about a change of assumptions about the role of government in American life. By signaling a determination to cut the growth of federal expenditure in areas other than military expenditure, by signaling a hostility towards the civil rights policies of previous administrations, and by signaling a more militant attitude towards the defense of American and Western interests internationally, President Reagan has created a distinctive synthesis of conservative economics, populism, and nationalism which has no exact counterpart in the politics of the right in Europe. The 1984 elections will reveal the extent to which either a Democratic candidate linked to a range of traditional constituencies or one allegedly free of such entanglements can compete against this mix. And it will reveal (although the true test will not come until the Senate elections of 1986, when the Reagan intake of 1980 is up for re-election) whether the Republican gains will be maintained. But elections are only the most easily measured aspect of the political system. What must continue to be of interest is the extent to which the experience of the period since 1974 has changed the values and priorities underlying the electorate's choice and the extent to which the right will maintain its influence on the agenda of American politics — at the federal, state, and local levels — throughout the 1980s.

NOTES

Introduction

1 For a comparison of trends in Britain and the United States with respect to conservative politics see N. Bosanquet, *After the New Right* (London, 1983). An introduction to the problems of nuclear strategy may be found in L. Freedman, *The Evolution of Nuclear Strategy* (London, 1981), and M. Mandelbaum, *Nuclear Future* (Ithaca, NY, 1983).

2 I intend to examine some of these issues in a forthcoming study of the American system of government.

3 The recent literature on Congress is voluminous. Especially useful is J. Sundquist, *The Decline and Resurgence of Congress* (Washington, DC, 1981).

4 On this speculation see R. Cohen, 'A Republican Plot?', *National Journal*, 23 August 1980, p. 1410.

5 For a useful overview of the mid-term elections see P. M. Williams, 'The U.S. Mid-Term Elections of 1982', *Electoral Studies*, 2. 2 (1983), 99–112.

6 On the various strategies for creating a new majority in American politics see K. Phillips, *The Emerging Republican Majority* (New York, 1969), and his later *Post-Conservative America: People, Politics and Ideology in a Time of Crisis* (New York, 1982); also S. M. Lipset (ed.), *Party Coalitions in the 1980s* (London, 1981).

7 On the newer issues of regional competition see R. J. Dilger, *The Sunbelt–Snowbelt Controversy* (New York, 1982); also K. Sale, *Power Shift: The Rise of the Southern Rim and Its Challenge to the Eastern Establishment* (New York, 1976).

8 The general change of mood, region, and generation at the end of the 1970s is usefully captured in D. Broder, *The Changing of the Guard: Power and Leadership in America* (New York, 1980).

9 E. J. Feulner, *Conservatives Stalk the House* (Ottawa, Ill., 1983), 11.

10 On this see D. M. Abshire and R. D. Nurnberger (eds.), *The Growing Power of Congress* (Washington, DC, 1981). D. M. Abshire was himself active in promoting a change in the foreign-policy climate as Chairman of the Georgetown Center for Strategic and International Studies (CSIS). He later headed the transition group on National Security. See M. Gordon, 'Right of Center Defense Groups — the Pendulum has Swung Their Way', *National Journal*, 24 January 1981, pp. 128–32.

11 On the role of finance in the election of 1980 see H. Alexander, *Financing the 1980 Election* (Lexington, Mass., 1983). On the role

of Senator Jackson see M. Novak, 'In Memoriam: Henry M. Jackson', *Commentary*, 77. 1 (1984), 48–50.

12 For a general appraisal of the neo-conservatives see P. Steinfels, *The Neo-Conservatives* (New York, 1979).

13 For a discussion of the implications of many of these developments from a left-of-center perspective see P. Green, *The Pursuit of Inequality* (New York, 1981).

14 See, for example, J. J. Kirkpatrick, 'Why We Don't Become Republicans', *Commonsense*, 2. 3 (1979).

15 For a favorable account of supply-side economics see J. Wanniski, *The Way The World Works* (New York, 1978), and G. Gilder, *Wealth and Poverty* (New York, 1981). Also of interest is a book by J. Kemp, one of the proponents of the major tax cut which occurred in the first year of the Reagan administration — *An American Renaissance* (New York, 1979). See also B. R. Bartlett, *Reaganomics: Supply-Side Economics in Action* (New York, 1982). For a hostile account see R. Lekachman, *Greed is Not Enough: Reaganomics* (New York, 1982). For a review of the effect of Reaganomics at mid-term see W. C. Stubblebine and T. D. Willett (eds.), *Reaganomics — a Mid-term Report* (Washington, DC, 1983). R. H. Fink, *Supply-Side Economics: A Critical Appraisal* (Frederik, Md., 1982), contains a selection of essays on American and British economic policy. Also of interest is F. Ackerman, *Reaganomics — Rhetoric* v. *Reality* (London, 1982). The more familiar free-market and monetarist approach of Milton Friedman and the Chicago school can be pursued in M. Friedman, *Capitalism and Freedom* (Chicago, 1962), and M. and R. Friedman, *Free to Choose* (London, 1980).

16 The style of some new-right campaigns is nicely conveyed in the account offered by one of its victims, T. McIntyre, *The Fear Brokers* (New York, 1979). McIntyre was the Senator from New Hampshire who was defeated by a new-right candidate in 1978 after the Senator's support for the Panama Canal Treaties and his general liberal record had been attacked. See also McIntyre's Senate speech on 1 March 1978, in which he draws attention to the tactics of the new right in New Hampshire.

17 The literature on recent American voting behavior is enormous; an excellent starting-point is S. Verba, J. Nie, and J. Petrocik, *The Changing American Voter* (Cambridge, Mass., 1976). A recent reassessment of the literature is to be found in M. P. Fiorina, *Retrospective Voting* (Cambridge, Mass., 1982). On voting and parties see also N. Polsby, *The Consequences of Party Reform* (Oxford, 1983). The 1980 elections are covered in A. Ranney (ed.), *The American Elections of 1980* (Washington, DC, 1981). On the question of turn-out at the mid-term elections see Williams, 'The U.S. Mid-Term Elections of 1982'. Dr Williams has estimated that turn-out will reach 41 per cent of the eligible population and has emphasized that 1982 was the first mid-term election for twenty years 'at which the turnout rose above that of four years earlier'.

[18] On the general relationship between a member and his state or district see R. F. Fenno, *Homestyle: House Members and Their Districts* (Boston, 1978). I have also benefited from the work done by M. Fiorina, J. Ferejohn, and B. Cain at the California Institute of Technology.

[19] On the general question of incentives to participate in politics see J. Q. Wilson, *Political Organization* (New York, 1973).

[20] For a general discussion of pressure-groups in America see R. J. Hrebenar and R. K. Scott, *Interest Group Politics in America* (Englewood Cliffs, NJ, 1982).

[21] See, for example, the treatment of the right-wing revival in A. Crawford, *Thunder on the Right* (New York, 1980).

[22] On the theme of family policy generally see G. Y. Steiner, *The Futility of Family Policy* (Washington, DC, 1981); also A. Merton, *Enemies of Choice: The Right to Life Movement and its Threat to Abortion* (Boston, Mass., 1981).

[23] C. Rossiter, *Conservatism in America: The Thankless Persuasion* (2nd rev. edn., London, 1982), 257.

[24] Ibid. 98.

[25] A. J. Cigler and B. A. Loomis, *Interest Group Politics* (Washington, DC, 1983).

[26] On general intellectual movements on the right see G. Nash, *The Conservative Intellectual Movement in America Since 1945* (New York, 1979).

[27] See, for example, Perry Deane Young's study *God's Bullies* (New York, 1982), where it is suggested that a number of the leading figures of the new right are themselves homosexual or, as in the case of Anita Bryant, have personal and psychological problems.

[28] J. R. Gusfield, *Symbolic Crusade: Status Politics and the American Temperance Movement* (London, 1980), 3.

[29] The Family Protection Bill was drafted in part by the Committee for the Survival of a Free Congress and introduced into the Senate in 1979 by Senator Paul Laxalt. It was later reintroduced by Senator Jepsen.

[30] On this aspect of modern Republicanism see L. Cannon, *Reagan* (New York, 1982).

[31] I am especially grateful to my graduate students Mr R. J. L. London and Mr D. Dreisbach for drawing my attention to a large amount of this literature.

[32] The Institute for Religion and Democracy was founded to resist the use by such bodies as the National Council of Churches of funds to further liberation movements. *This World* is a journal founded in 1981 to explore issues of religious and political significance. Both groups have received funding from the Scaife Foundation.

[33] A. Wohlstetter, 'Bishops, Statesmen, and Other Strategists on the Bombing of Innocents', *Commentary*, 75. 6 (June 1983), 16.

[34] On this see F. Greenstein (ed.), *The Reagan Presidency: An Early Assessment* (Baltimore, 1983), especially the article by Hugh Heclo and Rudolph Penner.

[35] An account of these clashes is contained in W. Greider, *The Education of David Stockman and Other Americans* (Washington, DC, 1982).

[36] See Cannon, *Reagan.*

[37] On the contradictions implicit in the tax revolts see R. Kluttner, *Revolt of the Haves: Tax Rebellions in Hard Times* (New York, 1980). On Proposition 13 see also C. Jones, 'Cutting Taxes in California', *Parliamentary Affairs*, 34. 2 (Winter 1981), 81–94.

[38] A statement of what the right wanted can be found in C. Heatherly (ed.), *Mandate for Leadership* (Washington, DC, 1981).

[39] The most important so far are the short collection by Greenstein, *The Reagan Presidency*, and J. L. Palmer and I. V. Sawhill, *The Reagan Experiment: An Examination of Economic and Social Policies under the Reagan Administration* (Washington, DC, 1982).

Chapter I

[1] See I. Kristol, *Reflections of a Neoconservative: Looking Back, Looking Ahead* (New York, 1983), p. ix.

[2] For an extended study of the ideas of the neo-conservatives see P. Steinfels, *The Neo-Conservatives* (New York, 1979); see also the useful article by Nigel Ashford, 'The Neo-Conservatives', *Government and Opposition*, 16. 3 (1981), 353–69.

[3] This point is made very forcefully in K. Phillips, *Post-Conservative America* (New York, 1982).

[4] The role of the media is provocatively covered in D. Halberstam, *The Powers That Be* (New York, 1979).

[5] On the role of ideology in American politics generally see L. Hartz, *The Liberal Tradition in America: An Interpretation of American Political Thought Since the Revolution* (New York, 1962).

[6] For personal accounts by a leading neo-conservative see N. Podhoretz, *Breaking Ranks: A Political Memoir* (New York, 1980), and id., *Why We Were in Vietnam* (New York, 1982).

[7] The literature on realignment is vast; an excellent starting-point is J. Sundquist, *The Dynamics of the Party System* (2nd edn., Washington, DC, 1983).

[8] For a discussion of the Communist Party see E. Latham, *The Communist Controversy in Washington: From the New Deal to McCarthy* (Cambridge, Mass., 1966). The CIO was founded as the Committee of Industrial Organisations in 1935; it changed its name to the Congress of Industrial Organisations in 1938.

[9] On the role of the Communist Party and the phenomenon of fellow-traveling in Europe and America in this period see D. Caute, *The*

Fellow-Travellers: A Postscript to the Enlightenment (London, 1973). On the role of communism in American life generally in this period, see also T. Draper, *The Roots of American Communism* (New York, 1957).

10 On the attitude of Edmund Wilson see his own account in E. Wilson, *The Thirties*, ed. L. Edel (New York, 1980).

11 J. Reed, *Ten Days That Shook the World* (New York, 1919).

12 On the break between *Partisan Review* and the Communist Party see Norman Podhoretz's first autobiographical work, *Making It* (2nd edn., New York, 1980). According to Daniel Bell, this book embarrassed all Podhoretz's friends when it appeared, but it does capture much of the background of the most prominent neo-conservative figures. Also relevant is Caute, *The Fellow-Travellers*. A useful discussion of the role of such magazines as *Partisan Review* is to be found in Lionel Trilling's 'The Function of the Little Magazine', in L. Trilling (ed.), *The Liberal Imagination: Essays on Literature and Society* (Harmondsworth, 1970), 102–12; the essay was first published as the introduction to W. Phillips and P. Rahv (eds.), *The Partisan Reader: Ten Years of* Partisan Review, *1933–44* (New York, 1946). In the twentieth century little magazines have been central to the development of avant-garde movements in art and literature in the United States as vehicles for expressing radical ideas in aesthetics and social criticism. See also 'The Little Magazines' in the *Times Literary Supplement*, 25 April 1968. A general selection of *Partisan Review* articles is contained in E. Kurzweil and W. Phillips, *A* Partisan Review *Reader* (London, 1983). On the general role of intellectuals in this period see W. Barrett, *The Truants: Adventures Among the Intellectuals* (New York, 1982); see also Kristol's essay 'Memoirs of a Trotskyist', in id., *Reflections of a Neoconservative*.

13 Eugene Lyons was a journalist who later wrote of the experiences of those who had been attracted to communism in the 1930s; see E. Lyons, *The Red Decade* (New York, 1941).

14 See M. Novak, *The Spirit of Democratic Capitalism* (Washington, DC, 1982); also the same author's *Confessions of a Catholic* (New York, 1983) and a variety of shorter pamphlets on the nature of capitalism.

15 Mary McCarthy was at one time the wife of Edmund Wilson. Her many books include *Memories of a Catholic Girlhood*, *The Group*, and *The Company She Keeps*. *The Oasis* provides a somewhat satirical account of New York intellectuals, and especially of Philip Rahv, her former lover.

16 See D. Bell, 'The Intelligentsia in American Society', in id., *Sociological Journeys: Essays 1960–1980* (London, 1980), 119–37; also A. Kazin, *New York Jew* (New York, 1978). Another account is given in Barrett, *The Truants*.

17 Bell, 'The Intelligentsia in American Society', pp. 119–37, especially p. 135.

[18] Ibid. 135.

[19] Ibid. 135.

[20] Trilling, 'The Function of the Little Magazine', p. 108.

[21] See, for example, Podhoretz, *Making It*.

[22] Some mention is made of the impact of the 1950s in Steinfels, *The Neo-Conservatives*, and there is an extensive and useful discussion of its impact on the conservative cause in America in G. Nash, *The Conservative Intellectual Movement in America* (New York, 1979). For an account of McCarthyism in American life see D. Caute, *The Great Fear* (New York, 1979), and the more specialized studies, such as D. Crosby, *God, Church and Flag: Senator McCarthy and the Catholic Church* (Chapel Hill, 1978), and T. Reeves, *The Life and Times of Joe McCarthy: A Biography* (London, 1983).

[23] In an aside Irving Kristol commented that Rosenberg was one of the two Stalinists he knew at New York's City College: Kristol, 'Memoirs of a Trotskyist', p. 7. The hearings on capital punishment took place before the Criminal Justice Sub-Committee of the House Judiciary Committee, December 1982. For a controversial reassessment of the case see R. Radosh and J. Milton, *The Rosenberg File: A Search for Truth* (London, 1983).

[24] See Reeves, *The Life and Times of Joe McCarthy*.

[25] L. Hellman, *Scoundrel Time* (London, 1976), 73–4.

[26] See Podhoretz, *Breaking Ranks*, p. 319, where Glazer's answer to Hellman is quoted.

[27] Ibid. 318.

[28] Ibid. 318.

[29] Irving Kristol's remarks were contained in an article in *Commentary* in March 1952. The quotation is taken from Steinfels, *The Neo-Conservatives*, p. 82.

[30] For a recent discussion of the consequences of reform for the major parties see N. Polsby, *The Consequences of Party Reform* (New York, 1983). For a discussion of the decline of party in America see D. Broder, *The Party's Over* (New York, 1972).

[31] D. Wrong, 'Not Very "Neo" Those Fellows', *Partisan Review*, 47 (1981), 96–103.

[32] G. Gilder, *Wealth and Poverty* (New York, 1981), 3.

[33] Novak, *The Spirit of Democratic Capitalism*.

[34] Ibid. 82.

[35] Ibid. 70.

[36] I. Kristol, *Two Cheers for Capitalism* (New York, 1978). The title may be a conscious echo of E. M. Forster's *Two Cheers for Democracy*. Forster had a seminal influence on Lionel Trilling and influenced the movement of many intellectuals away from Marxism.

[37] The problems of the Great Society initiatives have been reviewed in E. Ginzberg and R. M. Solow, *The Great Society: Lessons for the Future* (New York, 1974). See also J. Sundquist, *Politics and Policy: The Eisenhower, Kennedy and Johnson Years* (Washington, DC,

1968). For a recent assessment of what the role of the American federal government should be from an explicitly public policy school perspective see R. Zeckhauser and D. Leebaert, *What Role for Government? Lessons from Policy Research* (Durham, NC, 1983).

38 See N. Glazer, *Ethnic Dilemmas* (New York, 1983).

39 Bell, *Sociological Journeys*, preface, p. ix.

40 Ibid., p. xx.

41 For a review of the literature on affirmative action see J. C. Livingston, *Fair Game? Inequality and Affirmative Action* (San Francisco, 1979). For a hostile account of the Reagan approach from a right-of-center perspective see C. E. Finn, 'Affirmative Action Under Reagan', *Commentary*, 73. 4 (April 1982), 44.

42 *De Funis* v. *Odegaard*, 416 US 312 (1974), and *Bakke* v. *Regents of University of California*, 438 US 265 (1978), dealt with affirmative action in relation to law schools. *De Funis* was declared moot. *Bakke* was a complicated decision which did not strike down affirmative action programs. *United Steel Workers* v. *Weber*, No. 432 (1979), dealt with the legality of voluntary quotas for training opportunities. See C. Cohen, 'Justice Debased', *Commentary*, 68. 3 (1979), 43–53.

43 Interview with Nathan Glazer, Paris, 14 March 1983; see also the same author's *Ethnic Dilemmas*.

44 On busing generally see G. Orfield, *Must We Bus?* (Washington, DC, 1978).

45 E. Abrams, 'Beyond the Ethnic Polemic' [review of T. Sowell *et al.*, *American Ethnic Groups* (Washington, DC, 1979)], *The Public Interest*, 56 (1979), 129–33, at p. 132. For a hostile account of Sowell's role see J. Watts, 'The Case of the Black Conservative', *Dissent* (Summer 1982), 301–13.

46 For a further discussion of Moynihan's career see Steinfels, *The Neo-Conservatives*, and D. Schoen, *Pat: A Biography of David Patrick Moynihan* (New York, 1979).

47 Quoted in L. Rainwater *et al.*, *The Moynihan Report and the Politics of Controversy* (Cambridge, Mass., 1967). See also D. Moynihan and N. Glazer, *Ethnicity: Theory and Experience* (Cambridge, Mass., 1967).

48 D. Bell, *The Cultural Contradictions of Capitalism* (New York, 1978), 72.

49 Ibid. 54.

50 Kristol, *Reflections of a Neoconservative*.

51 Podhoretz, *Breaking Ranks*, p. 219.

52 Ibid. 219.

53 Especially in *Dictatorships and Double Standards: Rationalism and Reason in Politics* (New York, 1982); see especially the essay of the same name, ibid. 23–52.

54 Kristol, *Reflections of a Neoconservative*, p. xii.

55 Ibid., p. xii.

Chapter II

1 On this see P. M. Weyrich, 'Blue Collar or Blue Blood: The New Right Compared with the Old', in R. W. Whitaker (ed.), *The New Right Papers* (New York, 1982), 48–62.

2 On the conspiratorial aspects of the right in American history see S. M. Lipset and M. Raab, *The Politics of Unreason* (London, 1971). Richard Hofstadter's *The Paranoid Style in American Politics and Other Essays* (Chicago, 1979) remains a provocative and authoritative study of the right-wing mind. On the technique of expanding influence by infiltrating other organizations see T. McIntyre and J. C. Obert, *The Fear Brokers: Peddling the Politics of Hate* (New York, 1979), where Howard Phillips's 'The Crisis of Accountability and its Cure' is quoted on the subject.

3 For an excellent recent collection of essays with many pieces relevant to single-issue politics see A. J. Cigler and B. A. Loomis (eds.), *Interest Group Politics* (Washington, DC, 1983). On interest groups generally see R. J. Hrebenar and R. K. Scott, *Interest Groups in American Politics* (Englewood Cliffs, NJ, 1982).

4 See, for example, J. Kater, *Christians on the Right: The Moral Majority in Perspective* (New York, 1982).

5 See K. Rothmyer, 'Citizen Scaife', *Columbia Journalism Review* (July–August 1981). The article includes a summary of the Scaife donations.

6 On this see J. Bell, *Mr. Conservative: Barry Goldwater* (New York, 1962), and R. A. Kirk and J. McClellan, *The Political Principles of Robert A. Taft* (New York, 1967).

7 C. Rossiter, *Conservatism in America: The Thankless Persuasion* (2nd edn., London, 1982). On the teaching of evolution see D. Nelkin, *The Creation Controversy: Science or Scripture in the Schools* (London, 1982). Organizations which were rejuvenated included the Freeman Institute in Utah, where Cleon Skousen expanded his activities, and the John Birch Society. On the John Birch Society see B. R. Epstein and A. Forster, *Report on the John Birch Society, 1966* (New York, 1966), and the updated version by the same authors, *The Radical Right* (New York, 1967).

8 C. A. Moser, 'The New Right', *The Rockford Papers* (The Rockford Institute, November 1980).

9 Ibid.

10 L. Sabato, *The Rise of Political Consultants: New Ways of Winning Elections* (New York, 1981), provides an excellent introduction to the techniques employed by the new right. See also the review by G. R. Peele in *Electoral Studies*, 1. 2 (1982).

11 R. Viguerie, *The New Right: We're Ready to Lead* (Ottawa, Ill., 1981), 27–8.

12 Much of the discussion of direct mail here is based on a forthcoming article written jointly with Mr Nicholas O'Shaughnessy.

13 On this see the review cited above, n. 10.

14 On the general question of why people join organizations see J. Q. Wilson, *Political Organisation* (London, 1975). Some of the points made about the relationship between direct mail, political participation, and voluntary organization were suggested by reading R. K. Godwin and R. C. Mitchell, 'The Implications of Direct Mail for Political Organisations', paper presented to the American Political Science Association, 1982. I am grateful to Mr Godwin and Mr Mitchell both for permission to quote from their paper and for their help with my research in this area.

15 On the general theory of participation see R. W. Cobb and C. D. Elder, *Participation in American Politics: The Dynamics of Agenda-Building* (Boston, Mass., 1972).

16 On the general point about the relationship between single-issue groups and bargaining see M. R. Hershey and D. M. West, 'Single-issue Politics: Pro Life Groups and the 1981 Senate Campaign', in Cigler and Loomis (eds.), *Interest Group Politics*, pp. 31–59; see also Godwin and Mitchell, 'The Implications of Direct Mail for Political Organisations'.

17 A fair sample of the anti-abortion material which can be used in direct mail is reproduced as a set of color plates at the end of T. W. Hilgers and D. J. Horan, *Abortion and Social Justice* (Virginia, 1980). For a hostile overview of the Right to Life movement see A. Merton, *Enemies of Choice: The Right to Life Movement and its Threat to Abortion* (Boston, Mass., 1981). For a more dispassionate view see C. Schneider and M. Vinovskis, *The Law and Politics of Abortion* (Lexington, Mass., 1980).

18 Robin Beard was the Republican challenger to a one-term incumbent Democrat, Jim Sasser. Abortion became an issue because of Sasser's crucial tie-breaking vote on Senator Helms's anti-abortion amendment in 1982. Sasser, himself a supporter of the conservative position on school prayer, defeated Beard with 62 per cent of the vote to Beard's 32 per cent.

19 J. C. Roberts, *Conservative Decade* (New York, 1980).

20 On the new technology of direct mail see N. O'Shaughnessy and G. R. Peele, 'Mail and Markets' (forthcoming).

21 I am grateful to Margaret Latus for sharing her information on this subject and for the use of her unpublished paper 'Ideological PACs and Political Action'.

22 In 1983 much of the Republican Party's direct-mail consultancy was transferred to M. E. Lewis Associates.

23 See Sabato, *The Rise of Political Consultants*, p. 255.

24 The tax revolt is discussed in R. Kuttner, *Revolt of the Haves: Tax Rebellions and Hard Times* (New York, 1980).

25 L. Sabato, 'Political Consultants and Campaign Technology', in Cigler and Loomis (eds.), *Interest Group Politics*, pp. 145–68.

26 A comprehensive discussion of the role of money in the 1980 election is to be found in H. Alexander, *Financing the 1980 Election* (Lexington, Mass., 1983).

27 Sabato, *The Rise of Political Consultants*, p. 224.
28 Ibid. 221.
29 Ibid. 225.
30 On the right-to-work movement see the National Educational Association pamphlet *The Right to Work Revival: Far Right and Dead Wrong* (Washington, DC [1982?]). The topic is also covered in W. Hunter and T. Bonnett, *The New Right: A Growing Force in State Politics* (Washington, DC, 1980). General treatment can be found in A. Crawford, *Thunder on the Right: The New Right and the Politics of Resentment* (New York, 1980). Similar themes are covered in Roberts, *Conservative Decade*. The American Security Council has used direct mail to engage in general public campaigns on foreign-policy issues, whereas some of the other pressure-groups of the right which concentrate on foreign policy and international security (such as the Committee on the Present Danger) devoted themselves to élite persuasion and research.
31 Quoted in Sabato, *The Rise of Political Consultants*, p. 225. Hofstadter has emphasized the negative aspect of 'status politics', the term he used to describe the American right; see Hofstadter, *The Paranoid Style in American Politics and Other Essays*.
32 For a discussion of the changes introduced in the Democratic Party after the 1980 elections see the *National Journal*, 21 February 1981. I am also extremely grateful to Mr Michael Stead, Nancy Lieber, and other members of the staff of the Democratic National Committee for discussing the problems of party organization with me during 1983.
33 The law in this area is extremely complicated, and the best introduction is the Federal Election Commission's own material. On what Political Action Committees may do see *Campaign Guide for Corporations and Labor Organisations* (Washington, DC, 1982). Although separate segregated funds may be established by a variety of corporations, banks, and labor organizations, the solicitation of money is restricted and the rules governing solicitation by incorporated membership organizations differ from those for other organizations.
34 Edwin Feulner's own role in the new right can in part be gleaned from his book *Conservatives Stalk the House* (Ottawa, Ill., 1983).
35 *Buckley* v. *Valeo*, 424 US 1 (1976).
36 This was especially true in the 1982 Maryland Senate race.
37 Sabato, *The Rise of Political Consultants*, p. 270.
38 People for the American Way was founded to resist the increasing involvement of religious groups in political campaigns and against the attempts to impose a uniform morality on Americans.
39 See Chapter IV for a fuller discussion of this incident.
40 Americans for Democratic Action, *A Citizen's Guide to the Right Wing* (Washington, DC, 1978); quoted in McIntyre and Obert, *The Fear Brokers*, p. 76.
41 J. J. Kirkpatrick, 'Why We Don't Become Republicans', *Common-*

sense, 2. 3 (1979), 28. See also J. J. Kirkpatrick, *The New Presidential Élite: Men and Women in National Politics* (New York, 1976); also D. Broder, *The Party's Over* (New York, 1972), and id., *The Changing of the Guard: Power and Leadership in America* (New York, 1980). General discussion is also to be found in N. Polsby, *The Consequences of Party Reform* (New York, 1983), and W. Crotty and G. C. Jacobson, *Parties in Decline* (Boston, Mass., 1980).

42 Interview with Paul Weyrich, April 1982.

43 K. Sale, *Power Shift: The Rise of the Southern Rim and its Challenge to the Eastern Establishment* (New York, 1976).

44 *National Journal*, 2 May 1981, p. 779.

45 On the Reagan transition team see *National Journal*, 15 November 1980, pp. 1924-6.

46 R. N. Holwill (ed.), *The First Year* (Washington, DC, 1982), 1.

47 W. A. Johnson, 'Office of Presidential Personnel', in Holwill (ed.), *The First Year*, p. 8.

48 See R. P. Nathan, 'The Reagan Presidency and Domestic Affairs', in F. Greenstein (ed.), *The Reagan Presidency: An Early Assessment* (Baltimore, 1983), 48-81.

49 On the intellectual atmosphere of the right since 1945 see G. Nash, *The Conservative Intellectual Movement in America Since 1945* (New York, 1979). For general histories of the American right see M. Miles, *The Odyssey of the American Right* (New York, 1980). Also useful is the account by D. Reinhard, *The Republican Right Since 1945* (Lexington, Mass., 1983).

50 E. B. Jenkins, *Censors in the Classroom: The Mind Benders* (New York, 1979).

51 Ibid. See also the material published by the American Libraries Association.

52 For a recent overall study of American education see E. Boyer, *High School: An Agenda for Action* (New York, 1983); also D. Ravitch, *The Troubled Crusade: American Education 1945-80* (New York, 1983).

53 Hunter and Bonnett, *The New Right*.

54 Ibid.

55 Interview with Ron Godwin, Executive Director of Moral Majority (24 March 1982). (This interview was somewhat unusual in that it was conducted from the Moral Majority Offices in Washington by 'conference call' to Lynchburg, Virginia.)

56 N. Peirce and J. Hagstrom, *The Book of America: Inside Fifty States Today* (New York, 1983).

57 McIntyre and Obert, *The Fear Brokers*, chapter I ('Target: Home-Town America').

58 D. Danzig, 'The Radical Right and the Rise of the Fundamentalist Minority', in R. A. Rosenstone (ed.), *Protest from the Right* (Beverly Hills, Calif., 1968), 121 [originally in *Commentary* (April 1962), 291-8].

[59] J. Hadden and C. E. Swann, *Prime Time Preachers: The Rising Power of Televangelism* (Reading, Mass., 1981).

Chapter III

[1] For a very helpful bibliography see S. E. Ahlstrom, *A Religious History of the American People* (2 vols., New York, 1975); also R. Pierard, *Bibliography of the Religious Right in America* (privately circulated).

[2] P. Shriver, *The Bible Vote: Religion and the New Right* (New York, 1981). For a consideration immediately after 1980 see S. M. Lipset and E. Raab, 'The Election and the Evangelicals', *Commentary*, 71. 3 (March 1981).

[3] The arguments about the constitutional position are to be found in a number of academic and polemical writings. For a judicial summary see the decision of the Supreme Court in *Everson* v. *Board of Education*, 330 US 1 (1947), especially the arguments of Mr Justice Black and the dissenting arguments of Mr Justice Jackson and Mr Justice Rutledge. For arguments against Justice Black's historical interpretation and broad application of the no-establishment clause see R. L. Cord, *Separation of Church and State: Historical Fact and Current Fiction* (New York, 1982), and id., 'Understanding the First Amendment', *National Review* (22 January 1982), 26–32. Also of considerable interest are J. McClellan, *Joseph Story and the American Constitution* (Norman, Okla., 1971), and J. W. Whitehead, *The Separation Illusion* (Milford, Mich., 1977). The same author's *The Second American Revolution* (Elgin, Ill., 1982) gives further illustration of the thinking of the religious right on this and related issues. For a recent judicial opinion which looks at the basis of the constitutional separation of Church and State see *Jaffree* v. *Board of School Commissioners of Mobile County* (decided by the Federal District Judge W. Brevard Hand on 14 January 1983). The decision was inserted into the *Congressional Record*, 129. 4, on 26 January 1983, S. 139–S. 149. The insertion was made at the request of Senator Jesse Helms of North Carolina, who is one of the leading campaigners for the reintroduction of voluntary school prayer. The arguments about the extension of the Bill of Rights to the states can be found in H. J. Abraham, *Freedom and the Court: Civil Rights and Liberties in the United States* (4th edn., New York, 1982). See also M. Malbin, *Religion and Politics: The Intentions of the Authors of the First Amendment* (Washington, DC, 1981).

[4] On the ethos of the early settlers see P. Miller, *Errand into the Wilderness* (Cambridge, Mass., 1956).

[5] On the revival of creation science and the hostility to scientific modes of thought see D. Nelkin, *The Creation Controversy: Science or Scripture* (London, 1983). Arkansas's Balanced Treatment for Creation-Science and Evolution-Science Act (1981) was overturned

in *McLean* v. *Arkansas Board of Education*, decided in the US District Court, Eastern District of Arkansas, Western Division, opinion of William R. Overton, 5 January 1982. For a full account see *Science*, 215 (19 February 1982), 324–43; see also *Church and State*, 35. 2 (February 1982). For an account of the evolution controversy from a pro-creationist perspective see B. Keith, *Scopes II: The Great Debate. Creation versus Evolution* ([no place:] Huntington House, 1982). On fundamentalism, evangelicalism, and puritanism in American culture see J. D. Hunter, *American Evangelicalism: Conservative Religion and the Quandary of Modernity* (New Brunswick, 1983), and G. Marsden, *Fundamentalism and American Culture: The Shaping of American Evangelicalism 1870–1925* (New York, 1982). On the role of puritanism see L. Ziff, *Puritanism in America: New Culture in a New World* (London, 1973), and M. Walzer, *The Revolution of the Saints* (Cambridge, Mass., 1965).

6 For an account of the legal debate see as a useful starting-point F. Sorauf, *The Wall of Separation* (Princeton, 1976). Sorauf lists sixty-seven major cases handed down by the Supreme Court between 1951 and 1971. The most important would probably be reckoned to be those that relate to prayer and Bible-reading in schools (*Engel* v. *Vitale*, 370 US 421 (1962), and *Murray* v. *Curtlett*, 374 US 203 (1963)). Other important decisions concerned direct aid to religious schools (*Lemon* v. *Kurtzman*, 403 US 602 (1971), and *Dicenso* v. *Robinson*, 316 F. Supp. 112 (1970)). An extremely useful compendium of relevant cases may be found in R. T. Miller and R. B. Flowers, *Toward Benevolent Neutrality: Church, State and Supreme Court* (Waco, Texas, 1982).

7 *Bob Jones University* v. *United States*, No. 81-1, 644 F 2d 870 SC (24 May 1983). See also the companion case *Goldsboro Schools Inc.* v. *United States*, No. 81-3, 639 F 2d 147 (24 May 1983). In *Bob Jones* the Supreme Court held that for an institution to enjoy the obvious benefits of tax exemption it must 'serve a public purpose and not be contrary to established public policy'.

8 This approach can be found in F. H. Littel, *From State Church to Pluralism* (New York, 1962).

9 A. I. Katsh, *The Biblical Heritage of American Democracy* (New York, 1977); also C. Cherry, *God's New Israel: Religious interpretations of American Destiny* (Englewood Cliffs, NJ, 1971).

10 Quoted in Katsh, *The Biblical Heritage of American Democracy*, p. 131.

11 John Kennedy's Roman Catholicism was effectively shown to be no handicap in his search for the nomination when West Virginia, an overwhelmingly Protestant state, endorsed him in the primary, although Al Smith had in fact won in West Virginia's primary before being defeated in 1928.

12 The early American history of the Roman Catholic Church is covered in T. O'Gorman, *A History of the Roman Catholic Church in America* (New York, 1895). See also Ahlstrom, *A Religious History of*

the American People. Of interest is J. T. Ellis, *American Catholicism* (2nd edn., Chicago, 1969). See also J. Hennessy, *American Catholics: A History of the Roman Catholic Community in the United States* (New York, 1981). The nuclear debate is covered in R. Drinan, *Beyond the Nuclear Freeze* (New York, 1983), especially chapter 9, which covers the role of nuclear deterrence in the Roman Catholic tradition. For a different view see M. Novak, *Moral Clarity in a Nuclear Age* (New York, 1983), and the hostile review by J. M. Cameron, 'Nuclear Catholicism', in *New York Review of Books*, 30. 20 (22 December 1983), 38–42.

13 On the role of Jews in America see A. J. Karp, *The Jewish Experience in America: Selected Studies from the American Jewish Historical Society* (5 vols., New York, 1969). Also of interest is the same author's *Golden Door to America* (New York, 1976), which deals with the immigrant experience, and N. Glazer, *American Judaism* (Chicago, 1957).

14 See R. N. Bellah and P. E. Hammond, *Varieties of Civil Religion* (San Francisco, 1980).

15 For a general discussion of fundamentalism see J. Barr, *Fundamentalism* (London, 1977).

16 Marsden, *Fundamentalism and American Culture*, p. 4.

17 Ibid. 3.

18 Ibid., especially the introduction, pp. 3–8.

19 See, for example, Hunter, *American Evangelicalism*.

20 For a general history of religion in America see Ahlstrom, *A Religious History of the American People*. For a discussion of the manner in which evangelicals coped with cognitive and cultural dissonance see especially Hunter, *American Evangelicalism*. The Evangelical Church Alliance was incorporated in Missouri in 1928 as The World's Faith Missionary Association. It was later known as The Fundamental Ministerial Association and adopted its current name in 1958.

21 For a hostile view of the role of the World Council see the various publications of the Institute for Religion and Democracy.

22 Dean Kelley's argument is contained in *Why Conservative Churches Are Growing* (New York, 1977), 6.

23 Ibid. 21.

24 Ibid., especially pp. 33–5. For figures see C. Jacquet (ed.), *Yearbook of the American and Canadian Churches*. On the impact of Vatican II see Ahlstrom, *A Religious History of the American People*, especially ii. 503–27 (chapter 59); also J. Hitchcock, *The Decline and Fall of Radical Catholicism* (New York, 1971).

25 For a discussion of the recent growth of the evangelical Churches and sects see especially Ahlstrom, *A Religious History of the American People*, and Hunter, *American Evangelicalism*.

26 Quoted in Marsden, *Fundamentalism in American Culture*, p. 206.

27 J. Falwell, *Listen America* (New York, 1981), 12.

28 See Ahlstrom, *A Religious History of the American People*.

29 The encyclicals are discussed ibid. ii. 298–317. See also R. Aubert, *The Church in a Secularised Society* (*The Christian Centuries*, vol. v; London, 1978), and H. Jeddin, *The Church in the Industrial Age* (*History of the Church*, vol. ix; London, 1981). For a compendium of the statements of the American Catholic bishops on the social and political order between 1966 and 1980 see US Catholic Conference, *Quest for Justice* (Washington, DC, 1981).

30 An interesting test of attitudes occurred when the AWACS issue was debated. See M. Friedman, 'Awacs and the Jewish Community', *Commentary*, 73. 4 (April 1982), 29–33.

31 W. V. d'Antonio and J. Aldous (eds.), *Families and Religions: Conflict and Change in Modern Society* (Beverly Hills, Calif., 1983).

32 Quoted in Wakefield Washington Associates, *The American Family*, 1. 1 (December 1977–January 1978), 1.

33 Ibid. 2.

34 For an overview of family policy see G. Y. Steiner, *The Futility of Family Policy* (Washington, DC, 1981).

35 *Roe* v. *Wade*, 410 US 1973; *Doe* v. *Bolton*, 410 US 1973. Other major cases included *Maher* v. *Roe*, 432 US 464 (1977), *Bellotti* v. *Baird*, 443 US 622 (1979), and *Harris* v. *McRae*, 448 US 297 (1980).

36 Hearings have been held on various aspects of a Right to Life amendment. For example, see *Hearings before the Sub-Committee on Civil and Constitutional Rights of the Committee of the Judiciary* (House of Representatives), 94th Congress, Serial No. 46, Parts 1 and 2. SJ Res. 110 (the Hatch proposal) was rejected by full Senate on 28 June 1983.

37 In 1983 the Supreme Court reviewed a number of abortion-related issues as it considered a group of cases concerning restrictions on abortion such as the requirement of the humane disposal of the fetus and the examination of fetal tissue by two pathologists. See especially *City of Akron* v. *The Akron Center for Reproductive Health*, in *US Law Week*, 51 (1983), 4767. Of interest from the point of view of the right is Justice O'Connor's opinion in that case.

38 For a recent examination see N. Polsby, *The Consequences of Party Reform* (Oxford, 1983). On the abortion issue see M. R. Hershey and D. M. West, 'Single-issue Politics: Pro Life Groups and the 1981 Senate Campaign', in A. J. Cigler and B. A. Loomis (eds.), *Interest Group Politics* (Washington, DC, 1983), 31–59.

39 In early May 1980 Pope John Paul II ordered priests throughout the world to cease secular political activities. Congressman Drinan agreed to resign his seat, but the Massachusetts voters were angered by what was seen as interference by the Vatican in American politics. In late June Father Drinan gave his support to Barney Frank, a liberal Jewish Democratic candidate whose stand on moral issues was decidedly out of line with Roman Catholic teachings. See *New York Times*, 5 May 1980 and 6 May 1980; also 13 May 1980 and 23 June 1980. Father Drinan is himself a prolific writer and his

political position can be seen in his *Religion, The Courts and Public Policy* (New York, 1963) and 'State and Federal Aid to Parochial Schools', *Journal of Church and State*, 7 (Winter 1965), 67–77.

40 Barney Frank won by 60 per cent to 40 per cent in 1982, as opposed to 52 per cent to 48 per cent in 1980. The Frank–Heckler race was interesting both because of the amount of money spent and because of the family issues raised. Heckler was not supported to any great extent by the Republican National Committee and had to raise much of her own funds; she was outspent by Frank by $1,502,581 to $966,921. See M. Barone and G. Ujifusa, *Almanac of American Politics, 1984* (Washington, DC, 1983), 545–8.

41 Ibid. 737–9.

42 The textbook issue is discussed in Chapter II.

43 D. Nevin and R. E. Bills, *The Schools that Fear Built: Segregation Academies in the South* (Washington, DC, 1976), provides a useful investigation of the role of private schools in the South.

44 Ibid. See also Hunter, *American Evangelicalism*.

45 Stokes and Pfeffer had earlier made the point that the failure to resolve constitutionally the question of religious education in public schools was one of only two 'serious defects' in the American system of Church–State separation: A. P. Stokes and L. Pfeffer, *Church and State in the United States: Historical Development and Contemporary Problems of Religious Freedom under the Constitution* (3 vols., New York, 1950), iii. 722. On the role of Roman Catholic schools see A. Greeley *et al.*, *Catholic Schools in a Declining Church* (Kansas City, 1976).

46 On the topic of school see 'School Prayer: An Old Issue Surfaces Once Again', *Congressional Quarterly, Weekly Report*, 31 (4 August 1973), 2141–3; also 'The School Prayer Controversy', *Congressional Digest*, 5. 59 (December 1980), 289–314. Also useful is D. A. Ackerman, 'Prayer and Religion in the Public Schools: what is and is not permitted', *Congressional Research Services Report*, No. 80-156A, 28 January 1976. The Democratic Study Group Report, *Prayer in Public Schools* (Washington, DC, 1980), is helpful, as is C. E. Rice, *The Supreme Court and Public Prayer* (New York, 1964). An overview of the cases can be found in E. Brown, 'Quis Custodiet Ipsos Custodes? The School Prayer Cases', *Supreme Court Review* (1963). See also the various hearings before the Judiciary Committee. In addition, there is a certain amount of polemical literature on the subject, some of it of a banal kind (e.g. R. Warren and D. Schneider, *Mom They Won't Let Us Pray* (Chappaqua, NY, 1975)).

47 The role of the public schools became the focus of public debate in 1983 with the Report of the President's Commission for Excellence in Education.

48 The Michigan SRC survey, for example, suggests that school prayer is the least divisive social issue and that an overwhelming majority support voluntary school prayer. For a recent review of general attitudes to civil liberties, see H. McClosky and A. Brill, *Dimensions*

of Tolerance: What Americans believe about Civil Liberties (New York, 1983).

49 Sorauf, *The Wall of Separation.*

50 On these races see Barone and Ujifusa, *Almanac of American Politics, 1982.*

51 R. Viguerie, *The New Right: We're Ready To Lead* (Ottawa, Ill., 1981), especially pp. 155–74.

52 For a left-wing perspective on the Vietnam syndrome see M. T. Klare, *Beyond the Vietnam Syndrome: U.S. Interventionism in the 1980s* (Washington, DC, 1981). See also the remarks by J. Robison in his testimony before the House Judiciary Committee (June 1980). It may be worth noting that the Vietnam War provided some test cases for the courts by forcing them to determine when they would accept religious belief as a justification for conscientious objection under the free-exercise clause of the First Amendment: see *US* v. *Seeger*, 380 US (1965).

53 See, for example, Hearings of the Sub-Committee on Courts, Civil Liberties and the Administration of Justice on Prayer in Schools and Public Buildings, 29, 30 July, 19, 21 August, and 9 September 1980, House of Representatives, Serial No. 63.

54 For a general overview of the abortion issue see J. T. Burchaell (ed.), *Abortion Parley* (New York, 1980); also G. Y. Steiner, *The Abortion Dispute* (Washington, DC, 1983).

55 On the Board of PAW in 1982 were Dr Charles Bergstrom of the Lutheran Council; The Revd M. William Howard, President of the National Council of Churches of Christ in the USA; Rabbi Marc Tanenbaum of the American Jewish Committee; Mgr. George Higgins; the Episcopal Bishop of Massachusetts; and the President of Notre-Dame University; also included were Lane Kirkland, President of the AFL–CIO, and John Lindsay, former Mayor of New York.

56 For a useful discussion of the accommodation of modern American evangelicalism to the market of the consumer see Hunter, *American Evangelicalism*, especially chapter 6.

57 The vast majority of religious broadcasting in the United States is done by evangelicals. A *New York Times* article in January 1971 noted that members of The National Religious Broadcasters (which is affiliated to The National Association of Evangelicals) were responsible for three-quarters of the world's religious broadcasting: see *New York Times*, 28 January 1971.

58 A useful discussion of the figures is to be found in J. Hadden and C. E. Swann, *Prime Time Preachers: The Rising Power of Televangelism* (Reading, Mass., 1981). On the media evangelists generally see E. Jorstad, *The Politics of Moralism* (Minneapolis, 1981).

59 On the Carter campaign and the role of religion see P. D. Young, *God's Bullies: Power Politics and Religious Tyranny* (New York, 1982); also K. Phillips, *Post-Conservative America: People, Politics and Ideology in a Time of Crisis* (New York, 1982).

60 For an interesting discussion of the South see *National Journal*, 28

February 1981, p. 350.

61 I am indebted for much of my understanding of these early links between the new right and the religious right to the work done by Mr R. J. L. London.

62 On Billings see R. Babcock, 'Bob Billings: Christian Right's Inside Man', *Washington Post*, 25 March 1982. For an overview of educational policy since 1945 see D. Ravitch, *The Troubled Crusade: American Education 1945–80* (New York, 1983). For a discussion of the impact of Reagan on educational policy see J. L. Palmer and I. V. Sawhill (eds.), *The Reagan Experiment: An Examination of Economic and Social Policies under the Reagan Administration* (Washington, DC, 1982), especially pp. 329–59.

63 On Orrin Hatch see R. Vetterli, *Orrin Hatch: Challenging the Washington Establishment* (Chicago, 1982).

64 Barone and Ujifusa, *Almanac of American Politics, 1984*, pp. 47–8. Larry McDonald was killed in 1983 when a Korean passenger plane was shot down for straying into Soviet airspace. Stump's conversion to the Republican Party was one of only two conversions, although initially the GOP had thought that more conservative Democrats might change party.

65 See Christian Voice, *Report Card on Congress, 1980*.

66 On the Bauman case see Young, *God's Bullies*, especially pp. 132–52, which deals with the theme of hostility to homosexuality on the part of the right.

67 Bailey Smith made his remarks at the Religious Roundtable, National Affairs Briefing in Dallas, Texas, in August 1980. The meeting was attended by Ronald Reagan, who endorsed the attitudes of the group, though not the particular remarks of Bailey Smith. See Young, *God's Bullies*, pp. 201–2; also F. Conway and J. Sigelman, *Holy Terror: The Fundamentalist War on America's Freedoms in Religion, Politics and Our Private Lives* (New York, 1982), 167. Bailey Smith's remarks were quickly qualified by Jerry Falwell.

68 Jewish criticism of the NCC was fueled by that body's advocacy of recognizing the Palestine Liberation Organization. I am grateful to Mr Nate Perlmutter and Mr Irwin Suall of the Anti-Defamation League of B'nai B'rith for discussing their attitudes towards the religious right (interview, New York, 7 April 1982). I am similarly grateful to Rabbi Marc Tanenbaum of the American Jewish Committee for his comments (interview, New York, 7 April 1982). For Falwell's attitude to Israel see *Listen America*, pp. 93–8.

69 Ibid. 6.

70 J. Falwell (ed.), *The Fundamentalist Phenomenon: The Resurgence of Conservative Christianity* (New York, 1981), 188. Falwell's book is of interest especially for the commentary (largely in the endnotes) on other writers on fundamentalism.

71 Viguerie, *The New Right: We're Ready to Lead*, p. 161.

72 See Chapter II for further details.

73 Viguerie, *The New Right: We're Ready to Lead*, pp. 163–4.
74 See A. Wollner, 'Carter Cleric blasts Moral Majority', *Atlanta Journal/ Atlanta Constitution*, 12 October 1980. On the role of the new Christian right in President Carter's thinking see J. E. Carter, *Keeping Faith: Memoirs of A President* (London, 1982); on the general role of Bob Maddox I have relied on personal conversations with Mr Maddox and extensive notes given to Mr R. J. L. London.
75 Detailed material on the attitudes of evangelicals is very difficult to obtain. The *CPS 1980 Election Study* had some questions which permitted a rough examination of evangelical opinions and voting behavior. But because religious attitudes and practices do not coincide with objective denominational affiliation it is difficult to isolate conservative evangelicals, fundamentalists, or 'born-again' voters accurately.

Chapter IV

1 On the general significance of the elections of 1980 see A. Ranney (ed.), *The American Elections of 1980* (Washington, DC, 1981).
2 I am grateful to my student Mr Nicol Rae for a number of interesting contributions on the role of the liberal wing of the Republican Party. As far as the ideological impact of redistricting is concerned, it seems that the additional sun-belt members returned in 1982 were as likely to be moderates as either new-right Republicans or 'boll-weevil' Democrats.
3 On the Goldwater campaign generally see J. H. Kessel, *The Goldwater Coalition: Republican Strategies in 1964* (New York, 1968).
4 Quoted in E. J. Feulner, *Conservatives Stalk the House* (Ottawa, Ill., 1983), 154.
5 The literature on Congress is vast; useful starting-points are M. Foley, *The New Senate* (New Haven, 1980), and T. Mann and N. Ornstein, *The New Congress* (Washington, DC, 1981). See also D. M. Abshire and R. D. Nurnberger (eds.), *The Growing Power of Congress* (Washington, DC, 1981).
6 On this episode see the study of R. Vetterli, *Orrin Hatch: Challenging the Washington Establishment* (Chicago, 1982).
7 John Buchanan, a Republican, had become too liberal for his constituency and was defeated by Albert Lee Smith, who was himself defeated by a Democrat in 1982. Buchanan had apparently become increasingly sympathetic to blacks, and a combination of Albert Lee Smith's adherence to Reaganomics and Buchanan's vulnerability to the active Moral Majority caused his defeat. Albert Lee Smith's defeat was surprising, given the Republican tradition of the district. See M. Barone and G. Ujifusa, *Almanac of American Politics, 1984* (Washington, DC, 1983), 19; also interview with John Buchanan in Washington, 24 March 1982. Javits had long been a highly unusual liberal Republican, who, *inter alia*, cosponsored the War Powers

legislation of 1973. On Javits's philosophy see his own accounts in
J. Javits, *Order of Battle: A Republican Call to Reason* (New York,
1964), and J. Javits and D. Kellerman, *Who Makes War? The President versus Congress* (New York, 1973).

[8] On this see L. Cannon, *Reagan* (New York, 1982), 235.

[9] L. Sabato, 'Parties, PACs and Independent Groups', in T. E. Mann
and J. Ornstein (eds.), *The American Elections of 1982* (Washington,
DC, 1983), 72–110.

[10] Paul Sarbanes called on the Republican nominee, Laurence Hogan,
to get NCPAC out of Maryland, while Hogan responded that he was
tired of the contest being turned into a referendum on NCPAC.
See *Congressional Quarterly, Weekly Report*, 23 October 1982,
p. 2710.

[11] Richards actually announced his resignation in October 1982. Frank
Fahrenkopf was appointed to control the party's day-to-day management. On the whole episode see *Congressional Quarterly, Weekly
Report*, 13 November 1982 and 9 October 1982.

[12] Kessel, *The Goldwater Coalition.*

[13] M. Miles, *The Odyssey of the American Right* (New York, 1980).

[14] D. Reinhard, *The Republican Right Since 1945* (Kentucky, 1983),
especially pp. 1–14.

[15] See, for example, Nelson Polsby's comment that since the election
of 1968 the Democratic majority has only once been able to pull
itself together sufficiently to elect a President: N. Polsby, *The
Consequences of Party Reform* (New York, 1983), 89.

[16] Reinhard, *The Republican Right Since 1945*, p. 8.

[17] This point is also made by Reinhard.

[18] See G. H. Mayer, *The Republican Party 1854–1966* (2nd edn., New
York, 1967), p. ix.

[19] The term has been used by A. James Reichley in his stimulating
analysis of the Republicans in the Eisenhower, Nixon, and Ford
years. The categories used by Reichley are 'stalwarts', 'fundamentalists', 'moderates', and 'progressives': see A. J. Reichley, *Conservatives
in an Age of Change* (Washington, DC, 1981). Reinhard simply
uses a tripartite distinction between the factions.

[20] Cannon, *Reagan.*

[21] Reichley, *Conservatives in an Age of Change.*

[22] See Sinclair Lewis, *Main Street* (New York, 1920). Also of interest
is Lewis's *Babbitt* (New York, 1922).

[23] In the 98th Congress there were forty-five Roman Catholic Republicans in Congress — thirty-seven in the House and eight in the
Senate. See *Congressional Quarterly, Weekly Report*, 29 January
1983, p. 222.

[24] On this see Miles, *The Odyssey of the American Right*, especially
chapter 5.

[25] On this see J. T. Patterson, *Mr Republican: A Biography of Robert
A. Taft* (Boston, Mass., 1972), 80.

[26] See Reinhard, *The Republican Right Since 1945*, and Kessel, *The*

Goldwater Coalition.

27 For a history of recent Republican attitudes on the civil rights issue see Reichley, *Conservatives in an Age of Change.* For a liberal Republican perspective see J. Javits, *Discrimination: U.S.A.* (New York, 1960).

28 See Vetterli, *Orrin Hatch: Challenging the Washington Establishment,* especially pp. 139–52.

29 The intellectual developments on the right are well covered in G. Nash, *The Conservative Intellectual Movement in America Since 1945* (New York, 1979).

30 For an overview see Reinhard, *The Republican Right Since 1945.* For an analysis which focuses on the youth movement see E. Cain, *They'd Rather Be Right* (New York, 1963).

31 Reichley, *Conservatives in an Age of Change,* gives a full assessment of the policies of the Nixon years.

32 A full account is given in Cannon, *Reagan.* See also F. Clifton White, *Why Reagan Won: The Conservative Movement 1964–81* (Chicago, 1981), especially pp. 151–91.

33 On this see Joshua Muravchik's essay, 'The Senate and National Security: A New Mood', in D. N. Abshire and R. D. Nurnberger (eds.), *The Growing Power of Congress* (Washington, DC, 1981), 199–282. A variety of groups formed during this period to switch foreign policy in a more conservative direction. See *National Journal,* 24 January 1981, pp. 128–32, for an overview. Some of them are more fully discussed in Chapter VI.

34 See Cain, *They'd Rather Be Right.*

35 On Taft see Patterson, *Mr. Republican.* On the role that the South might play in a realignment see K. Phillips, *The Emerging Republican Majority* (New Rochelle, 1969).

36 For a discussion of family issues see Chapters II and III.

37 See *Congressional Quarterly, Weekly Report,* 16 October 1982, p. 2675.

38 See Feulner, *Conservatives Stalk the House.*

39 On the Bow Group's role see R. Rose, 'Parties, Factions and Tendencies in Britain', *Political Studies,* 12 (1964), 33–46.

40 On the Senate see Foley, *The New Senate.*

41 On the general role of the Republican Study Committee see Feulner, *Conservatives Stalk the House.* On the role of staff see M. Malbin, *Unelected Representatives: Congressional Staff and the Future of Representative Government* (New York, 1980).

42 On this see Abshire and Nurnberger (eds.), *The Growing Power of Congress.*

43 On this see Barone and Ujifusa, *Almanac of American Politics, 1984.*

44 Abshire and Nurnberger (eds.), *The Growing Power of Congress.*

45 Vetterli, *Orrin Hatch: Challenging the Washington Establishment.*

46 On Rockefeller's career see R. M. Connery and G. Benjamin, *Rockefeller of New York: Executive Power in the State House* (Ithaca, NY, 1979). Some of Rockefeller's attitudes towards government

and politics are set out in *Selected Issues and Positions of Nelson A. Rockefeller, Nominee for Vice President of the United States* (House of Representatives Judiciary Committee, 93rd Congress, 2nd Session, November 1974).

47 *Congressional Quarterly, Weekly Report*, 4 December 1982, p. 2973.

48 On the role of governors generally see L. Sabato, *Goodbye to Good-Time Charlie* (Lexington, Mass., 1982).

49 President Reagan's proposals for the reform of the federal system were contained in the Address to Congress on the State of the Union, 26 January 1982.

50 See *Congressional Quarterly, Weekly Report*, 13 November 1982.

51 On this see Barone and Ujifusa, *Almanac of American Politics, 1984*, pp. 545–7.

52 The magazine was started in 1978.

53 See Sabato, 'Parties, PACs and Independent Groups'.

54 See *Congressional Quarterly, Weekly Report*, 23 October 1982.

55 See Barone and Ujifusa, *Almanac of American Politics, 1982*.

56 *Congressional Quarterly, Weekly Report*, 23 October 1982.

57 Ibid.

58 Ibid.

59 Ibid.

60 *Congressional Quarterly, Weekly Report*, 31 December 1983, p. 2789. In 1983 Democrats united on partisan votes more frequently, according to this analysis, than in any year since 1954, when *Congressional Quarterly* started making such calculations.

Chapter V

1 For a study of the Reagan Presidency which focuses on Reagan's personal attitudes as a source of his views on social and domestic policy, see L. Cannon, *Reagan* (New York, 1982). A more hostile account is to be found in R. Dugger, *On Reagan: The Man and His Presidency* (New York, 1983). Mr Dugger's study relies heavily on the transcripts of a number of broadcasts which Reagan made in the late 1970s. These broadcasts, in Dugger's view, indicate a much more extreme and ideological aspect of Reagan's personality than was allowed to appear after 1980.

2 There have been two major assessments of Reagan's policies so far — F. Greenstein (ed.), *The Reagan Presidency: An Early Assessment* (Baltimore, 1983), and J. L. Palmer and I. V. Sawhill (eds.), *The Reagan Experiment* (Washington, DC, 1982).

3 For an overall view of America's handling of the problem of poverty see J. T. Patterson, *America's Struggle Against Poverty* (Cambridge, Mass., 1981).

4 The cuts and their impact are extensively handled in J. W. Ellwood (ed.), *Reductions in U.S. Domestic Spending: How They Affect State and Local Governments* (London, 1982). Although I have

relied to a large extent on Ellwood for a discussion of the basis of Reagan's social policy, it should be noted that the budget figures produced there are not always the final ones.

5 Some of the points were made earlier in G. R. Peele, 'The Reagan Administration and Social Policy', in C. Jones and J. Stevenson (eds.), *The Yearbook of Social Policy in Britain, 1982* (London, 1983), 321–51.

6 The topic is covered in a number of works, including J. Sundquist, *The Decline and Resurgence of Congress* (Washington, DC, 1982).

7 This point is made in the introduction to S. E. Collender, *The Guide to the Federal Budget* (Washington, DC, 1982).

8 See W. Greider, *The Education of David Stockman and Other Americans* (New York, 1982), especially chapter 4.

9 On the unfairness issue see Dugger, *On Reagan*, pp. 285–312.

10 See Greider, *The Education of David Stockman and Other Americans*, chapter 4.

11 On this see *Congressional Quarterly, Weekly Report*, 14 August 1982 and 11 September 1982.

12 Quoted in *Congressional Quarterly, Weekly Report*, 11 September 1982, p. 2237. Silvio Conte was an extremely experienced member of the House Appropriations Committee.

13 On this general theme see S. Hess, *Organising the Presidency* (Washington, DC, 1976). For a reassessment of the Eisenhower Presidency see F. Greenstein, *The Hidden Hand Presidency: Eisenhower as Leader* (New York, 1982). A useful overview of domestic policy in the Eisenhower, Kennedy, and Johnson years is J. Sundquist, *Politics and Policy: the Eisenhower, Kennedy and Johnson Years* (Washington, DC, 1968).

14 On Kennedy see Hess, *Organising the Presidency*; also L. W. Koenig, *The Chief Executive* (New York, 1975), and C. M. Brauer, *John F. Kennedy and the Second Reconstruction* (New York, 1977).

15 J. E. Carter, *Keeping Faith: Memoirs of A President* (London, 1983). On the earlier years see also B. Adams and K. Kavanagh-Baran, *Promise and Performance: Carter Builds a New Administration* (Lexington, Mass., 1980). From the inside both Z. Brzezinski, *Power and Principle: Memoirs of The National Security Adviser 1977-81* (London, 1983), and W. (Hamilton) Jordan, *Crisis: The Last Year of the Carter Presidency* (London, 1982), are of interest.

16 See Cannon, *Reagan*, for a discussion of Reagan's work habits and intellectual interests, especially the early chapters and chapter 22.

17 This point is made very forcibly in Dugger, *On Reagan*, chapter 2, which he entitles 'The Board of Directors of the United States'.

18 See, for example, the arguments produced in the Heritage Foundation publications, including R. H. Holwill (ed.), *A Mandate for Leadership, Report: The First Year* (Washington, DC, 1981).

19 See Hess, *Organising the Presidency*. Other discussions are to be found in R. Pious, *The American Presidency* (New York, 1979),

and R. Rose, *Managing Presidential Objectives* (New York, 1976). See also M. Medved, *The Shadow Presidents: The Secret History of the Chief Executives and their Top Aides* (New York, 1979). Two of Carter's aides published their own thoughts on the need for priorities: see B. R. Heinemann and C. Hessler, *Memorandum for the President: A Strategic Approach to Domestic Affairs in the 1980s* (New York, 1980).

20 For a general discussion see Dugger, *On Reagan*.

21 See the overview of Reagan's first year put out by the White House Office of Public Affairs and the Republican National Committee, *The Reagan Presidency: A Review of the First Year* (Washington, DC, 1981); also the review by the Heritage Foundation in Holwill (ed.), *A Mandate for Leadership*.

22 David Stockman gave a number of off-the-record interviews to William Greider which were subsequently published in *Atlantic Monthly* magazine. They detail his thoughts about the budget and reveal the extent to which he had doubts about the logic of Reagan's economic strategy. They also provide insight into the politics of budget-making in contemporary America. Stockman offered his resignation when the revelations appeared, but it was not accepted. Two useful articles on Reagan's managerial style are to be found in *National Journal*, 19 July 1980 and 17 January 1981.

23 See Dugger, *On Reagan*, especially pp. 25-42, and Cannon, *Reagan*. Also of interest are the comments in the special issue of *National Journal*, 25 April 1981 (containing an analysis of the new decision-making structure), and ibid., 4 April 1981, pp. 564-8, 11 April 1981, pp. 605-10, 11 July 1981, pp. 1242-8, and 23 January 1982, p. 140.

24 The distinction is made by R. Nathan, 'The Reagan Presidency in Domestic Affairs', in Greenstein (ed.), *The Reagan Presidency*, pp. 48-81. See also Nathan's account of Nixon's use of executive orders and non-legislative method in *The Administrative Presidency: Richard Nixon and the Plot that Failed* (New York, 1976). Nathan Glazer makes the point that much of the apparatus of affirmative action has been introduced not by Congress but by executive order: see N. Glazer, *Ethnic Dilemmas* (London, 1983).

25 Greider, *The Education of David Stockman and Other Americans*, p. 19.

26 The 1981 budget attempted severe cuts in urban renewal programs.

27 See Nathan, 'The Reagan Presidency in Domestic Affairs'.

28 Presidential popularity may be charted from the surveys in the AEI journal *Public Opinion*. It declined steadily from a 60 per cent approval rating in July 1981 to 37 per cent in January 1983, but the decline was not as precipitous as Carter's: *Public Opinion*, February–March 1983, p. 38.

29 The Federal Reserve Board began tightening its control of the money supply in 1979 as a way of controlling interest rates. The independence of the Board means that neither the President nor

Congress normally tries to make policy for the Board. Basic facts about the workings of the Federal Reserve Board can be gained from its own publications: see Federal Reserve Board, *The ABCs of the Federal Reserve System* (Washington, DC).

30 On the Thatcher administration see P. Riddell, *The Thatcher Government* (London, 1983).

31 Greider, *The Education of David Stockman and Other Americans*, pp. 49–50.

32 These are American billions. In fact both British and US statistics employ this usage: $1 billion = $1,000 million. For a discussion of Reagan's first budget see A. Pechman, *Setting National Priorities: The 1982 Budget* (Washington, DC, 1982).

33 For an overview of the welfare policies of the United States see G. Y. Steiner, *The State of Welfare* (Washington, DC, 1971), and id., *The Futility of Family Policy* (Washington, DC, 1982).

34 Stockman apparently wanted to cut the Pentagon budget but was not allowed to do so: see Greider, *The Education of David Stockman and Other Americans*, especially pp. 23–5. The details of the budgetary process are discussed in A. Schick, *Congress and Money* (Washington, DC, 1980), and Collender, *The Guide to the Federal Budget*. Reagan's first budget, which contained a substantial package of cuts, was obtained by the use of the reconciliation procedure to prevent Congress taking it apart on an item-by-item basis. Congress and the administration develop their own versions of a budget, but then negotiate over the details. What was highly unusual about the 1982 budget was that it was passed on the basis of a bipartisan compromise (known as Gramm–Latta II) which gave the administration the majority of the budget proposals it required, while Congress abandoned its own budget proposals.

35 On this see R. M. Ball, *Social Security Today and Tomorrow* (New York, 1978), and, for a right-of-center view, P. J. Ferrara, *Social Security: The Inherent Contradictions* (San Francisco, 1980). An overview of the policy-making process in this field is to be found in M. Derthick, *Policy-Making for Social Security* (Washington, DC, 1979).

36 This is certainly Dugger's view: see Dugger, *On Reagan*, especially pp. 43–69 and 285–312.

37 The term 'specific grants' is used in Britain for these kinds of grants, but the American phrase is 'categorical grant', a term used in Britain for those grants where central government imposes an obligation on the Local Authority to provide a service (as, for example, in the case of the police force). On block grants generally see Palmer and Sawhill (eds.), *The Reagan Experiment*.

38 On the new federalism from Nixon onwards see M. Reagan and J. G. Sanzone, *The New Federalism* (Oxford, 1981).

39 Address to Congress on the State of the Union, 26 January 1982.

40 Ibid.

41 Ibid.

42 Steiner, *The State of Welfare*, p. 20.

43 J. T. Patterson, *America's Struggle Against Poverty* (Cambridge, Mass., 1981), 163.

44 See the *International Herald Tribune*, 28 January 1982, which reprinted the leader of the *Washington Post*.

45 See, for example, the comments by Pearl Robinson in the Urban League publication *The State of Black America* (New York, 1982).

46 See *Congressional Quarterly*, *Weekly Report*, 11 September 1982, p. 2237.

47 A full discussion is to be found in Palmer and Sawhill (eds.), *The Reagan Experiment*. See also E. Bardach and R. A. Kagan, *Going by the Book: The Problem of Regulatory Unreasonableness* (Philadelphia, 1982), for a discussion of the arguments about deregulation. The AEI journal *Regulation* is a useful source of information on the regulatory process.

48 On the role of James Watt see Dugger, *On Reagan*, pp. 70–99. Watt was forced to resign in 1983 and was replaced by William Clark.

49 For a critical review of affirmative action see J. C. Livingston, *Fair Game? Inequality and Affirmative Action* (San Francisco, 1979). On attitudes towards civil liberties in America see H. McClosky and A. Brill, *Dimensions of Tolerance: What Americans Believe About Civil Liberties* (New York, 1983). See also, for example, the comments of C. E. Finn, 'Affirmative Action Under Reagan', *Commentary*, 73. 4 (April 1982).

50 For a discussion of affirmative action in relation to ethnicity see N. Glazer, *Ethnic Dilemmas* (London, 1983); also Finn, 'Affirmative Action Under Reagan'.

51 See P. Robinson in *The State of Black America*.

52 See also the useful discussion in Dugger, *On Reagan*, pp. 237–58.

53 The original IRS ruling was backed in a Supreme Court case in 1970 — *Coit* v. *Green* — and had led to the removal of the charters of a small number of schools. The IRS policy became more aggressive in 1975-7 as the IRS observed the increase in the number of schools designed, in its opinion, to avoid integration yet so organized as not to formally bar racial minorities (interview with Jerome Kurtz, Washington, 31 March 1982). See also *Bob Jones University* v. *US*, No. 81-1, 644 F 2d 870 SC (24 May 1983), and *Goldsboro Christian Schools Inc.* v. *US*, No. 81-3, 639 F 2d 147 SC (24 May 1983).

54 Tightening AFDC regulations of course went against the trend of reducing government regulations and red tape. AFDC was, however, an unpopular program considered open to abuse and fraud.

Chapter VI

1 For an overview of American foreign policy under Reagan see, for example, K. A. Oye, 'International Systems Structure and American

Foreign Policy', in K. A. Oye, R. J. Lieber, and D. Rothchild (eds.), *Eagle Defiant: United States Foreign Policy in the 1980s* (Boston, Mass., 1983), 3-32. Another overview is provided in F. Greenstein (ed.), *The Reagan Presidency: An Early Assessment* (Baltimore, 1983): see the chapters by S. Huntington ('The Defense Policy 1981-2', pp. 82-116) and I. M. Destler ('The Evolution of Reagan's Foreign Policy', pp. 117-58).

2 N. Podhoretz, 'The Neo-Conservative Anguish over Reagan's Foreign Policy', *New York Times Magazine*, 2 May 1982.

3 This aspect of the Reagan administration is commented on in R. Dugger, *On Reagan: The Man and His Presidency* (New York, 1983), 268-84.

4 See the comments in Oye, Lieber, and Rothchild (eds.), *Eagle Defiant*.

5 See Dugger, *On Reagan*, p. 350.

6 The 'evil empires' speech was delivered to an audience of evangelical Christians in Orlando, Florida, on 8 March 1983; see *New York Times*, 9 March 1983.

7 See Kenneth Oye's essay (above, n. 1).

8 On this see M. Gordon, 'Right of Center Defense Groups — The Pendulum has swung their Way', *National Journal*, 24 January 1981, pp. 128-32.

9 Z. Brzezinski, *Power and Principle: Memoirs of the National Security Adviser 1977-81* (London, 1983), especially pp. 17-78 and 513-47.

10 Quoted in R. J. Hrebenar and R. K. Scott, *Interest Groups in American Politics* (Englewood Cliffs, NJ, 1982), 228, quoting *Congressional Quarterly, Weekly Report*, 12 May 1979.

11 On the significance of public opinion in foreign policy see W. Schneider, 'Conservatism, Not Interventionism: Trends in Foreign Policy Opinion, 1974-82', in Oye, Lieber, and Rothchild (eds.), *Eagle Defiant*, pp. 33-64.

12 On this aspect of Reagan see the biographical studies by L. Cannon, *Reagan* (Washington, DC, 1982), and Dugger, *On Reagan*. It is an important part of Dugger's argument that Reagan's anti-communism is both extreme and deep-rooted.

13 See *National Journal*, 24 January 1981.

14 On this see R. Brownstein and N. Easton, *Reagan's Ruling Class: Portraits of the President's Top One Hundred Officials* (Washington, DC, 1982), 3; also *National Journal*, 24 January 1981, pp. 128-32.

15 W. Scott Thompson *et al.*, *Defending America: Toward a New Role in the Post-Détente World* (New York, 1977). The later collection is W. Scott Thompson (ed.), *National Security in the 1980s: From Weakness to Strength* (San Francisco, 1980).

16 See Christian Voice, *Report Card on Congress*, *1980*.

17 See Dugger, *On Reagan*, pp. 370-2, on this point; also A. Doak Barnett, *U.S. Arms Sales: The China-Taiwan Tangle* (Washington, DC, 1982), and G. Hsiao and M. Witunski, *Sino-American*

Normalization and its Policy Implications (New York, 1983).

[18] On the role of foreign policy in the 1980 elections see A. Ranney (ed.), *The American Elections of 1980* (Washington, DC, 1981).

[19] Schneider, 'Conservatism, Not Interventionism: Trends in Foreign Policy Opinions, 1974–82'.

[20] Ibid.

[21] On the background to foreign-policy divisions in the United States, especially on the right, see M. Miles, *The Odyssey of the American Right* (New York, 1980).

[22] Brzezinski makes the point that the 'chemistry' between Baker and Carter was so incompatible that even in discussion of subjects where they were of like mind the result was unproductive (*Power and Principle*, p. 545).

[23] See Cannon, *Reagan*, p. 317.

[24] On the background to the Adelman affair see J. Fallows, 'The Agony of Kenneth Adelman', *Atlantic Monthly*, July 1983.

[25] For a hostile critique of this aspect of United States foreign policy see Dugger, *On Reagan*, pp. 350–92. Between 1981 and 1984 there were major struggles between President and Congress over aid to Nicaragua, El Salvador, and Guatemala in particular. In 1983 there was also internal Congressional wrangling as the Congressional Committees with foreign-policy jurisdiction failed to pass authorizing legislation for aid programs, which were then dealt with *de facto* by the Appropriations Committees. See *Congressional Quarterly, Weekly Report*, 26 November 1983, pp. 2485 ff.

[26] For a background to the events in Latin America see A. Lowenthal in Oye, Lieber, and Rothchild (eds.), *Eagle Defiant*.

[27] S. Hersh, *Kissinger: The Price of Power* (New York, 1983). The Kissinger Commission reported in January 1984, and the report has been published as *The Report of the President's National Bipartisan Commission on Central America* (New York, 1984).

[28] The legislative veto was declared unconstitutional in *Immigration and Naturalization Service* v. *Chadha* (1983) SC. A discussion of the role of the legislative veto in the increasing control of American foreign policy by Congress is to be found in T. Frank and E. Weisband, *Foreign Policy by Congress* (New York, 1979).

[29] The point is made by R. Dugger in *On Reagan*. See also *Congressional Quarterly, Weekly Report*, 2 October 1982, p. 2469. Senator Percy and Senator Pell apparently both wrote to Reagan on 22 September urging him to use the War Powers Act in relation to Lebanon and trigger Congressional participation in the maintenance of troops there.

[30] On the peculiar character of the American foreign-policy process see M. Beloff, *Foreign Policy and the Democratic Process* (Baltimore, 1954).

[31] For a discussion of NCPAC see Chapter III; also T. Mann and N. Ornstein, 'The Republican Surge in Congress', in Ranney (ed.), *The American Elections of 1980*, pp. 263–302.

[32] On the Congressional races generally in 1980 see B. Hinckley, *Congressional Elections* (Washington, DC, 1981).

[33] See Cannon, *Reagan*; also H. Kissinger, *The White House Years* (Boston, Mass., 1979).

[34] See Brzezinski, *Power and Principle*.

[35] S. Nunn in Scott Thompson (ed.), *National Security in the 1980s*, pp. 375-95, at p. 375.

[36] W. W. Kaufmann, 'The Defense Budget', in J. A. Pechman (ed.), *Setting National Priorities: The 1982 Budget* (Washington, DC, 1981), 135. For a general discussion see Nunn, 'Defense Budget and Defense Capabilities'.

[37] Kaufmann, 'The Defense Budget', p. 137.

[38] For a discussion of defense estimates see Kaufmann, 'The Defense Budget'.

[39] For another estimate of defense spending see Huntington, 'The Defense Policy 1981-2'; also Kaufmann in Pechman (ed.), *Setting National Priorities*.

[40] See, for example, *Congressional Quarterly, Weekly Report*, 11 September 1982, pp. 2047-8, where the doubts of many GOP members on the President's priorities are described.

[41] See Committee on the Present Danger, *Is the Reagan Defense Program Adequate?* (Washington, DC, 1982).

[42] On this see the discussion in Dugger, *On Reagan*.

[43] For Mrs Kirkpatrick's views on Central America see especially the two essays 'Human Rights in El Salvador' and 'Human Rights in Nicaragua', as well as the 1982 statements in the United Nations Security Council. All are reprinted in J. J. Kirkpatrick, *The Reagan Phenomenon — and Other Speeches on Foreign Policy* (Washington, DC, 1983). On human rights in Latin America see L. Schultz, *Human Rights and United States Policy Towards Latin America* (Princeton, 1981).

[44] On this aspect of American policy see A. Lowenthal in Oye, Lieber, and Rothchild (eds.), *Eagle Defiant*.

[45] Though for an interesting discussion of the relative strength of the Jewish and Arab lobbies see M. Friedman, 'Awacs and the Jewish Community', *Commentary*, 73. 4 (April 1982), 29-33. The article is of particular interest because it underlines the attitudes of the new Christian right to the sale; according to the author, '26 out of 28 Senators associated with the Christian right' voted for it. They included Roger Jepson of Iowa, who had hitherto voted to stop the sale.

[46] See Destler, 'The Evolution of Reagan's Foreign Policy'.

[47] For a sensitive overview of the differences between Europe and the United States see M. Kahler, 'The Diplomatic Consequences of Mr Reagan', in Oye, Lieber, and Rothchild (eds.), *Eagle Defiant*, pp. 273-309.

Conclusion

[1] Oliver Wendell Holmes, letter to the Harvard Liberal Club, 1920.
[2] The point is forcibly made in K. Phillips, *Post-Conservative America: People, Politics and Ideology in a Time of Crisis* (New York, 1982).

BIBLIOGRAPHICAL ESSAY

It would be impossible to give a complete bibliography for all the topics touched upon in the book. However, some suggestions for further reading are given here in the hope that they may aid those readers who would like to follow some of the themes in greater depth. A useful reference work for anyone concerned with American studies is F. Freidel (with R. K. Showman), *The Harvard Guide to American History* (rev. edn., Cambridge, Mass.: Belknap Press of Harvard University Press, 1974). Also helpful is T. J. Johnson, *Oxford Companion to American History* (New York: Oxford University Press, 1966).

On electoral politics an invaluable source is the *National Journal* publication, *The Almanac of American Politics*, which is published every two years. The *National Journal* itself is an excellent fount of information about the details of party politics and policy. The *Congressional Quarterly, Weekly Report* is also a very useful source of information on political issues.

Many of the books referred to in the notes have been included here (but not the articles and occasional pieces mentioned). Some additional works have also been included where this has seemed appropriate. Rather than follow the sequence of the chapters, it has seemed more useful to group the books under four headings: (i) General and Intellectual History (including the role of the neo-conservatives); (ii) Party Politics and the New Right; (iii) Religion and the Religious Right; (iv) Policy Issues, Domestic and Foreign.

(i) General and Intellectual History

A general history of the intellectual development of the American right is to be found in G. Nash, *The Conservative Intellectual Movement in America since 1945* (New York: Basic Books, 1979). This book should be supplemented with the study by P. Steinfels, *The Neo-Conservatives: The Men Who Are Changing America's Politics* (New York: Simon and Schuster, 1979); an earlier work from a critical standpoint is A. Coser and I. Howe (eds.), *The New Conservatives* (New York: Quadrangle, 1974).

L. Hartz, *The Liberal Tradition in America: An Interpretation of American Political Thought since the Revolution* (New York: Harcourt Brace, 1962), is a useful study, explaining the dominance of liberal ideas in the political culture of the United States. Also of interest from the point of view of general background are the writings of Richard Hofstadter, including *The Paranoid Style in American Politics and Other Essays* (Chicago: University of Chicago Press, 1979).

The works of individual neo-conservatives are important sources for tracing the development of their ideas, although the British reader may find some difficulty in obtaining the articles and essays contributed to various American magazines and newspapers. Irving Kristol's collection, *Reflections of a Neoconservative: Looking Backwards, Looking Ahead* (New York: Simon and Schuster, 1983), gives a useful indication of the topics which Kristol has taken up in the past thirty years. His *Two Cheers for Capitalism* (New York: Basic Books, 1978) is an important statement. His earlier work, *On the Democratic Idea in America* (New York: Harper and Row, 1972), brings together Kristol's essays between 1967 and 1971. The special bicentennial issue of *The Public Interest*, which was edited with Nathan Glazer and published as *The American Commonwealth 1976* (New York: Basic Books, 1976), contains a collection of essays from various writers close to the neo-conservative movement.

Many of Nathan Glazer's essays on the theme of ethnicity have been drawn together in *Ethnic Dilemmas* (New York: Simon and Schuster, 1983). A work of immediate interest to readers on both sides of the Atlantic is Glazer's collection (edited with Ken Young) *Ethnic Pluralism and Public Policy* (London: Heinemann Educational Books/Policy Studies Institute, 1983). Earlier works include *Remembering the Answers: Essays on the American Student Revolt* (New York: Basic Books, 1970), which makes explicit the role of the student riots in transforming Glazer from a 'mild radical' to a 'mild conservative', and *Affirmative Discrimination: Ethnic Inequality and Public Policy* (New York: Basic Books, 1975), which details Glazer's arguments against affirmative action.

Earlier works of Glazer which retain their interest for the scholar of American intellectual history include his contribution to Clinton Rossiter's series on the role of communism in American life, *The Social Basis of American Communism* (New York: Harcourt Brace, 1961). In the same series Theodore Draper's *The Roots of American Communism* (New York: The Viking Press, 1957) illuminates the role of the American Communist Party between the wars. The editor of the series is Clinton Rossiter, whose own *Conservatism in America: The Thankless Persuasion* (2nd edn., Westport, Conn.: Greenwood, 1981) is an elegant and lucid study of the subject. Also of interest is Glazer's early study of the character of American Jewry, *American Judaism* (Chicago: University of Chicago Press, 1957).

Much of Daniel Patrick Moynihan's work has been concerned with ethnicity, and some of it has been conducted in conjunction with Nathan Glazer. Their *Beyond the Melting Pot* (Cambridge, Mass.: MIT Press, 1965) and the collection done a decade later, *Ethnicity: Theory and Environment* (Cambridge, Mass.: Harvard University Press, 1975), are useful sources. Moynihan's own books detail different episodes of his political career. *Maximum Feasible Misunderstanding: Community Action in the War on Poverty* (New York: The Free Press, 1970) details his experience with the Great Society poverty programs, while *The Politics of a Guaranteed Income: The Nixon Administration and the Family Assistance Plan* (New York: Random

House, 1973) describes the political controversy surrounding his period as a domestic-policy adviser to Richard Nixon. *A Dangerous Place* (Boston, Mass.: Atlantic Little Brown, 1978), written with Suzanne Weaver, documents his period at the United Nations.

Moynihan has also brought together several of his articles in two collections — *Coping: Essays on the Practice of Government* (New York: Random House, 1973) and *Counting Our Blessings: Reflections on the Future of America* (London: Secker and Warburg, 1980), which draws together pieces published over the 1970s.

Moynihan's career is covered in a personal biography by D. Schoen, *Pat: A Biography of Daniel Patrick Moynihan* (New York: Harper and Row, 1979). The controversy over the report on the Negro family is the subject of L. R. W. Yancey, *The Moynihan Report and the Politics of Controversy* (Cambridge, Mass.: MIT Press, 1967).

The flavor of Daniel Bell's work can be gleaned from his collected essays of 1980, which are published under slightly different titles in the United Kingdom and in the United States. See D. Bell, *Sociological Journeys: Essays 1960–1980* (London: Heinemann, 1980), published in the United States as *The Winding Passage: Essays and Sociological Journeys* (Cambridge, Mass.: Harvard University Press, 1980). Among his other works which are of interest are *The Cultural Contradictions of Capitalism* (New York: Basic Books, 1976).

Norman Podhoretz's autobiographical works, *Making It* (1st edn., 1967; 2nd edn., New York: Harper and Row, 1980) and *Breaking Ranks: A Political Memoir* (New York: Harper and Row, 1980), are important documents in any attempt to appreciate the style of neo-conservatism in America. Podhoretz's later book, *Why We Were in Vietnam* (New York: Simon and Schuster, 1983), is useful for understanding the tone of his criticism of American foreign policy.

Jeane Kirkpatrick's articles and speeches have been usefully brought together in two collections, *Dictatorships and Double Standards: Rationalism and Reason in Politics* (New York: Simon and Schuster, 1982) and *The Reagan Phenomenon and Other Speeches on Foreign Policy* (Washington, DC: AEI, 1983). Her earlier writings are more specialized pieces of political science, but a useful insight into her views on party reform can be found in *The New Presidential Élite: Men and Women in National Politics* (New York: Russell Sage, 1976).

Michael Novak's writings are voluminous, but the fullest statement is his *The Spirit of Democratic Capitalism* (New York: Simon and Schuster, 1982). A more personal apologia is to be found in *Confessions of a Catholic* (New York: Harper and Row, 1983).

The background to the arguments which have engaged the neo-conservatives is to be found in a number of detailed policy studies and histories. The literary and political world of the inter-war and war period is captured in the diaries of Edmund Wilson, edited by L. Edel (published in New York by Farrar, Straus, and Giroux, and in London by Macmillan): *The Twenties: From Notebooks of the Period* (1975); *The Thirties: From Notebooks of the Period* (1980); *The Forties*

(1983). Lionel Trilling's *The Liberal Imagination: Essays on Literature and Society* (Harmondsworth: Peregrine, 1970) documents cultural concerns of the time. W. Barrett, *The Truants: Adventures Among the Intellectuals* (New York: Doubleday, 1982), captures nicely the leading personalities of the New York literary and political milieu.

Readers who wish to acquire the flavor of *Partisan Review*, the magazine which was so central to the literary and political world from which many neo-conservatives emerged, could start with E. Kurzweil and W. Phillips, *Writers and Politics: A* Partisan Review *Reader* (London: RKP, 1983). Mary McCarthy's works, especially *The Oasis*, also capture something of the New York environment at that time. The specific Jewish quality of the New York intelligentsia is reflected in A. Kazin, *New York Jew* (New York: Knopf, 1978).

The debate about communism in the immediate post-war period can be followed in two books by David Caute, *The Fellow-Travellers* (London: Weidenfeld, 1973) and *The Great Fear* (New York: Simon and Schuster, 1978). Other studies relevant to McCarthyism include T. Reeves, *The Life and Times of Joe McCarthy: A Biography* (London: Blond and Briggs, 1983), and D. F. Crosby, *God, Church and Flag: Senator Joseph R. McCarthy and the Catholic Church 1950–1957* (Chapel Hill: University of North Carolina Press, 1978).

An account of one who was a partisan of the left in the McCarthy period can be found in L. Hellman, *Scoundrel Time* (Boston, Mass.: Little Brown, 1976).

The debates about the Great Society programs can be augmented by reading D. A. Levitan, *The Great Society's Poor Law* (Baltimore: Johns Hopkins Press, 1969), and E. Ginzberg and R. Solow (eds.), *The Great Society* (New York: Basic Books, 1974). A useful policy study is also to be found in J. Sundquist, *Politics and Policy: The Eisenhower, Kennedy and Johnson Years* (Washington, DC: The Brookings Institution, 1968).

The impact of free-market and supply-side economics on political thought can be traced in M. Friedman, *Capitalism and Socialism* (Chicago: University of Chicago Press, 1962), and the same author's book (written with Rose Friedman), *Free to Choose: A Personal Statement* (New York: Harcourt Brace, 1980).

Supply-side theories can be traced in J. Wanniski, *The Way the World Works: How Economics Fail and Succeed* (rev. edn., New York: Simon and Schuster, 1983), and G. Gilder, *Wealth and Poverty* (New York: Basic Books, 1981).

(ii) Party Politics and the New Right

There are obviously an enormous number of general works on American parties and the party system. In seeking to understand the current state of the American parties readers may wish to refer to R. Scott and R. Hrebenar, *American Parties in Crisis* (2nd edn., New York: John Wiley, 1984), and F. Sorauf, *Party Politics in America* (4th edn.,

Boston, Mass.: Little Brown, 1980). David Broder provides an informed and lively account of developments with a trained journalist's eye in *The Party's Over* (New York: Harper and Row, 1972) and *The Changing of the Guard: Power and Leadership in America* (New York: Simon and Schuster, 1980). Kevin Phillips's works are of interest since he is a long-time observer of the potential for partisan realignment. Especially important are *The Emerging Conservative Majority* (New Rochelle: Arlington House, 1969) and *Post-Conservative America: People, Politics and Ideology in a Time of Crisis* (New York: Random House, 1982).

More specialized works on American party politics include Nelson Polsby, *The Consequences of Party Reform* (New York: Oxford University Press, 1983). Also of major interest is W. Crotty and G. Jacobson (eds.), *American Parties in Decline* (Boston, Mass.: Little Brown, 1980).

Finance is covered in the various works of Herbert Alexander; of especial interest from the point of view of this book is *Financing the 1980 Election* (Lexington, Mass.: Lexington Books, 1983). On the role of political consultants see L. Sabato, *The Rise of Political Consultants: New Ways of Winning Elections* (New York: Basic Books, 1981).

Studies of election trends are numerous, but especially helpful are A. Ranney (ed.), *The American Elections of 1980* (Washington, DC: AEI, 1981), and P. Abramson, J. Aldrich, and D. Rohde, *Change and Continuity in the 1980 Elections* (rev. edn., Washington, DC: Congressional Quarterly Press, 1983). See also T. E. Mann and N. Ornstein, *The American Elections of 1982* (Washington, DC: AEI, 1983).

Morris Fiorina's study, *Retrospective Voting in American National Elections* (London: Yale University Press, 1981), offers a revision of the theory of voting behavior.

The Republican Party is well covered in J. A. Reichley, *Conservatives in an Age of Change: The Nixon and Ford Administrations* (Washington, DC: The Brookings Institution, 1981). Reference should also be made to two studies of Ronald Reagan — L. Cannon, *Reagan* (Washington, DC: Putnam Publishing Group, 1982), and R. Dugger, *On Reagan: The Man and His Presidency* (New York: McGraw-Hill, 1983).

Specifically on the American right see M. Miles, *The Odyssey of the American Right* (New York: Oxford University Press, 1980), and D. Reinhard, *The Republican Right since 1945* (Kentucky: University of Kentucky Press, 1983).

On the new right R. Viguerie, *The New Right: We're Ready to Lead* (Ottawa, Ill.: Caroline House, 1981), and R. W. Whittaker, *The New Right Papers* (New York: St Martin's Press, 1982), are useful sources, as is E. J. Feulner, *Conservatives Stalk the House* (Ottawa, Ill.: Green Hill, 1983).

A. Crawford, *Thunder on the Right: The New Right and the Politics of Resentment* (New York: Pantheon, 1981), is a stimulating overview of the new right and can be supplemented by J. Roberts, *The Conservative Decade: Emerging Leaders of the 1980s* (Westport, Conn.: Arlington House, 1980).

From a hostile perspective T. J. McIntyre and J. C. Obert, *The Fear Brokers: Peddling the Hate Politics of the New Right* (New York: The Pilgrim Press, 1979), is of especial interest because McIntyre as a Senator was subjected to the new right's tactics.

(iii) Religion and the Religious Right

Readers who want a comprehensive history of the role of religion in American life could hardly do better than to use S. E. Ahlstrom's authoritative two-volume study, *A Religious History of the American People* (New York: Image Books, 1975), which also contains an excellent bibliography. Also useful is the annual *Yearbook of the American and Canadian Churches*, edited by C. H. Jacquet (Nashville: The Abingdon Press).

Constitutional questions relating to Church and State in the United States are well covered in A. P. Stokes and L. Pfeffer, *Church and State in the United States* (3 vols., New York: Harper and Row, 1950), and F. Sorauf, *The Wall of Separation: The Constitutional Politics of Church and State* (Princeton: Princeton University Press, 1976). See also H. J. Abraham, *Freedom and the Court: Civil Rights and Liberties in the United States* (4th edn., New York: Oxford University Press, 1982). An excellent case-book with an introduction is R. T. Miller and R. B. Flowers, *Toward Benevolent Neutrality: Church, State and Supreme Court* (Waco, Texas: Markham Press Fund, 1982). A survey of popular attitudes on civil liberties is contained in H. Mc-Closkey and A. Brill, *Dimensions of Tolerance: What Americans Believe about Civil Liberties* (New York: Russell Sage Foundation, 1983).

The issues raised by the separation of Church and State are covered from a revisionist perspective in R. Cord, *Separation of Church and State: Historical Fact and Current Fiction* (New York: Lambeth Press, 1982), and J. W. Whitehead, *The Separation Illusion* (Milford, Mich.: Mott Media, 1982). The same author's *The Second American Revolution* (Elgin, Ill.: David C. Cook, 1982) gives a further indication of the revisionists' attitudes towards the American constitution.

The various influences in American life are covered by S. E. Ahlstrom's *A Religious History of the American People* (above). The influence of puritanism is covered in P. Miller, *Errand into the Wilderness* (Cambridge, Mass.: Harvard University Press, 1956). Also of interest are L. Ziff, *Puritanism in America: New Culture in a New World* (New York: Viking Press, 1973), and M. Walzer, *The Revolution of the Saints* (Cambridge, Mass.: Harvard University Press, 1965).

Evangelicalism is covered in J. D. Hunter, *American Evangelicalism: Conservative Religion and the Quandary of Modernity* (New Brunswick: Rutgers University Press, 1983). Fundamentalism is covered in G. Marsden, *Fundamentalism and American Culture: The Shaping of American Evangelicalism 1870–1925* (New York: Oxford University Press, 1982). A useful study of the phenomenon of fundamentalism is J. Barr, *Fundamentalism* (Philadelphia: The Westminster Press, 1978).

The biblical inheritance of American democracy is covered in A. Katsh, *The Biblical Heritage of American Democracy* (New York: Ktav, 1977), and C. Cherry, *God's New Israel: Religious Interpretations of American Destiny* (Englewood Cliffs, NJ: Prentice Hall, 1971).

The Roman Catholic Church is treated in a number of studies, but especially useful are J. Ellis, *American Catholicism* (2nd edn., Chicago: University of Chicago Press, 1969), and J. Hennessy, *American Catholics: A History of the Roman Catholic Community in the United States* (New York: Oxford University Press, 1981). A nineteenth-century study is T. O'Gorman, *A History of the Roman Catholic Church in America* (9 vols., New York: ACHS, 1895).

The Jewish experience is covered in A. J. Karp, *The Jewish Experience in America: Selected Studies from the American Jewish Historical Society* (5 vols., New York: Katz Publishing House, 1969), and the same author's *Golden Door to America* (New York: Viking Press, 1976) (which deals with the experience of America's Jewish immigrants).

Overviews of American religious history can be found in F. H. Littel, *From State Church to Pluralism: A Protestant Interpretation of Religion in American History* (New York: Macmillan, 1971).

The theme of civil religion is tackled in R. N. Bellah and P. E. Hammond, *Varieties of Civil Religion* (San Francisco: Harper and Row, 1980).

The new religious right is covered in a variety of monographs and studies. Of particular interest are E. Jorstad, *The Politics of Moralism* (Minneapolis: Augsburg Publishing House, 1981), and J. Hadden and C. E. Swann, *Prime Time Preachers: The Rising Power of Televangelism* (Reading, Mass.: Addison Wesley, 1981), which both have a substantial amount of material on the electronic Church. J. Kater, *Christians on the Right: The Moral Majority in Perspective* (New York: Seabury, 1982), looks at the role of the new right and religious right.

J. Falwell's *Listen America* (New York: Bantam, 1981) conveys the flavor of his thought.

On policy-related issues W. V. Antonio and J. Aldous (eds.), *Families and Religions: Conflict and Change in Modern Society* (Beverly Hills, Calif.: Sage, 1983), provides some insights into the different approaches of the various religions to family issues. Father Robert Drinan's *Religion, The Courts and Public Policy* (New York: McGraw-Hill, 1963) is important as a reflection of the thought of someone who has been at the center of religious and political controversy in the United States. D. Nevin and R. E. Bills, *The Schools That Fear Built: Segregation Academies in the South* (Washington, DC: Acropolis, 1977), is a stimulating examination of the role of private Christian schools. It may be complemented by A. Greeley *et al.*, *Catholic Schools in a Declining Church* (Kansas City: Sheed and Ward, 1976).

School prayer is the subject of much polemical literature, including R. Warren and D. Schneider, *Mom, They Won't Let Us Pray* (Chappaqua, NY: Chosen Books, 1975).

The impact of religion on politics is covered in P. Shriver, *The Bible Vote: Religion and the New Right* (New York: The Pilgrim Press, 1981).

(iv) Policy Issues, Domestic and Foreign

Domestic policy under the Reagan administration is discussed in F. Greenstein (ed.), *The Reagan Presidency: An Early Assessment* (Baltimore: Johns Hopkins Press, 1983). See also J. L. Palmer and I. V. Sawhill (eds.), *The Reagan Experiment: An Examination of the Economic and Social Policies of the Reagan Administration* (Washington, DC: The Urban Institute, 1982). The impact of Reagan's policies is discussed in J. W. Ellwood (ed.), *Reductions in U.S. Domestic Spending: How They Affect State and Local Governments* (New Brunswick: Transaction Books, 1982). The personnel of the Reagan administration are discussed in R. Brownstein and N. Easton, *Reagan's Ruling Class: Portraits of the President's Top One Hundred Officials* (New York: Pantheon Books, 1982).

The construction of the budget and the economic arguments surrounding Reagan's policies can be gleaned from W. Greider, *The Education of David Stockman and Other Americans* (New York: E. P. Dutton, 1981). An assessment of the difficulties in controlling Congressional expenditure is to be found in D. S. Ippolito, *Congressional Spending* (Ithaca, NY: Cornell University Press, 1981). An explanation of the way the budget process operates is contained in S. E. Collender, *The Guide to the Federal Budget* (Washington, DC: North-East–Midwest Institute, 1982); see also A. Schick, *Congress and Money: Budgeting, Spending and Taxing* (Washington, DC: The Urban Institute, 1980).

J. Pechman's series *Setting National Priorities* (Washington, DC: 1981) contains useful material on elements of each budget. L. Berman, *The Office of Management and Budget and the Presidency 1921–1979* (Princeton: Princeton University Press, 1979), contains a useful overview of the OMB prior to Reagan. P. Light, *The President's Agenda: Domestic Policy Choice from Kennedy to Carter with Notes on Ronald Reagan* (Baltimore: Johns Hopkins Press, 1982), makes a contribution to the understanding of how American policy is formed.

Questions about the general role of government are raised in R. J. Zeckhauser and D. Leebaert (eds.), *What Role for Government? Lessons for Public Policy Research* (Durham, NC: Duke University Press, 1983).

Deregulation is covered in M. Weidenbaum, *The Future of Business Regulation* (New York: AMACOM, 1979), and E. Bardach and R. A. Kagan, *Going by the Book: The Problem of Regulatory Unreasonableness* (Philadelphia: Temple University Press, 1982). An earlier study still of interest is J. Q. Wilson, *The Politics of Regulation* (New York: Basic Books, 1980). C. De Muth, 'Constraining Regulatory Costs: The White House Review Programs', *Regulation*, 4 (Jan.–Feb. 1980), is of interest for the perspective of an insider who master-minded part of the Republican strategy.

Aspects of social policy are covered in J. T. Patterson, *America's Struggle Against Poverty* (Cambridge, Mass.: Harvard University Press, 1980), and various works by G. Y. Steiner. Of especial interest from the point of view of this book are G. Y. Steiner, *The State of Welfare* (Washington, DC: The Brookings Institution, 1971), and id., *The Futility of Family Policy* (Washington, DC: The Brookings Institution, 1981). Also relevant is the symposium edited by Steiner, *The Abortion Dispute and the American System* (Washington, DC: The Brookings Institution, 1982). Abortion itself is covered in a number of works, including J. T. Burchaell (ed.), *Abortion Parley* (New York: Andrews and McMeel, 1980), and A. Merton, *Enemies of Choice: The Right to Life Movement and Its Threat to Abortion* (Boston, Mass.: The Beacon Press, 1981).

Social security issues are covered in R. M. Ball, *Social Security Today and Tomorrow* (New York: Columbia University Press, 1978), and P. Ferrara, *Social Security: The Inherent Contradiction* (San Francisco: Cato Institute, 1978).

Environmentalism is covered in R. Arnold, *At the Eye of the Storm: James Watt and the Environmentalists* (Chicago: Regnery Gateway, 1982).

A comparative dimension is provided in C. Jones and J. Stevenson (eds.), *The Yearbook of Social Policy in Britain, 1982* (London, Routledge and Kegan Paul, 1983).

Foreign-policy issues are covered succinctly in K. A. Oye, R. J. Lieber, and D. Rothchild (eds.), *Eagle Defiant: United States Foreign Policy in the 1980s* (Boston, Mass.: Little Brown, 1983). Background can be found in the memoirs of various key politicians significant in foreign and national security policy during the 1970s. Especially useful is Henry Kissinger's *The White House Years* (Boston, Mass.: Nelson, Brown, & Co., 1979). This could be supplemented by S. Hersh, *Kissinger: The Price of Power. Henry Kissinger in the Nixon White House* (London: Faber and Faber, 1983). Zbigniew Brzezinski's *Power and Principle: Memoirs of the National Security Adviser 1977–81* (London: Weidenfeld and Nicholson, 1983) covers the foreign-policy issues of the Carter period.

The debate about America's national security can be followed in the journal *International Security*; W. Scott Thompson, *National Security in the 1980s: From Weakness to Strength* (San Francisco: Institute for Contemporary Studies, 1980), gives the flavor of the controversies at the end of the 1970s.

On human rights in Latin America L. Schultz, *Human Rights and United States Policy Towards Latin America* (Princeton: Princeton University Press, 1981), is a useful study.

The process of constructing foreign policy in the United States is covered in a number of works, but especially helpful are T. Franck and E. Weisband, *Foreign Policy by Congress* (New York: Oxford University Press, 1979), and the earlier study by Max Beloff, *Foreign Policy and the Democratic Process* (Baltimore: Johns Hopkins Press, 1954).

INDEX

Abdnor, James:
    repudiation of NCPAC tactics 64
abortion 8, 10, 11, 44, 72, 75, 91, 95,
        96, 98, 99, 132, 142, 145, 165, 192
    anti-abortion 58, 76, 95, 143
    'Hyde Amendment' 145
    legislation 94, 136
    liberal bill 119
    Medicaid 145
    national campaign 73
    opposition to 142
    pastoral letter 95
    public funding 119
    Religious Coalition for Abortion
        Rights 101
    religious opinion 100
    Supreme Court: *Doe* v. *Bolton*
        93; *Roe* v. *Wade* 93
Abscam scandal 95, 112
absolutism, resistance to 83
academic autonomy 39
academic freedom 32
Accuracy in Media 54
Adelman, Kenneth:
    Director of Arms Control 176
Advanced International Studies In-
        stitute:
    foreign policy 171
affirmative action 33, 37, 40, 163
    demand for 39
    regulations affecting 164
Afghanistan, Soviet invasion of 170,
        180
Aid to Families with Dependent
        Children:
    eligibility requirements 155
    regulations 166
    responsibility for 158
    state aid 159
Airborne Warning and Control System
        (AWACS) 69
Algren, Nelson 22
Allen, Richard:
    Committee on the Present Danger
        172
    National Security Adviser 172, 173

Allott, Gordon Llewellyn:
    busing 66
alternative life-styles 32
American Churches:
    constitutional discussion 84
    role of 84
American civilization, fragility of 33
American Civil Liberties Union:
    communist interest in 22
    criminal procedure 163
American Committee for Cultural
        Freedom:
    CIA funding 31
American Communist Party:
    pro-Stalinist attitude 23
American Conservative Union 74
    fundamentalist schools, tax status
        of 108
American Enterprise Institute:
    public policy research 53, 163
American free-enterprise system 35
American Independent Party 67
Americanism:
    Bible, link with 102
    conservative causes, link with 102
    'heresy' 90
    new chosen people 99
American Jewish Committee:
    Commentary 75
American Legislative Exchange Council
        52, 54
    new right, connnection with 75
    social issues 74
    state legislators' support 76
    state-level politics 74
    Suggested State Legislation 75
American Lutheran Church 88
American Security Council:
    direct-mail strategy 61, 171
    SALT II 171
Americans for Common Sense 12
    opposition to right wing 101
'Americans United':
    Protestant fundamentalism 98
Andersen, Hans Christian 73
Anglican Church 82

Angola, Soviet intervention in 180
anti-Europeanism 128, 187
anti-nuclear sentiment 183
anti-Semitism 76, 91, 107, 113
appropriations bills:
  anti-abortion riders 93
  'Hyde amendment' 145
  non-germane riders 145
  social policy riders 145
Arbitron and Nielson 104
Arendt, Hannah 24
arms control 182, 183
  agreements 170
  negotiations 176
  opposition to agreements 171
Arms Control and Disarmament
    Agency:
  vetoing of appointments 70, 176
arms negotiations 104, 172, 182
arms sales 177
Armstrong, Ben:
  National Religious Broadcasters 116
  religious broadcasting 104
  Religious Roundtable 116
army mental standards 41
Assemblies of God 87, 88
Atlantic Alliance 1, 174, 185

B-1 bomber 181
Bagnal, Anne:
  election campaign 142
Baker, Howard:
  Carter, Jimmy (support for) 175
  Democratic Party, deals with 144
  legislation 121
  legislative leader 144
  marriage 129
  Panama Canal Treaties 137, 175
  Senate agenda 69
  Senate leader 175
  strategy 144
  successor to 132
Baker, James
  criticism of 68, 70
  influence of 150
  Moral Majority 119
  personnel management 150
Bakke v. *Regents of University of*
    California 39
Bakker, Jim:
  Federal Communications Com-
    mission investigation 104

The PTL Club 104
Baptist congregations:
  private schools 96
Baptist pastors:
  Moral Majority 76, 113
  new-right pressure-groups 97
Baptist traditionalism, and funda-
    mentalism 85
Baumann, Robert Edmund:
  forced to resign 112
Bayh, Birch:
  electoral defeat 7, 77
  women, equal rights to 77
Bazelon, David 25
Beard, Robin:
  election campaign 58, 142
  social issues 142
Beckett, John D.:
  Intercessors for America 116
  Religious Roundtable 116
Bell, Daniel 24, 25, 27
  community, sense of 39
  counter-culture, analysis of 46
  culture, conservative with respect
    to 44
  culture, treatment of 80
  culture shapes economy 45
  economic determinism, rejection of
    45
  economy, socialist with respect to
    44
  ethnicity, definition of 38
  individualism 44
  morality, treatment of 80
  politics, liberal with respect to 44
  Public Interest, The 37
  puritanism 44
  religion 43, 80
  work ethic 89
Bell, Jeffrey:
  direct mail 59
  election campaign 123
Bellow, Saul 24
Bible 113
  Americanism, link with 102
  authority of 82
  conservative causes, link with 102
  conservative views of 86
  free-enterprise system 89
  'inerrance' 90
  tenets 100
Bible Belt 91
Bible instruction (in public schools) 98

biblical morality 12
  return to 45
  State subject to 100
biblical precepts:
  social norms 72
  yearning for 81
bigotry 107
Billings, Robert (Bob) 114
  Bob Jones University degree 108
  Hyles–Anderson College 108
  Religious Roundtable 116
  schools, racial integration in 97
Bill of Rights:
  First Amendment 81
  Fourteenth Amendment 81
bipartisan consensus 122
bipartisan foreign policy 175
blacks:
  desegregation 160
  morality 43
  poverty 41
  social problems 42
  Voting Rights Act (1965) 164
  welfare benefits 160
Blacks for Reagan 127
Black Silent Majority 116
Blackwell, Morton:
  foreign policy luncheons 74
Bob Jones University 82, 108
'boll-weevils' 3, 144
'born-again' Christians:
  electoral data 118
bourgeois-capitalist system 50
Bow Group (UK) 134
Breaking Ranks (Podhoretz) 29
Britain: *see* United Kingdom
British Empire 128
broadcasting, religious 101
Brock, William:
  direct mail 140
  election campaign 140
  election candidates 140
  Panama Canal Treaties 175
  party loyalty 129
  Republican National Committee 139, 140
  Republican Party revival 4
  successor to 173
brokerage 1
Brookings Institution:
  public policy research 53
Brown, Jerry:
  federal government, role of 15

Brown v. *Board of Education of Topeka* 160
Brzezinski, Zbigniew:
  bipartisan foreign policy 175
  détente, Soviet interpretation of 179
  foreign policy, comments on 169
  National Security Adviser 169
Buchanan, John:
  election defeat 118, 123
  Moral Majority 118
Buckley, William 56
  cosmopolitan conservatism 78
  intellectual conservatism 55
Buckley v. *Valeo* 63
Bush, George:
  party loyalty 129
  social style 67
  support for 150
  Task Force on Regulatory Relief 162
busing 40, 72, 73, 165, 192
Butcher–Forde 59

Cabinet, American, influence of 150
Cade, Charles:
  Moral Majority, impact of 76
Califano, Joseph:
  families and national wellbeing 92
California Law and Order Commitee 74
  direct mail 59
Campbell, W. Glenn:
  Committee on the Present Danger 172
  Intelligence Oversight Board 172
'Campus Crusade' 100
Candidate Management College 140
capitalism 44
  creativity 34
  finance capitalism 79
  free society, necessary for a 36
  Gospel 89
  laissez-faire capitalism 50: and rejection of social gospel 89
  moral concerns 34
  moral superiority 45
  New American right 71
  political concerns 34
  theoretical justification of 33
Caribbean, American position in 168
Carlucci, Frank:
  foreign-policy manager 175

carol-singing (in public schools) 98
Carter, Jimmy:
    administration 99, 136, 169, 170,
        171, 172, 173, 180, 182, 183,
        184: human rights policies
        of 47; other policies of 167; and
        schools (racial integration of) 96
    Afghanistan 170
    armed forces 180
    arms control agreements 170
    arms limitations 169
    arms negotiations 172, 182
    'born-again' Christian 106
    Central America 184
    Civil Service admissions tests 164
    cold war 170
    Congressional liaison staff 145
    defense budget 172, 180–2
    Democratic Party and Church/
      religious groups 117
    détente 180
    economic policy 169
    election campaign 106
    federal government, role of 15
    foreign policy 170, 171, 172, 180,
      184: *détente* 179; human rights
      strategy 176; moral dimension
      176; opposition to 169, 173
    government regulations 162
    human rights 47, 183, 184
    Iran (US Embassy crisis) 170
    judicial appointments 118
    Labor Law Reform Bill 136
    Latin America 170
    Middle East 170
    MX missile 174
    National Security Adviser 169
    NATO 180
    Panama Canal 170
    Panama Canal Treaties 137, 175
    Presidency 93, 149
    rearmament 170
    religious convictions 117
    religious right, opposition of 103
    Rhodesia/Zimbabwe 170
    SALT II 170
    secondary picketing 136
    security 169
    social welfare 155
    Southern America 184
    Soviet Union 169, 170
    strategic balance 172
    support for 175

    Taiwan Enabling Act (1979) 112
    Taiwan Treaty 172
    USA's military position 170
    Vice-President, role of 150
    Washington Court of Appeals 118
    White House Conference on Families
      92
Case, Clifford:
    election campaign (new-right
      challenge) 173
Cather, Willa:
    censorship 73
caucus, role of 134
censorship:
    homosexual writers 73
    see also textbook censorship
Center for Strategic and International
    Studies 54
Central America:
    human rights 184
    policy towards 86, 174
Central Intelligence Agency 179
    American Committee for Cultural
      Freedom 31
    Encounter 31
    role 164
Chafee, J. 138
Chamberlin, William Henry:
    Human Events 70
Chamber of Commerce, and picketing
    136
child abuse laws 77
Child Development Act 135
China 112, 124
    Republican Party policy 174
    Senators' attitudes to 111
    Taiwan 112
    USA, relations with 112, 172
    USSR, relations with 38, 173
    Vietnam, relations with 38
Christian Broadcasting Network 103
Christian candidates 10
Christian Century 89
Christian Freedom Foundation 135
    donations to 108
    free-market economic views 107
Christian fundamentalist commu-
    nity:
    new right, links with 106
Christianity 85
    Marxist forces, attacks from 112
    teachings of 86
Christian morality, imposed 117

Christian republic 117
Christians and politics 11
Christian schools 96, 98, 164
Christian symbols, and pluralist society 35
Christian values, and schools 99
Christian Voice 10, 102, 106
  China 112
  Congressional Advisory Board, membership of 110
  culture, treatment of 80
  direct mail 111
  election strategy 111
  foreign policy 11
  government expenditure (Kemp–Roth amendment) 112
  government taxes 112
  morality, treatment of 80
  religion, treatment of 80
  Report Card on Congress 111
  Rhodesia 112
  social issues 112
  Southern Rim 110
  Taiwan 112
  Taiwan Treaty 172
Church, the:
  broadcasting 101
  'conservative' Churches 85, 89, 90
  disestablishment 87
  ecumenical Churches 86
  electronic Church 78, 104
  'fundamentalist' Churches 85
  particularism 90
  political involvement 81
  right-wing political coalition 85
  social gospel 89
  State, relationship with 12
  'strict' Churches 85
Church, Frank:
  Christian Voice 112
  CIA 179
  criticism of 112
  election campaigns 7, 118, 179
  foreign policy 179
  Foreign Relations Committee 179
  Moral Majority 118
  NCPAC opposition 179
  Senatorial score-card 112
  Vietnam War 179
Churches of God 87
church membership 84
Church of England 82
Church of God (Cleveland, Tenn.) 88

Church of Jesus Christ of the Latter Day Saints: *see* Mormon Church
Church of the Nazarene 87
church schools:
  aid to 98
  federal control 96
  support 99
  tax-exempt status 96
Church–State relationship 98, 117
City College (New York) 41
civil liberties 3, 31, 166
  affirmative action 163
  groups 97
  Protestant Christian schools 97
  right-wing activity, effect of 11
civil rights 127
  Church involvement 10
  filibuster 147
  groups 8
  movements 42
Civil Service:
  admissions tests 164
  population, representative of 164
Claiborne, Clay:
  Black Silent Majority 116
  Religious Roundtable 116
Clark, William 48
class divisions 28
Clawson, Del:
  Republican Study Group 135
coalition-building 1
Cohen, Elliott 24
cold war 27
  emphasis on 170
  liberalism, effect on 30
  transformation of conservatism 28
collectivism 6, 146
Commager, Henry Steele 29
Commentary 25, 29, 37
  cultural traditionalism 100
Committee for a Free World 167
Committee for American Principles 12
Committee for the Defeat of Jacob Javits 123
Committee for the Survival of a Free Congress 52, 53, 135
  defense-policy briefings 171
  direct-mail strategy 59
  foreign-policy briefings 171
  growth of 108
  new-right pressure-group 141
  social issues 116

Committee on the Present Danger 54
  arms negotiations 172
  Carter administration, criticism of 172
  defense budget 172, 182
  membership, and government appointments 172
  SALT II, opposition to 171
Common Market:
  pro-Arab 187
  Venice Declaration 187
Common Sense 141
communism 13, 22, 25, 26, 45, 117
  anti-communism 23, 31, 48, 130, 173, 174
  anti-communist liberalism 29
  communist forces 184
  communists 31, 77: ex-communists 30; Stalin, defense of 30
  European attitude 186
  hostility to 184
  nuclear freeze 168
  subversion 124
  threat of 71
Communist Party 22
communist States:
  internal structures 38
community, sense of 39, 43
Comprehensive Education and Training Act, criticism of 13
compromise 1
'Compromise is sin' 79
Conable, Barber:
  Kemp–Roth bill 126
  partisan postures, opposition to 122
  tax-cutting initiatives 126
  Ways and Means Committee 122
conference, role of 134
Congregational Church 83
Congregationalism 82
Congress:
  executive, relationship with 147
  White House Conference on Families, joint resolution 92
Congress of Industrial Organisations, communist interest in 22
Congressional Budget and Impoundment Control Act (1974) 147
Congressional Campaign Committee, contributions to 61
Congressional Club:
  new-right pressure-group 141
Congressional Quarterly:

'debate of the decade' 170
new right (social issues) 133
SALT II 170
Conlan, John:
  election campaign 107
Connally, John 67
conservatism:
  contemporary American 18
  cosmopolitan 78
  political conservatism 87
  populist constituency and 192
  radical conservatism 146
  rejection of 163
  revived conservatism 17, 167, 168
  Thatcher brand 153
  transformation of 28
Conservative Caucus 52
  moral issues 95
  strategy 109
conservative causes 120
Conservative Christianity 110
conservative Christians:
  organizational developments 104
  social issues 112
conservative Churches:
  Bible 'inerrance' 90
  sin, expiation of 89
conservative coalition 2, 144
  election success 20
Conservative Digest 56, 69
  O'Connor, Sandra Day 119
  'President Reagan's first broken promise' 119
  public expenditure cuts 148
  Supreme Court appointment 119
conservative evangelicals 11, 89
Conservative Party (UK):
  Bow Group 134
  Republican Party, comparisons 125
conservatives, as 'silent majority' 57
conservatives, old-line:
  defeatism 55
conservative views 86
Constitution, and established Church 81
consumer protectionism 162
containment 176
Conte, Silvio:
  presidential veto 148
Coors, Joseph 54
  ALEC 75
  Heritage Foundation 53
  Research and Analysis 53

Coors, Joseph (*cont.*):
    Schuchman Foundation 53
Corrupt Practices Act (1925) 63
Coughlin, Father 102
Council for American Private Edu-
    cation, and Department of Edu-
    cation appointment 109
Council of State Governments 75
Council on Foreign Relations 77
counter-culture:
    definition 5
    hostility to 45
    significance of 46
    Vietnam War 99
'counterfeit culture' 45
Crane, Philip 67, 75
    new-right hero 142
    Republican Study Group 135
    support for 142
Cranston, Alan 74
creationism 73
creation-science movement 119
crime 5, 36
    action against 166
    black problem 24
Cruise missiles, siting of 188
cultural issues 145
cultural nihilism:
    literary criticism 100
    sexual behavior 100
cultural traditionalism 100
culture:
    new-right concern 80
    religion 44
Curtis, Carl:
    new-right appointees 137
    Republican Conference 137
    Select Committee on Committees
        137

Daily Telegraph 70
d'Amato, Alfonse:
    election campaign 123
Danzig, David:
    fundamentalism 78, 79
Darwinism 86
dealignment (electoral) 191
Deaver, Michael:
    influence of 150
defeatism:
    conservatives, old-line 55
Defending America 172
defense 3, 16

budget 131, 154, 175, 176, 181:
    deficiencies 172; opposition to
    181, 182
    expenditure 136
    policy 61, 186: assertive 61;
        reorientation of 167
    Senate attitude to 136
De Funis v. *Odegaard* 39
democracy 30, 183
    fragile 48
democratic capitalism 35
    Anglo-American system 36
    cultural level 34
    defense of 32
    market economy 34
    political system 34
    Roman Catholic perspective 34
    spiritual inheritance 33
Democratic–Farmer–Labor Party:
    welfare programs 75
Democratic National Committee:
    direct-mail facilities 62
Democratic Party 120, 125, 192
    appropriations bills 145
    Budget Committee 144
    candidates, and direct-mail facilities
        62
    church/religious groups liaison
        117, 171
    criticism of 142
    Democratic ethnics 127
    Democratic Studies Group 135
    demoralization of 6
    economic strategy, criticism of 144
    economy, record on 142
    electoral support 192
    family issues, record on 142
    finances 140, 145
    foreign policy, record on 142
    government appointments, op-
        position to 176
    House Democrats (Committee ap-
        pointments) 144
    House of Representatives, control 2
    internal divisions 3, 124
    internationalist 128
    moderates and 192
    'new politics' 5, 65
    new-right similarities 106
    new-right threat (secularism) 116
    Panama 171
    partisan identity 144
    party democracy, internal 66

polarization of 31
Reagan program, ideological sympathy with 152
Republican Party, deals with 144
resurgent 72
Roosevelt vision 5
SALT II 171
social issues 142
Vietnam War 46
democratic polity 45
Democratic Studies Group:
model for Republican Study Group 135
democratic theory (method of mobilization) 58
'denominational orthodoxies', and fundamentalism 85
denominations, major 86
Denton, Jeremiah:
election success 99, 123
Roman Catholic 99
deregulation 15, 162
economic strategy 162
government, role of 162
impetus for 163
Derwinski, Edward J.:
loses seat 135
Republican Study Group 135
desegregation 33, 37, 39
'destabilization syndrome' 183
détente 131, 171
pro-*détente* 179
rejection of 179
Dickinson, Emily 73
Dickson, Everett 129
'Dictatorships and Double Standards' (Kirkpatrick) 48
Dingman, Richard:
Christian Freedom Foundation 135
Kingston Group 135
Religious Roundtable 116
Republican Study Committee 116, 135
direct mail 65, 105, 111
computerized 7
financial balance-sheet 61
fund-raising 4, 56, 60, 62
importance of 101
mobilization, method of 58
new right 59, 62, 107
potential donors 74
social issues 72

technology 60
Dirkson, Everett 129
disease, black problem of 42
disestablishment 83
Dissent 25
divorce rate 91
Dixiecrats 3
Dolan, Terry:
National Conservative Political Action Committee 52
tax laws, manipulation of 64
Dole, Robert:
legislation 121
public expenditure cuts, criticism of 148
Senate Finance Committee 148
domestic issues:
economic prosperity 152
inflation 152
domestic policy 20
domestic public expenditure, cuts in 142, 154
domestic social programs 138
Donovan, Raymond:
affirmative action 164
Dornan, Robert:
Christian Voice 110
draft, resistance to 32
Dreyfus trial 27
Drinan, Robert:
withdrawal from politics 95
drug addiction, black problem of 42
dual-use technology 187
Dugan, Bob:
National Association of Evangelicals 116
Religious Roundtable 116

Eastern Establishment 3, 67, 77
East European community, American 26
Eberle, Bruce 59
Eberle (Bruce) and Associates 61
Citizens for Reagan Committee 59
economic achievement 71
economic *détente* 186
economic equality 39
economic policy 1, 3, 13, 14, 71, 138, 162, 165, 169, 186
new-right concern 71
Reagan program 152
economic prosperity 152

economic recovery 71
Economic Recovery Tax Act (1981)
    153
economics and politics 37
economic strategy 69
    criticism of 144
economic theory:
    free-market 6
    monetarist 6
    supply-side economics 6
economic warfare 186
    political weapon 187
economies, mixed 45
economy 91, 104, 131
    criticism of 142
    fund-raising 72
    government intervention 126, 162
ecumenical Churches, and social
        gospel 89
ecumenical movement, membership
        of 87
education 16
    block grants 156
    disadvantaged, provision for 156
    electoral dealignment and 191
    'explosion' of higher 32
    free enterprise 75
    handicapped, provision for 156
    intelligence tests 40
    programs, number of 157
Eisenhower, Dwight 194
    Presidency 149
    presidential nomination 129
elections:
    financial strategies 4
    fragmentation of 62
election technology (direct mail) 62
electoral law:
    changes in 4, 7, 8
    fund-raising 60
    reforms 60, 62
electoral redistricting 140
electronic Church: see Church, the
Eli Lilly Foundation:
    ALEC 75
El Salvador:
    American aid 176
    American support 177
    Honduras, relations with 185
    human rights 176
    military aid 177, 185
    USA diplomatic representation
        184

emancipation 27
employment:
    election theme 142
    intelligence tests 40
Encounter 25
    CIA funding 31
Ender, Thomas:
    ambassador to El Salvador 185
energy conservation programs 157
energy policy 3
environment, and intelligence 40
environmentalism 162
    rejection of 163
Episcopalian Church 82, 83
    membership 87, 88
equality, substantive (government
        promotion of) 152
equality before the law 42
equality of opportunity 39, 42
equality of outcome 39
Equal Rights Amendment 165
    opposition to 9, 74, 104, 116
ethic of abstinence 44
ethic of individual self-realization
        44
Ethics and Public Policy Center:
    foreign policy 171
ethics groups:
    political involvement 42
ethnic identity, interest in 38
ethnicity 25, 33, 37
    content 39
    definition of 38
    understanding of 38
ethnic origins 78
ethnic pluralism, as force for stability
        39
Europe:
    anti-nuclear sentiment 183
    defense of 1
    foreign policy 187
    nuclear umbrella 49
    pro-Arab 187
    protest movements 12
    religious orthodoxy 81
    Republican Party policy towards
        174
    security 49
Europeanism: see anti-Europeanism
evangelical Christians, political re-
        sponsiveness of 109
evangelical Churches 10
evangelicalism 85

evangelical Protestantism 127
evangelical right, and role of federal
    government 14
evangelicals:
    abortion 94
    family issues 91
    membership 87
    National Association of 116
    social issues 91
evangelicals, conservative 192
    direct-mail campaign 97
    new-right mobilization of 80
    populism 78
evangelical views 86
evangelists, and broadcasting 102
Evans, M. Stanton:
    ALEC 74
    American Conservative Union 74
    Ronald Reagan, meeting with 70
Evans, Rowland 119
evolution 11
    rejection of 85
    teaching of 55: hostility to 81
extreme right, as 'silent majority' 57
extremism 45

factionalism 129
Falwell, Jerry 10, 12
    American populism 78
    Christian schools 96
    free-enterprise system 114
    Israel, support for 113
    Liberty Baptist College 102
    Listen America 89
    Moral Majority 114
    Old-time Gospel Hour 102, 104
    patriotism 114
family 42, 43
    American vision of 93
    defense of 72
    definition of 93
    federal public policy 92
    homosexual families 93
    instability, black problem of
        42
    institution of 25
    issues 71, 132, 142, 145: new-
        right definition 11; potentially
        divisive 91
    role of 92
Family Assistance Plan 135
Family Protection Bill 11
federal aid grants 157

federal budget 104
    defense in 181
federal bureaucracy, expansion of 36
Federal Communications Commission
    104
federal courts' jurisdiction 132
Federal Election Campaign Act (1971)
    63
    amendments (1974) 60
    'independent expenditure loophole'
        63
Federal Election Commission 64, 105
federal expenditure 3
    domestic 2
    growth of 154
federal government:
    the country's problem 14
    expenditure 153
    role 13, 14, 15, 22, 32, 36
federalism 15, 139, 159
federal legislative contests 139
federal policy 5
Federal Register 162
Federal Reserve Board, monetary
        policy of 153
fellow-travelers: Stalin, defense of 30
'fellow-traveling liberalism' 29
female vote, and Supreme Court
        appointment 119
feudal past, values of 34
Feulner, Edwin J.:
    ALEC 74
    Heritage Foundation 74, 135
    Political Action Committees,
        business investment in 63
    Republican Study Committee 74,
        133, 135
    Ronald Reagan, meeting with 69
Fiedler, Leslie 24
filibuster 147
First Amendment:
    free exercise clauses 81
    no establishment clauses 81
food stamps:
    eligibility requirements 155
    responsibility for 158
Ford, Gerald 194
    administration, policies of 167
    détente, opposition to 179
    foreign policy ('moral amendment')
        177
    government regulations 162
    party loyalty 129

Fore, Daniel:
  anti-Semitism 76
foreigners 77
foreign policy 1, 3, 17, 20, 69, 72,
    104, 111, 127, 137, 152, 165,
    170, 175, 186
  approach to 33
  arms limitation 169
  arms sales 177
  AWACS sale 145
  bipartisan foreign policy 175
  constraints 168
  containment 176
  criticism of 142
  defense budget 176
  détente 177
  direction of 4
  disagreements 21
  double standards of discussion 47
  'fortress America' 128
  human rights 177
  idealistic grounds 176
  isolationism 128
  liberalism, effect on 28
  moral dimension 176
  moralism 177
  National Security Adviser (com-
    ments) 169
  neo-conservative recognition 48
  new right 71, 74
  opposition to 169
  pragmatism 177
  questions 133
  realism 49
  realpolitik 176
  regional divisions 174
  reorientation of 167
  revived conservatism, roots of 168
  subversive activity 177
foreign-policy élites, traditional 48
Foreign Relations Committee 174
  Director of Arms Control (ap-
    pointment delayed) 176
'fortress America' 28, 128
Founding Fathers 81
Fourteenth Amendment:
  Bill of Rights 81
Frank, Barney:
  election campaign 95, 140
Frank, Waldo 22
Free Congress Research and Education
  Foundation 74
  Initiative and Referendum Report 75

freedom 30, 183
freedom of speech 164
free enterprise 13, 45
free market 13, 152
  economists 163
  federal government, role of 14
  free-marketeers 7
  new American right 71
  policy 6
  principles 148, 163
  theories 166
free world, leadership of 29
Friedman, Milton 13
  economic theories 6, 45
From Weakness to Strength 172
Fuller, Charles E.:
  Old Fashioned Revival Hour 102
fundamentalism:
  anti-Semitism 113
  Baptist traditionalism 85
  centrality to religious history 86
  Church–State relationship 98
  conservatism 78
  'denominational orthodoxies' 85
  direct-mail campaign 97
  evangelicalism 85
  holiness movements 85
  meaning of 85
  millenarianism 85
  modernity, constraints of 85
  organizational developments 104
  pietism 85
  political 79
  populism 78
  private schools 96
  Reformed confessionalism 85
  religious 79
  revivalism 85
  social attitudes 79
  social gospel, rejection of 89
fundamentalist Christianity 110
  abortion 91
  school prayer 91
fundamentalist Churches 10
fundamentalist movement 100
fundamentalists:
  abortion 11, 94, 118
  family issues 91, 118
  judicial appointments 118
  new-right mobilization of 80
  Old Testament prohibitions 101
  political awareness 118, 192
  social issues 91

fundamentalist schools, political
    controversy over 97
fundamentalist sects:
    American right, alliance with 89
fundamentalist theology 102
fundamentalist values, strength of 81
Fundamentals 89
fund-raising:
    direct-mail 60
    politics of 60

Garn, Jake:
    conservative legislator 132
    MX missile 174
    Republican Party Committee 137
    Select Committee on Committees,
        appointments 137
gay rights 173
General Revenue Sharing Scheme
    (1972) 156
Gilder, George:
    capitalism 33, 34, 35
    supply-side theories 13
    Wealth and Poverty 6, 33
Glazer, Nathan 25, 29
    community, sense of 39
    ethnicity 37
    religion 43
Goldberg, Arthur:
    Secretary of Labor 41
Goldwater, Barry 55
    campaign strategy 121
    election campaign 56, 131: media
        impact 20; right-wing activities
        54
    moral issues, role in political debate
        of 133
    philosophy of 106
    political coalition (1964) 121
    role of 130
    social agenda, opposition to 71
    social issues 133
government:
    expenditure (Kemp–Roth amend-
        ment) 112
    role of 162
Graham, Billy 102
Gramm, Phil:
    Budget Committee 144
    Republican Party membership 144
Grand Old Party: *see* Republican Party
Grassley, Charles:
    NCPAC tactics, repudiation of 65

Great Britain: *see* United Kingdom
Great Depression 152
    federal response 159
'great fear' 29
Great Society:
    Aid to Families with Dependent
        Children 155
    job training schemes 155
    legislation 4
    Medicaid 155
    popular rejection 12
    programs 131, 155: criticism of
        36, 42; expenditure 181;
        filibuster protection 147; policy
        flaws 5
    tradition 5
    years of frustration 36
Grenada, American invasion of 178
Grey, Robert:
    Nuclear Weapons, Assistant Director
        in charge of 175
Gross National Product (GNP):
    defense as percentage of 175, 181,
        182
Group Research 105
Gun Owners of America:
    direct mail 59
    founder 52, 74
Gusfield, J. R. 11
'gypsy moths' 148

Haig, Alexander:
    Defense appointment 173
    foreign policy 184, 187
    pro-Israeli 187
Hammett, Dashiell:
    Moscow trials 22
    prose style 30
Hanighen, Frank:
    Human Events 70
Harriman, Averell 41
Harrington, Michael 5
Hart, Gary 191
Hatch, Orrin:
    abortion 94, 130
    Christian Voice 110
    conservative legislator 132
    criticism of 122
    personality, effect of 136
    Republican Conference 137
    Select Committee on Committees
        137
    Supreme Court 130

Hatfield, Mark:
  isolationism, pacific 138
  nuclear freeze 138, 174
  private schools 139
  tuition tax credits 139
  Vietnam War 138
Hayakawa, Sam:
  social issues 71, 133
Hayek, Friedrich von 6
health 156
Heckler, Margaret:
  election campaign 95, 140
hedonism 44, 45
Hellman, Lillian 29, 30
Helms, Jesse:
  abortion 130, 136
  Agriculture Bill 136
  Congressional Club 141
  effect of 136
  European Affairs, Sub-Committee
    on 175
  Foreign Relations Committee 175
  Panama Canal Treaties 175
  personality 136
  Republican Right 133
  school prayer 136
  social agenda 71
  State Department appointments
    175
Hemingway, George 30
Heritage Foundation 63, 69, 74, 105
  appointments 135
  conservatives, list of reliable 68
  financial support 54
  'new right' institute 53
  Policy Review 70
  public expenditure cuts 148
  State Department appointments
    175
Himmelfarb, Gertrude 25
Hiss, Alger 27, 28
Hofstadter, Richard 24
  American politics, paranoid style
    of 77
Hogan, Laurence 65
Holiness Groups 87
holiness movements:
  fundamentalism 85
holiness sects 90
Holmes, Oliver Wendell 191
Holwill, Richard 68
'home town America' 78
homosexuality 11, 44, 77, 133, 193

homosexuals 10
  censorship 73
  Congressman's resignation 112
  families 93
  religious opinion 100
  rights 72, 76, 173
Honduras:
  El Salvador, relations with 185
  USA military aid 185
Hook, Sidney 23, 24
Hoover Institute for the Study of War,
    Peace, and Revolution 53
Hoover Institution 54
Horn of Africa, Soviet intervention
    in 180
House Conservative Forum 152
House Judiciary Committee, and school
    prayer 100
Howe, Irving 24, 29
Human Events 70
human rights 183, 184
  administration strategy 176
  Central America 176
  El Salvador 176
  foreign policy, effect on 170
  policies 47
Humbard, Rex:
  American populism 78
Humphrey, Gordon:
  election 109
  Religious Roundtable 116
Hyde, Henry:
  abortion 145
'Hyde Amendment':
  abortion 145
  Medicaid 145
Hyles–Anderson College 108

ideological conservatism 130
Iklé, Fred:
  Committee on the Present Danger
    172
  Defense appointment 172
immigration:
  puritan theocracy 81
imperialism 47
impoundment 15
income tax: *see* taxation
independent conservative party 120
'independent expenditure loophole'
    63
independent third party:
  new right 67

individualism 13, 44, 49
inequality 37, 40
  patterns of 39
inflation 91, 152, 153, 180
Initiative and Referendum Report 75
inner cities 36
Institute for Contemporary Studies 53, 54
  Defending America 172
  From Weakness to Strength 172
Institute for Foreign Policy 171
Institute for Foreign Policy Analysis 171
Institute for Religion and Democracy 12
intellectual right 26, 172
intellectuals 77
intelligence, environment and 40
Intelligence Quotient (IQ), race and 40
intelligence services 136, 178
intelligence tests controversy 40
Intercessors for America 116
Internal Revenue Service 105
  direct-mail campaign against 97
  legal authority 165
  private schools, tax status of 96, 108, 164, 165
inter-racial marriage 54, 77, 82
Iran, US Embassy seizure in 170
isolationism 128, 138, 193
isolationist impulse, right-wing purging of 28
isolationists 129, 173
Israel 47
  Moral Majority support 113
  USA, relations with 49, 91, 168, 187
Israel, ancient:
  American parallels 91
  historical experience 100
item veto 157

Jackson, Henry 137, 180
  arms control agreements 171
Jacksonian Democrats, and new-right Republican alliance 4
James, Pendleton 68
Japan 174
Jarmin, Gary:
  Report Card on Congress 111
Jarvis, Howard:
  Proposition 13 (direct-mail

strategy) 59
Jarvis–Gann Proposition 16
Jasper, Claude 66
Javits, Jacob:
  election defeat 123
  internationalist 138
  liberal Republican 138
  Rhodesia 112
Jehovah's Witnesses:
  legitimacy of 83
  membership 87, 88
Jennings, Bryan William:
  populism 79
Jewish intellectual community 24
Jewish novel, the 24
Jews 127
  Moral Majority 112
job training schemes 155
John Birch Society:
  Monthly Opinion 108
John Reed Clubs 23
Johnson, Lyndon 5
  administration 42
  Great Society programs 147, 155
Johnson, Willie 68
Judaism 84
judges 165
Justice Department 164

Kaisich, John 142
Kaufmann, William 181
Kazin, Alfred 24
Kelly, Dean:
  Churches, conservative theological 89
  ecumenical movement 87
Kelly, Richard:
  Abscam scandal 11
  Christian Voice Senatorial score-card 112
Kemp, Jack:
  supply-side theories 13
Kemp–Roth amendment 112
Kemp–Roth bill 126
Kennedy, Edward:
  nuclear freeze 138, 174
Kennedy, John F.:
  administration 41
  assassination 42
  Presidency 149
  presidential election 83

Keynesianism 126
  criticism of 6
Keynesian 'revolution' 126
Kingston Group 135
Kirk, Russell 56
Kirkpatrick, Jeane 66
  Cabinet appointment 167, 172,
    183
  Committee on the Present Danger
    172
  democracy 183
  'destabilization syndrome' 183
  'Dictatorships and Double Stan-
    dards' 48
  foreign policy 47, 184
  freedom 183
Kissinger, Henry:
  détente 177, 179
  foreign policy 177
  see also Kissinger Commission
Kissinger Commission:
  Central America (human rights
    record) 176, 177
'Kissinger-style détentist thinking'
    70
Klu Klux Klan:
  anti-Catholic 83
Kristol, Irving 25, 27, 29, 41
  American liberalism 31
  capitalism, defense of 35, 36
  culture, treatment of 80
  democratic polity 45
  free market 37
  Israel, USA support for 49
  morality, treatment of 80
  neo-conservatism, 'godfather' of 36
  neo-conservative label 19
  pornography 46
  Public Interest, The 37
  religion, treatment of 80
  Soviet Union, resistance to 48
  Two Cheers for Capitalism 33

labor organizations:
  civil rights groups, cooperation with
    8
Lacy, William 61
Laffer, Arthur:
  supply-side theories 13
laissez-faire free-market economies
    126
Lancaster House Agreement (1979)
    112

Lasky, Melvin 24
Latin America:
  American response 168
  policy towards 170, 178
law and order 72, 73, 192
  racial overtones 3
Laxalt, Paul:
  conservative legislation 132
  MX missile 174
  Republican Party chairmanship
    123, 132
League of Nations 128
Lebanon 187
  American aid 178
  American withdrawal 178
  Beirut massacre 178
Lee, Gary:
  education cuts 161
Lefever, Ernest:
  State Department appointment
    176
legal services 163
Legal Services Corporation 166
legislative process, greater profes-
    sionalization in 134
Legislative Reorganization Act (1970)
    134
Lehmann, John:
  Cabinet appointment 172
  Committee on the Present Danger
    172
Lewis, Sinclair:
  Main Street 127
liberalism 3, 7, 49
  American 27, 31
  defensiveness 55
  family policy 93
  imperialism 47
  McCarthysim 29
  transformed 28
  trend 40
  Vietnam War 46
liberal Republicanism:
  stronghold 109
Liberty Baptist College:
  graduates' placements 102
libraries 6
Life Amendment Political Action
    Committee 52
life-style:
  alternative 32
  government authority 133
Lincoln, Abraham 127

Lincoln Institute 127
Lipset, Seymour Martin 25
literacy, in Christian schools 98
literature 25
Lodge, Henry Cabot:
  mailing campaign for 56
Lofton, John 69
London School of Economics 41
Long, Huey:
  populism 79
  southern demagogue 77
Longinqua Oceani (1895) 90
Lott, Trent:
  legislation 121
loyalty (party) 129, 190
Lugar, Richard:
  National Republican Senatorial
    Committee 138
Lutheran Church 87, 88
Lyons, Eugene:
  'the red decade' 23

McAteer, Ed 106
  Christian Freedom Foundation
    107
  Conservative Caucus 109, 115
  evangelicals 115
  Moral Majority 114
  Religious Roundtable 115, 116
McCarthy, Joe 29
  communism 31
  politics 77
McCarthy, Mary 24
McCarthyism 27, 31
  backlash against 28
  conservative Christian parallels
    117
  liberalism, effect on 30
  neo-conservative support 29
  populist tradition, link with 30
McCarthy symposiums 29
McClure, James 132
Macdonald, Dwight 23
McDonald, Larry:
  Christian Voice 110
  Democratic Party 110
  John Birch Society 110
McGovern, George:
  election defeat 7
  mailing campaign 56
McIntyre, Thomas:
  'home town America' 78
Maddox, Robert:

Church/religious groups, liaison
    with 117
Church–State constitutional sepa-
    ration 117
  McCarthyism 117
  Moral Majority 117
  new right 117
  Southern Baptist Churches 117
Madeiros, Humberto (Cardinal):
  pastoral letter on abortion 95
Madison, James:
  Church of England 82
Madison Group 171
Main Street 11, 26
Main Street (Lewis) 127
Malamud, Bernard 24
Manatt, Charles:
  Democratic Party chairmanship
    123
  direct-mail facilities 62
  PACs, electoral role of 123
Marcus, Steven 25
market, role of 45
marketing, direct-mail 57
market mechanism 13
Marx, Karl 23
Marxism 23, 38
Marxist forces:
  Christianity, destruction of 112
Marxist ideologies 33
Mathias, C. 138
media:
  Democratic bias 56
  importance 192
  liberal bias 56
  religion 79
Medicaid:
  abortion 145
  eligibility requirements 155
  government responsibility 158
  'Hyde Amendment' 145
  spending cuts 139
Medicare 155
  federal government funding 158
medieval past, values of 34
Meese, Ed:
  nominated as Attorney-General
    150
  conservative loyalist 150
  Moral Majority, significance of
    119
Menorah Journal 25
Michel, Robert 121

Middle East:
  American policy 170
  European attitude to 187
  oil crisis 187
  politics, contemporary 91
military:
  budget 138
  expansion 152
  expenditure, European attitude to 186
  interventions 173
millenarianism 85
Milton, John 73
minority interests 138, 163
modernism 85
monetarism 14
monetary policy:
  Federal Reserve Board 153
  money supply 14, 153
money 64
Montgomery, Sonny:
  Christian Voice 110
  Democratic Party 110
  foreign policy 110
Monthly Opinion 108
moral decline, and political decline 100
moralism 129
moral issues 11, 71, 145
  incentive to political involvement 8
  political debate, role in 133
  political effects of 94
morality 93, 133
  neo-conservative analysis 45
  new-right concern 80
  political impact 95
moral law, conformity to 83
Moral Majority 10, 97, 101, 102, 106, 108
  Baptist pastors 76, 113
  child abuse laws 77
  clergy, affiliation of 76
  criticism of 117
  crusade to save America 114
  culture, treatment of 80
  electoral influence 118
  family 52
  education 115
  electoral involvement 115
  homosexual rights, opposition to 76
  interdenominational organization 112

Israel, support for 113
  law 115
  membership 76
  morality, treatment of 80
  Moral Majority Report 115
  PAC 115
  'pro-family Bible believing coalition' 115
  religion, treatment of 80
  Republican Party, infiltration of 73
  significance of 119
  social issues 52
  voter registration 115
Moral Majority Foundation:
  tax-deductible and tax-exempt 115
Moral Majority Inc.:
  tax-exempt political form 115
Moral Majority Legal Defense Fund 114
Moral Majority Report 115
moral perversion 103
moral questions:
  new-right activists 99
  power of 94
morals, code of 25
moral values 33
  questioning of 73
  traditional 92
Morley, Felix:
  Human Events 70
Mormon Church:
  legitimacy of 83
  membership 87, 88
  theology 80
Moscow trials 22
Moser, Charles 55
Moynihan, Daniel:
  blacks, problems of 42
  black poverty 41
  policies 20
  social mobility 43
  social policy 160, 161
  UN, Ambassador to 47
'Mr Republican' 128
Mutual Assured Destruction (MAD) 188
Muzorewa, Abel 112
MX missile 174, 181

Nader, Ralph 53
National Christian Action Coalition 80
  fundamentalist schools 108
  religious and political right 106

National Conference of State Legislatures 75
National Conservative Political Action Committee (NCPAC) 52, 141
  Church, Frank (targeted for defeat) 179
  direct mail 60
  election campaign 123
  electoral tactics 20
  expenditure 64
  importance of 7
  moral issues 95
National Council for Catholic Bishops: pastoral letter 12
National Council of Catholic Charities: White House Conference on Families 92
National Council of Churches: White House Conference on Families 92
National Council of Churches of Christ in the United States 86
National Gay Task Force: White House Conference on Families 92
National Governors' Association 158-9
National Governors' Conference 139
national health insurance 104
nationalism 28, 38
National Journal:
  'truth-seekers' 67
National Merit Scholarships 41
National Religious Broadcasters Association 104, 116
National Republican Senatorial Committee:
  appointments 138
  campaign funds 138
National Rifle Association 74
National Right to Work Committee 61
national security policy 170
  regional divisions 174
National Strategy Information Center 171
natural justice 163
Nazi Germany 46
negative campaigns 72, 193
negative expenditures 64
Nelson, Gaylord 7
neo-conservatism 19, 20, 26
  affirmative action 163
  CETA, criticism of 13
  contemporary 22

definition 19
foreign policy 46
'godfather' 37
government appointments 167
ideological controversies 27
journals 25
morals, code of 25
role of 21
social policy 160-1
neo-conservatives 1, 7, 17, 22, 54
  activists 99
  affirmative action 163
  American role in the world 46
  anti-communism 46, 48
  anti-Europeanism 187
  anti-USSR sentiment 170
  blacks, treatment of 42
  busing 40
  class 38
  cold war 170
  contemporary issues 43
  creed 6
  cultural traditionalism 100
  data, collection of 41
  definition 5
  distinctive orientation 50
  ethnicity 38
  federal government, role of 14
  foreign policy 48, 49
  government appointments 167
  intellectuals 34: concerns of 80; debate/policy research 51
  McCarthyism 29
  opposition to 170
  pro-Israel 187
  public policy, aspects of 37
  race 38
  realism, emphasis on 27
  religious values 44
  Republicanism and 192
  SALT II 170
  social policy 36, 160-1
  special concerns of 33
  writers 23, 24, 30: higher education 'explosion' 32
  younger generation 20
neutralist movement 12
New Deal 15, 22, 125, 146, 156, 190
  economy, intervention in 131
  hostility to 129, 130
  Republican support 138
  tradition 5
New Frontier 5

new issue agenda 70
new left 31, 43
'new nationalism' 168
New Republic 25
new right 1, 8, 9, 12, 17, 105, 119
   agenda 71
   ALEC, connections with 75
   anti-USSR sentiment 170
   campaigning, emphasis on 55
   Christian fundamentalist community,
     links with 106
   cold war 170
   community mobilization 73
   completely 'new' claim 107
   concerns of 80
   Congressional Club 141
   conservation 163
   conservative evangelicals 116:
     mobilization of 80
   constituency 58
   consumer movement 163
   CSFC 141
   definition 7, 51, 52
   Democratic Party, similarities to
     106
   deregulation 163
   determination 54
   direct mail 56, 59, 74, 107:
     advantages of 57; fund-raising
     62
   distinguishing features of 54
   electoral impact 141
   electoral strategy 138
   environmentalism 163
   family issues 91
   family policy 93
   Federal Election Campaign Act
     (1971) 60
   fundamentalists 116: mobilization
     of 80
   fund-raising, emphasis on 55
   'home town America' 78
   'independent expenditure loophole'
     63
   independent third party 67
   intellectual conservatism, separation
     from 55
   Israel, defense of 113
   leaders: church members, mobili-
     zation of 87; populist senti-
     ments 78
   legislative action, agenda for
     165

   Moral Majority planning meetings
     114
   moral values, traditional 92
   NCPAC 141
   neglected majority 61
   oil crisis (1973) 187
   Old Right, distinctions between
     55
   opposition to 170
   outlook 79
   PACs 64
   paranoia 66
   party system, hostility to 65
   personalities 70
   picketing 136
   populism 54, 77, 78, 193
   populist conservatism 65
   pressure-groups 97, 141
   public interest movement 163
   religion 44
   religious leaders, mutual interest
     84
   religious right: alliance with 10;
     integration with 118; links with
     135
   Religious Roundtable 115
   Republican Party: distrust of 67;
     internal divisions 124; links
     with 135
   research institutes 53
   Roman Catholic membership:
     electoral success 99
   SALT II 170
   sectarianism 67
   self-destructiveness 67
   sexual morality 11
   social issues 72, 91, 112, 133,
     165
   success of 101
   tactics 60, 78, 193
   technology 107
new-right activists, and moral questions
   99
new-right groups:
   Republican candidates 142
new right–religious right:
   élites, movements between 105
New Right Report 56
new-right Republicans:
   Jacksonian Democrats, alliance 4
New York:
   Establishment Republicans 110
   intellectual subculture 24

Jewish intellectual community 24:
   journals 25
New Yorker, The 24
New York Review of Books 24
New York Times 167
Nicaragua 185
Nickles, Don 99
1960s counter-culture 10
Nitze, Paul:
   Chief Negotiator for Theater
      Nuclear Forces 172
   Committee for the Present Danger
      172
Nixon, Richard M. 194
   administration: conspiratorial style
      178; second 135; policies
      167
   Child Development Act 135
   China diplomatic relations with
      172
   Family Assistance Plan 135
   federalism 15
   federal system 157
   General Revenue Sharing Scheme
      (1972) 156
   government regulations 162
   Great Society programs 14
   personal staff, role of 150
   presidential candidacy 131
Nixonian new federalism 156
Nofziger, Lyn 75
non-internationalists 173, 174
North American Baptist Conference 88
North Atlantic Treaty Organization
   (NATO) 187
   armed forces 180
   demoralization of 186
   nuclear attack on 188
   Republican Party policy 174
north-eastern internationalists 129
Novak, Michael 24, 35
   democratic capitalism, defense of
      33
   federal government obligations 161
   Spirit of Democratic Capitalism 34
Novak, Robert 119
Nozick, Robert 6
nuclear defense, of Western Europe
   186
nuclear freeze 138
   Catholic Bishops 84
   communist involvement 168
   resolution 174

nuclear issue, Church involvement in
   10; *see also* anti-nuclear sentiment
nuclear strategy 1
   MAD 188
   NATO 188
numeracy, in Christian schools 98
Nunn, Sam:
   defense expenditure 180, 181
   USA's misplaced priorities 180
nutrition programs, eligibility requirements 155

O'Connor, Sandra Day:
   abortion 118–19
   Supreme Court appointment 118,
      119
Office of Management and Budget 148,
   150, 162, 181
Office of Policy Planning and Research,
   appointments 41
oil crisis (1973) 187
Old Fashioned Revival Hour 102
'Old Glory' 102
old right, distinction from new right 55
Old Testament:
   authority of 82
   prohibitions 101
Old-Time Gospel Hour 102
organized labor:
   growth of 126
   PACs 62
O'Sullivan, John 69, 70

pacifist movement 12
Packwood, Bob 138
Panama, relations with 171
Panama Canal 72
   status of 170
Panama Canal Treaties 131
   opposition to 137, 175
   state legislatures 75
   support for 175
parental authority 73
Parents Without Partners:
   White House Conference on Families
      92
Parker, Dorothy 22
parochial schools:
   state finance 96
   Supreme Court 82
particularism 90
partisan preference 28, 118

partisan realignment 22
Partisan Review 22, 23, 25, 47
　intellectual freedom, values of 29
party dealignment, new right and 66
party politics, coalitions in 124
party system, new-right hostility to
　65
party whipping 134
paternalism 37
peace movements 5
　European attitude to 186
Pentecostal Groups 87
People for the American Way 12
　election tactics 117
　PACs' financial accountability 64
　right wing, opposition to 101
Percy, Charles Harting:
　foreign policy 111
　Foreign Relations Committee 174
　Taiwan Enabling Act (1979),
　　amendment 111
Perle, Richard 171
　Assistant Secretary of Defense for
　　International Security Policy
　　171
　Committee on the Present Danger
　　172
Pershing missiles 188
Persian Gulf, American position in
　168
personal responsibility 45
Perspective, The:
　arms negotiations 104
　economy 104
　Equal Rights Amendment 104
　Federal Budget 104
　foreign policy 104
　national health insurance 104
　price controls 104
　SALT II 104
　wage controls 104
Pew, J. Howard:
　Christian Freedom Foundation
　　108
　Monthly Opinion 108
Pfeffer, Leo 97
Phillips, Howard 55, 114
　Conservative Caucus 52, 109
　evangelical right 109
　Moral Majority 113
　Religious Roundtable 116
Phillips, Kevin:
　'new right' 51

southern strategy 3
Phillips, William 24
picketing 136
pietism, and fundamentalism 85
pluralism 35, 84
pluralist society 72
　Christian symbols 35
Plymouth Rock Foundation 116
Podhoretz, Norman 25, 29
　Breaking Ranks 29
　foreign policy 167
　Hellman, Lillian, criticism of 30
　Israel, USA support for 49, 187
　'movement', the 46
　'new nationalism' 168
　religion 43
　social mobility 43
　Vietnam War 47: meaning of 21
Poland 168
policy-making, 'dual approach' in
　151
policy research 141
policy topics, related to race 41
Political Action Committees (PACs)
　65, 194
　connected 63
　corporate 63
　direct-mail strategy 59
　financial accountability 64
　ideological 62
　Moral Majority 115
　multi-candidate 63
　new right 64
　non-connected 63
　role of 62
　single-issue 62
　support for candidates 8
political atomism 147
political consultants 65
　importance of 62
political decline, and moral decline
　100
Political Gun News 56
political system, moral basis of 33
political values, questioning of 73
politics:
　economics, priority over 37
　marketing side of 56
　money, role of 64
　paranoid style 77
　party loyalty 65
　relationship to religion 17, 43, 106
pollution control 157

population:
minorities 84
segmentation 57
populism 163, 166, 193
the left 77
new right 54, 77, 78, 193
reforming spirit of 79
religious right 193
'populist' 77
populist conservatism, and new right
65
populist sentiments, and new-right
leaders 78
populist tradition:
McCarthyism, link with 30
pornography 10, 46, 72
positive discrimination 39
poverty 16, 36, 37, 42
federal obligation to reduce 155
prayer in schools 98, 133
pressure-groups;
importance 192
multi-purpose 52
price controls 104
private enterprise 152
private schools 139
tax status 164
'pro-family Bible believing coalition'
115
prohibition 127
Church involvement 10
movement, analysis of 11
Proposition 13 (1978) 15, 16, 73
direct-mail strategy 59
protectionism 126
Protestant Christian Schools:
'segregation academies' 96, 97
Protestant fundamentalism:
'Americans United' 98
Protestantism 127
American nineteenth-century 86
dominance of 83
'Protestants and Others United for the
Separation of Church and State'
98
PTL Club, The 104
public-choice theorists 7
public education 74
Public Interest, The 25, 37
intelligence tests 40
public opinion polls 16
public policy 143, 146
crucial issues 133

family, impact on 92
research institutes 53
schools' racial integration 96
public schools 98
Puritan heritage 10
puritanism 44
ideological derivation from 83
puritan theocracy, and immigration 81

Quayle, Dan 143
NCPAC tactics, repudiation of 64
Quie, Albert 122

race 3, 38
IQ and 40
policy topics related to 41
socially divisive 39
racial equality 38
racial integration 40, 43, 96
racialism 40
radicals, and Vietnam War 46
Rahv, Philip 24
Reagan, Ronald 1, 141
abortion 165
administration 16–19, 67, 71, 121,
144, 147, 148, 150–2, 154–8,
160, 162–7, 169, 171–8, 181,
182, 185, 187, 188, 194
affirmative action 163, 164
Aid to Families with Dependent
Children 158: regulations 166
Airborne Warning and Control
System (AWACS), sale of 145
allies 174
American military position 170
anti-communism 171, 173, 184
appointments 69, 167, 172
arms control 171, 182
arms sales 177
Atlantic Alliance 185
B-1 Bomber 181
blacks, and welfare benefits 160
black support 127
budget 145, 147, 156, 157, 167
bureaucracy, infiltration of 151
candidacy 20, 67
Caribbean 168
Central America 184, 185
China 111
civil liberties 163, 166
coalition 119, 146
collective decision-making 151
collectivism 146

Committee on the Present Danger 172
communication 151
communists 168
Congress, liaison with 151
Congressional Republican Party, relations with 145
conservatism, radical 146, 147
conservative Christians, liaison with 108
criticism of 68, 148, 161
defense 172
defense budget 154, 181, 182
defense expenditure 181
defense policy 167, 186
delegation 149
Democrats' ideological sympathy 152
deregulation 162
direct personal taxation 153, 154
domestic issues 152
domestic policy 166
domestic politics 167
domestic public expenditure 154
dual-use technology 187
early success 3
economic objectives 144
economic package 153, 161
economic policies 13, 14, 138, 152, 162, 186, 194
economic program 165
economic prosperity 152
Economic Recovery Tax Act (1981) 153
economic strategy 144, 148, 166: supply-side economics 126
economic warfare 187
education 157: block grants 156
election campaign 108, 121, 146: Christian right, liaison with 97; *détente* 131
electoral success 2, 12, 20, 146
El Salvador 177, 185: human rights 176
energy conservation 157
Europe 187
exploiting Main Street 11
federal aid 157
federal budget 159
federal expenditure 153, 154
federal government 163
federalism 139, 159
food stamps 158

foreign aid 177
foreign policy 21, 145, 167, 172, 173, 176–8, 184–8: continuity 169; criticism of 168
foreign-policy issues 152
forgotten man, the 15
freedom of speech 164
free-market economic theories 166
government: regulations 162; role of 162
Grenada invasion 178
health block grants 156
Heritage Foundation 54: lists of reliable conservatives 68
Human Events 70
human rights 177, 182
industry 163
inflation 152
intelligence services 178
international issues 167
IRS case 165
Israel 168, 187
judicial appointments 118
Kissinger Commission 177: Central America, aid to 176
Latin America 168
Lebanon 178, 187
legislative program 143
Medicaid 158: spending cuts 139
Medicare 155, 158
military aid 178
military expansion 152
military expenditure 173
military force, use of 177
military intervention 178
minority interests 138
monetary policy, influence on 153
Moral Majority, importance to 119
MX missile 174, 181
National Governors' Conference 139
nationalism 194
national security 173
NATO, USA role in 188
neo-conservatism, influence of 169
New Jersey Senate Primary 123
new right 69, 123, 148
nuclear freeze 168
OMB 162, 181
Persian Gulf 168
personal staff 150
personnel 175

Poland 168
policies 145, 175
policy-making ('dual approach')
    151
pollution control 157
populism 163, 166, 194
poverty, reduction of 155
Presidency, style of 149, 151
private schools 164
public expenditure cuts 148
public policy 146
public policy research institutes,
    links with 53
Reaganism 166, 184
rearmament 170
relief programs, state responsibility
    for 158
religion/religious groups, electoral
    impact of 80
religious liaison officer 74
religious right, support of 103
Republicanism 146
Republican Party 118: chair-
    manship 123; relations with
    145, 192; support 144; unity
    123
retirement benefits 154
SALT II 182
Saudi Arabia 187
school prayer 165
Shah of Iran 182
social issues 165
social policy 161
social safety-net programs 155
social security 154, 155: reforms,
    criticism of 41
social services 157: block grants
    156
social welfare 154: federal with-
    drawal 155
Soviet expansionism 173
State of the Union (1982) 157,
    159
strategic defense 182
strategic forces 181
sub-Cabinet councils 150
subversive activities 177-8
support for 148
Supreme Court 118, 165: ap-
    pointments 119
Taiwan 111, 173
Task Force on Regulatory Relief
    150, 162

transition team 171, 175
Trident II 181
'truth-seekers' 67
'truth squads' 175
unemployment 152, 160: pay 155
United Nations, appointments to
    48
USSR, and international relations
    185
values of 180
veto, use of 148
Vice-President, role of 150
Voting Rights Act (1965) 164
War Powers Act (1973) 178
welfare benefits 150
welfare provision 158
Welfare State 146
welfare system 166
women's rights 138
Reaganism 70, 184
legacy of 166
realignment (electoral) 191
realism, neo-conservative emphasis on
    27
realpolitik 176
reapportionment 73
rearmament 170
'red decade' 23
redistricting 95
Reed, John:
    Ten Days That Shook the World
    23
Reformed confessionalism 85
regional background 28
relief programs, responsibility for 158
religion 33, 127
    effect on political culture 10
    establishment of State religions 82
    Founding Fathers 81
    importance of 25
    media 79
    neo-conservative analysis 45
    new-right concern 80
    political role of 119
    politics, relationship with 17, 43,
        106
    role of 12
    secularism 84
    unity in culture 44
religious affiliation, its electoral
    significance 80
religious beliefs, undermined by books
    73

religious broadcasting 102–4
religious causes 10
Religious Coalition for Abortion Rights 101
religious groups:
  political involvement 42
  Supreme Court appointment, opposition to 119
religious leaders:
  new right, mutual interest 84
  politics, involvement in 71
religious orthodoxy (in Europe) 81
religious pluralism, and secular polity 82
religious revivals 10
religious right 17, 44, 51, 52, 80, 119
  activation of 99
  direct mail 101
  family issues 91
  foreign policy, criticism of 172
  legislative action, agenda for 165
  mobilization 101
  Moral Majority planning meetings 114
  moral values, traditional 92
  new right: alliance with 10; élites, movements between 105; integration with 118
  outlook 79
  populism 193
  Religious Roundtable 115
  Republican Party, links with 135
  sexual morality 11
  social issues 91, 112, 165
Religious Roundtable 106
  abortion 116
  culture, treatment of 80
  moral issues 80, 115
  national defense 116
  planning session, first 116
  prayer in schools 116
  private schools 116
  religion, treatment of 80
  sex in the media 116
religious tests 81
religious values 35
  capitalism, relationship with 24
Report Card on Congress, issues 111
Reporter 41
Republican Conference 137
Republican Governors' Conference 139

Republicanism 145
  collectivism 146
  neo-conservatives and 192
  populist constituency and 193
  protection of 132
  radical conservatism 146
  rejection of 146
  right-wing support for 174, 193
  Welfare State 146
Republican National Committee 121
  appointments 139
  Candidate Management College 140
  Common Sense 141
  contributons to 60
  election campaign 141: strategy 140
  local elections division 140
  1980 elections 4
  policy research 141
  publicity 141
  unity 122
  Winchell (Stephen) Associates (direct mail) 59
Republican Party (Grand Old Party):
  abortion 130, 133
  agenda 143
  Airborne Warning and Control Systems (AWACS) 145
  anti-communism 130
  anti-Europeanism 128
  'boll-weevils' 144
  British Conservative Party 125
  British Empire, alliance with 128
  budget 145
  Candidate Management Committee 140
  candidates 141: social policy statements 142
  capital 125
  Chairmanship 123
  China 111, 124
  Christian Voice, and Congressional Advisory Board 110
  civil rights 127, 130
  Common Sense 141
  communist subversion 124
  Congressional Club 141
  Congressional Republican Party 145
  conservative: campaign 121; coalition 144; policies 106; Republicans 135
  country club values 78

CSFC 137, 141
Democratic Party: criticism of 142;
   deals with 144
developments 120
direct mail 4
distrust of 67
domestic social programs 138
dynastic elements 129
economic issues 71
economic motivation 66
economic policy 14, 138
economic strategy, criticism of 144
economy 126, 142
electoral campaign 141, 179
electoral candidates 123, 140
electoral redistricting 140
electoral strategy 142
electoral success 12, 120, 191-2
employment 142
ethnic composition 127
evangelical Protestantism 127
factionalism, pattern of 124
factions 17
family issues 91, 93, 142, 145
federalism 139
federal legislative contests 139
finance 140, 145
foreign policy 127-8, 142, 145:
   criticism of 173; internal
   divisions 123, 174; record on
   177; unanimity on 173
'fortress America' 128
free enterprise 93
fund-raising 141
gay rights 163
'gypsy moths' 148
historical origins 127
ideological emphasis 122
ideological input 73
institutionalization of the right
   134
internal divisions 143
internal ideological differences
   139
internal unity 144
internationalism 138
isolationism 128, 138
Kemp-Roth bill 126
legal aid, opposition to 163
legislation 122
liberal-progressive wing 138-9,
   144, 145
liberal Republicans 137: public

expenditure cuts, criticism of
   148
loyalty to 129
mainstream Republicans 137-8
Main Street 126
Medicaid 139
military budget 138
minority racial groups 163
minority rights 138
moderates and 192
National Governors' Conference
   139
national organization 4
National Republican Senatorial
   Committee 138
NCPAC 141
new areas of dominance 110
New Deal 125, 138: hostility to
   130
new right 65, 124: relations with
   52
nuclear freeze 138
organization 121
organized labor 126
Panama Canal Treaties 137
People's Party 61
policies 20
political philosophy 137
populism 163, 192
post-war period, immediate 124
power within 110
presidential nomination 129
prohibition 127
protectionism 126
public policy 143
Reagan, Ronald, relations with
   145
Reaganism, legacy of 166
regional divisions 174
religion 127
Republican Conference 137
Republican Governors 139
Republican National Committee
   121-2, 139, 140-1
Republican Policy Committee 137
'Republican professionals' 137
Republican Study Committee 121,
   134: appointments 135; impact/
   effect of 136
Republican right 130-3, 137-8:
   defense budget 131; economy
   131; Goldwater, Barry 131;
   Great Society Programs 131;

Republican Party (*cont.*):
    homosexuality 133; 95th
      Congress 137; States' rights
      132 (critical of 130); taxation
      133; youth, appeal to 132
    'Republican Year' 143
    Senate, control of 2
    social issues 91, 142–3, 145
    social status 127
    Southern Rim 121
    Steering Committee in the Senate
      121
    strategy 110
    supply-side economics 6, 126
    support, geographic movement of
      193
    Supreme Court 130
    Taft-Eisenhower battle 129
    Taiwan 111
    tariffs 126
    taxation 126, 138
    tendencies: liberal–progressive 125;
      mainstream 125; right 125
    two-party competition 111
    unemployment 13
    Vietnam War 138
    'Volvo Republicans' 145
    Wasps 127
    Watergate 120, 145
    Women's liberation 138, 163
Republican Policy Committee ap-
    pointments 137
Republican Study Committee 69, 74,
    116, 121, 133
    appointments 135
    development of 133
    impact/effect of 136
    institutionalization of the right
      134
    membership 3, 134
    new right, links with 135
    religious right, links with 135
'Republican Year' 143
Research and Analysis, financial sup-
    port of 53
retirement benefits 154
reverse discrimination 38
revivalism, and fundamentalism 85
Rhodesia/Zimbabwe 112, 170
Richards, Richard:
    PACs, electoral role of 123
    Republican Party chairmanship
      123

resignation 123
retirement 132
Richardson, H. L. (Bill):
    ALEC 74
    California Law and Order Com-
      mittee 74
    Gun Owners of America 52, 74
    Gun Owners of California 74
    Washington, DC (proposed state
      of) 75
right, institutionalization of 134
Right to Life:
    issue 95
    movement 9
right-to-work 74
    campaign against 136
    picketing 136
Roberts, Oral 78
Robertson, Pat:
    religious broadcasting 102
    700 Club 103
    The Perspective 104
    viewing figures 104
Robison, James 10, 12
    'Campus Crusade' 100
    religious broadcasting 102, 104
    United States, collective sin of 100
Rockefeller, Nelson
    internationalist 138
    liberal Republican 138
    political liberalism 67
Rockefeller (family) 77, 110
'Rocky Mountain conservatives':
    abortion 132
    family issues 132
    women's liberation 132
Rogers, Adrian:
    Religious Roundtable 116
    Southern Baptist Convention 116
Roman Catholic Church:
    abortion 94, 95
    anti-Catholicism, death of 98
    bishops, and nuclear freeze debates
      84
    conservative disposition 43
    education, private 96, 98
    legitimacy of 83
    membership 87–8
    papal encyclicals: *Longinqua
      Oceani* (1895) 90; *Testem
      Benevolentiae* (1899) 90
    parochial school system 97
    political presence 84

social philosophy 34
Vatican II (effects on member-
ship) 87
Roman Catholicism, in nineteenth
century 90
Roman Catholics 11, 24
electoral successes 127
Moral Majority 112
Roosevelt vision 5
Rosenberg, Harold 24
Rosenberg trial 28
Rossiter, Clinton 10
comments on conservative dilemma
9
'the thankless persuasion' 55
Rostow, Eugene:
Director of Arms Control ('resig-
nation') 176
Roth, Philip 27
Roth, William:
supply-side theories 13
Roundtable 106, 115
Rusher, Bill 56
Ryskind, Alan 70

Sabato, Larry 61
Sale, Kirkpatrick 67
SALT II 61, 182
opposition to 59, 74, 104, 170,
171
ratification 170
Sarbanes, Paul:
election campaign 123
NCPAC, as election issue 123
Saudi Arabia:
American surrogates 168
AWACS, sale to 69
USA, relations with 187
Save Our Children, and textbook
censorship 73
Scaife, Richard:
Heritage Foundation, funding of
53
Scaife Foundation, and ALEC 75
Schafly, Phyllis:
anti-Equal Rights Amendment 116
Religious Roundtable 116
Schapiro, Meyer 24
Schneider, William 173
School Boards (as new-right targets)
73
school prayer 91, 165

House Judiciary Committee 100
legislation 136
national campaign 73
non-denominational, voluntary
98
Supreme Court 66, 82
schools:
Christian values 99
integration 40
problems 96
sex education 10
Schuchman Foundation 53
Schuller, Robert 78
Schwartz, Delmore 24
Scoundrel Times 29
Scrantons 78, 129
Scripture study (in public schools)
98
secular humanism 10, 11, 117
resistance to 103
state philosophy 100
suspect 73
transforming attitudes 98
secularism 116
religion 84
secular liberalism 10
secular polity, and religious pluralism
82
secular State 81
'segregation academies' 97
Select Committee on Committees
(appointments) 137
self-control 44
self-reliance 13
Semitism: *see* anti-Semitism
Senate:
Finance Committee 148
Foreign Relations Committee 179
Judiciary Committee: abortion 94
Steering Committee: abortion 136;
defense expenditure 136;
foreign policy, effect on 137;
impact/effect of 136; intelligence activities 136; school
prayer 136; USSR, attitude to
136
Senate races 193
Senatorial Campaign Committee,
contributions to 61
700 Club 103
Seventh Day Adventists 110
legitimacy of 83
membership 87

sex education 73
sexual morality 11, 44, 91
Shannon, James:
  election campaign 95
Shaw, E. Clay:
  social welfare 161
Shultz, George:
  government appointment 184
'silent majority', as a conservative
    constituency 57
Siljander, Mark:
  election campaign 142
sin, expiation of 89
single-issue constituencies 58
single-issue groups 65
  federal government, role of 14
'single-issue politics' 8
slavery 82, 127
Smith, Al:
  Klu Klux Klan reaction to 83
Smith, Bailey (Revd):
  anti-Semitism 113
Smith, Christopher:
  abortion 142
  election campaign 95
Smith, William French:
  affirmative action 163, 164
  Justice Department policies 163,
    164
social attitudes (fundamentalist) 79
social change 125
  dislocative 71
social democracy 45
social equality 39
social evils 127
social gospel, importance of 89
socialism 45
  dolorous idiom 34
social issues 13, 71, 96, 116, 143,
    145, 165
  conservative Christians 112
  criticism of 142
  direct mail 72
  divisive 68, 69, 91
  new right 72, 112, 193
  new-right definition 11
  religious right 112
social mobility 43
social norms, and biblical precepts 72
social policy 1, 17
  candidates' statements 142
  deficiencies 36
social security 16, 154

programs, cuts in 155
social security issues, and direct mail
    57
social security reform, criticism of 42
social services:
  block grants 156
  programs, number of 157
social status 127
social welfare 13, 161
  responsibility for 155
  tradition of 154
Sojourners 117
Sonneland, John:
  election campaign 142
South Africa, policy towards 86
South-East Asia 177
Southern Baptist Convention 87, 88
  anti-Semitism 113
Southern Baptists, and religious
    schools 98
southern political culture 3
Southern Rim 110, 121, 132
  power-shift to 3
Sowell, Thomas 40, 41
Spender, Stephen 25
Spirit of Democratic Capitalism, The
    (Novak) 34
Stalin, Joseph 22, 30
Stalinism 23, 30
  anti-Stalinists 47
Stark, John Paul:
  election campaign 142
State–Church relationship 12
state constitutions, and budget 157
State Department:
  Human Rights Division (ap-
    pointment blocked) 176
  'Kissinger-style détentist thinking'
    70
  pro-*détente* 179
  role of 183
  suspicion of 183
State of the Union (1982):
  federal system 157
state religion 82
states' rights 132
Staton, David:
  election campaign 142
Staton, Mick:
  election campaign 95
status 78
'stealth' aircraft 181
Steering Committee 121, 133

Stennis, John Cornelius:
   Rhodesia, sanctions against 112
Stewart, Lyman:
   Fundamentals 89
Stewart, Milton:
   Fundamentals 89
Stewart, Potter 118
Stockman, David 147
   budget cuts 151
   defense priorities 181
   economic policies, criticism of 150
   expenditure cuts 148
   influence of 150
   Office of Management and Budget
      148: appointment 150, 181
   tax cuts 153
Stokes, Anson Phelps:
   church schools 97
strategic forces 181
Strauss, Leo 10
strict separationists 12
Stump, Bob:
   Christian Voice 110
   Democratic Party 110
   Republican Party 110
   Seventh Day Adventist 110
subversive activity 177, 178
Suggested States Legislation 75
sun-belt 3
supply-side economics 6, 14, 126
   arguments 152
   literature 33
   theories 13
   Wealth and Poverty 33
supply-siders 7
   federal government, role of 14
   tax cuts 153
Supreme Court:
   abortion 130
   appointments 118
   Bob Jones University, tax status 108
   Buckley v. *Valeo* 63
   Church and State, theory of 81
   civil rights 130
   Doe v. *Bolton* 93
   first female appointment 119
   intelligence tests 40
   IRS 165
   parochial schools 82
   private schools 165
   Roe v. *Wade* 93
   school prayer 66, 82
   social and political change, agent

     of 147
   tax status 165
   textbook censorship 73
   Warren Court 130
Symms, Steve 132
   NCPAC tactics, repudiation of 65

Taft, Robert 55
   anti-European 129
   'Mr Republican' 128
   party support 129
   presidential nomination 129
   Republicanism, protection of 132
Tafts 78
Taiwan:
   arms sales to 173
   Senators' attitudes to 111
   USA: relations with 172, 173;
     support 112
Taiwan Enabling Act (1979), amend-
     ment 111
Taiwan Treaty 172
Talcott, John:
   Plymouth Rock Foundation 116
   Religious Roundtable 116
tariffs 126
Tarrance, Lance:
   CSFC 116
   Religious Roundtable 116
Task Force on Regulatory Relief 150
   Executive Order 162
taxation 6, 13, 14, 133, 138, 193
   base rate 153
   direct 153, 154
   inflation 153
   Kemp–Roth Bill 126
   personal 153: UK 153
   progressive 152
   state, constitutional amendments 75
tax exemption 114
tax rebellions 126
Teague, Kathy:
   Free Congress Research and Edu-
     cation Foundation 74
'telethons' 57
television, new-right use of 107
television evangelists 102
   abortion 118
   family issues 118
   judicial appointments 118
   political awareness 118
Ten Days That Shook the World (Reed)
   23

Tennessee Baptist Foundation 107
Terrell, Norman:
    Nuclear Weapons, Deputy Director
        in charge of 175
Testem Benevolentiae (1899) 90
textbook censorship 96
    book-banning campaign 76
    Supreme Court 73
textbook selection 73
Thatcher, Margaret:
    American right, sympathy with
        186
    conservatism 147, 153
    inflation 153
    personal taxation 153
theology:
    conservatism 87
    liberalism 87
    modernism 90
    radical (effect on political culture)
        82
Third World, democratic development
    of 176
This World 12
Thompson, Frank:
    Abscam scandal 95
Thompson, Mike:
    direct mail 74
Thompson and Associates 74
Trans-Siberian pipeline, USA op-
    position to 188
Trident II 181
Trilateral Commission, the 77
Trilling, Lionel 23, 24, 27, 29
    Partisan Review 25
Trotskyism 23
trusts 162
'truth-seekers' 67
'truth squads' 175
Tsongas, Paul:
    Rhodesia sanctions 112
Tufts 41
tuition tax credits 139
Ture, Norman:
    supply-side theories 13
Two Cheers for Capitalism (Kristol)
    33

unemployment 13, 16, 91
    black problem 42
    federal government role 160
    Great Depression 152
    pay 155

    rate 152
UNESCO 183
unilateralism 188
    definition 28
Union of Soviet Socialist Republics
    28, 176
    adventurism 170
    Afghanistan 170, 180
    aggression 170, 186
    Angola 180
    armed forces 180
    arms control agreements 170
    arms limitation 169
    attitudes to 22
    China: conflicts with 38; *rap-
        prochement* 173
    cold war 170
    détente 131, 180: interpretation of
        179
    economic *détente* 186
    expansionism 173
    Horn of Africa 180
    international relations, influence on
        185
    navy 180
    nuclear forces 180
    Senate attitude to 136
    Siberian gas pipeline 188
    USA attitude to 182
    USA relations with 169, 188
unions:
    anti-union causes 61
United Church of Christ 87
United Kingdom 1, 30
    Cabinet 147
    Civil Service 147
    Government 147
    Parliament 147
    party loyalty 65
United Methodist Church 87, 88
United Nations 47, 183
United Presbyterian Church 87, 88
United States:
    biblical morality 100
    military position in the world 170
    world policeman 168
    world role 99
university autonomy, challenge to 32
urban renewal programs 151
USSR: *see* Union of Soviet Socialist
    Republics
Utopianism 27
Utopian society 35

'value-related' issues 66
Vance, Cyrus:
    pro-*détente* 179
Van Cleave, William:
    Arms Control and Disarmament
        Agency appointment 70
    defense policy (and budget) 175
    Weinberger, Caspar, dispute with
        68
Vandenberg, Senator:
    internationalist 128
Vatican, and priest's withdrawal
    from politics 95
Vatican II, effects on church member-
    ship 87
Venice Declaration, European attitude
    to 187
Vice-President:
    role of 150
    Task Force on Regulatory Relief
        150
Vietnam 49
    Cambodia, conflicts with 38
    China, conflicts with 38
Vietnam era, and taboos 178
Vietnam War 46, 179, 180
    American troops 138
    anti-American sentiment 47
    attitudes to 31
    collective sin, result of 100
    counter-culture 99
    Great Society program expenditure
        181
    military expenditure 181
    resistance to 32
    spiritual erosion 99
Viguerie, Richard 74
    American Independent Party 67
    Conservative Right 69
    direct mail 56, 58
    evangelical right 109
    magazine publication 56
    Moral Majority 113, 114
    new right as 'new' 107
    origins 77
    philosophy of 105
    Religious Roundtable 116
    Republican Party 65, 67
    Roman Catholic 99
'Volvo Republicans' 145
voter registration, and Moral Majority
    115
Voting Rights Act (1965) 164

wage controls 104
Wald, Patricia:
    judicial appointment 118
Wallace, George 77
Wallop, Malcolm 132
Wall Street 126
    hatred of 79
Wall Street Journal 6
Walzer, Michael 32
War Powers Act (1973) 178
Warren Court 130
Washington Court of Appeals, ap-
    pointments 118
Washington Post:
    welfare provision (national stan-
        dards) 159, 160
Wasps 127
Watergate 4, 120, 145
    election law reforms 60
    reaction to 180
    result of collective sin 100
Watt, James 163
    Government appointment 163
Ways and Means Committee 122
Wealth and Poverty (Gilder) 6, 33
Weaver, Richard 10
Weber (United Steel Workers v.) 39
Weber, Max:
    capitalism, definition of 34
Weber, Vin:
    election campaign 142
Weicker, L. 138
Weinberger, Caspar:
    Defense appointment 173, 175
    defense policy, and budget 175
    foreign policy 187
    pro-Arab 187
welfare 5, 15
    European attitude to 186
    expenditure 152, 158
    federal guidelines 156
    government intervention, selective
        37
    payments 156
    programs 75
    racial overtones 3
    services 156
    system (AFDC regulations) 166
Welfare State:
    paternalism 37
    presidential dislike of 13
    rejection of 146
Western Europe, defense of 186

Western Society, modern, atomization
of 38
Weyrich, Paul 53, 55
ALEC 74
appointment 137
CSFC 52, 108, 171
evangelical right 109
foreign policy 135
Free Congress Research and Edu-
cation Foundation 74
independent conservative party
120
Moral Majority 113, 114
new right 71, 107
origins 77
Religious Roundtable 116
Republican Party: country club
values 78; pragmatism 66
Roman Catholic 99
tax laws, manipulation of 64
White House Conference on Families,
Congress endorsement of 92
Williams, Rogers:
freedom of religion 81
Williams, Tennessee 73
Wilson, Edmund 22
Wilson, Woodrow:
mailing campaign 56
Winchell (Stephen) Associates:
Republican National Committee

(direct mail) 59
Winter, Tom 70
women 145
role of 9
women's liberation 10, 132
hostility to 163
religious opinion 100
women's rights 138
work ethic 44
divine plan 89
World Council of Churches:
Central America, USA policy
towards (criticized) 86
revolutionary regimes, aid to 86
South Africa, USA policy towards
(criticized) 86
Wrong, Dennis 32
Wycliffe Bible Translators 116

*Yearbook of the American and
Canadian Churches* 86
Young Americans for Freedom 53, 74,
78
conservative policies 106
Republican Right 131
right-wing activists 54
youth organizing 132

Zimbabwe: *see* Rhodesia/Zimbabwe